A Bay Ridge Life

A Bay Ridge Life

BY: BOB LANE

MILL CITY PRESS

Mill City Press, Inc.
2301 Lucien Way #415
Maitland, FL 32751
407.339.4217
www.millcitypress.net

Printed in the United States of America

Library of Congress Control Number:

Paperback ISBN-13: 9781662806360
Dust Jacket ISBN-13: 9781662806377
Ebook ISBN-13: 9781662806384

TO MY MIRACULOUS WIFE, GAIL
I CAN'T IMAGINE LIFE WITHOUT HER

A BAY RIDGE LIFE

Many books have been written over the years about life in New York City. Me, I'm from Brooklyn. That's spelled B-R-O-O-K-L-Y-N. More specifically, BAY RIDGE, Brooklyn, the center of the known universe.

That may be somewhat of an exaggeration, but only slightly so.

I mean, how bad could it be when about a third of the Brooklyn Dodgers called it home in the decade of the fifties.

Duke Snider, Pee Wee Reese, Preacher Roe, Carl Erskine, Rube Walker, Russ Meyer, Bobby Morgan, and Bill Antonello all went home to sleep in Bay Ridge after games at Ebbets Field.

Bill Antonello was a reserve outfielder on the '53 team. His father was the superintendent of an apartment house three blocks from where I lived on Ovington Avenue. A true Bay Ridge native son.

I believe that his apartment house was plowed under by good old Robert Moses to make way for the approach road to the Verrazano Bridge.

That building, and hundreds of others, was obliterated in the early 60's, virtually destroying the Scandinavian Community in Bay Ridge. Thanks, Mr. Moses!

All in all, however, Bay Ridge was truly a great place in which to grow up.

This narrative will attempt to relate the experiences of a young man coming of age in a time that I honestly feel was much more innocent and better in just about every way.

I hope my children and grandchildren will enjoy the story of the early life journey of their "Silly Grandpa".

It was with them in mind that I began to chronicle my adventures with no intention of ever publishing the tale.

Eventually, those to whom I showed the manuscript convinced me to do so.

The final version contains lots and lots of pictures which is somewhat unusual.

But, since it's my life, I can do whatever the hell I want.

Hope everybody enjoys the ride, I sure have.

TABLE OF CONTENTS

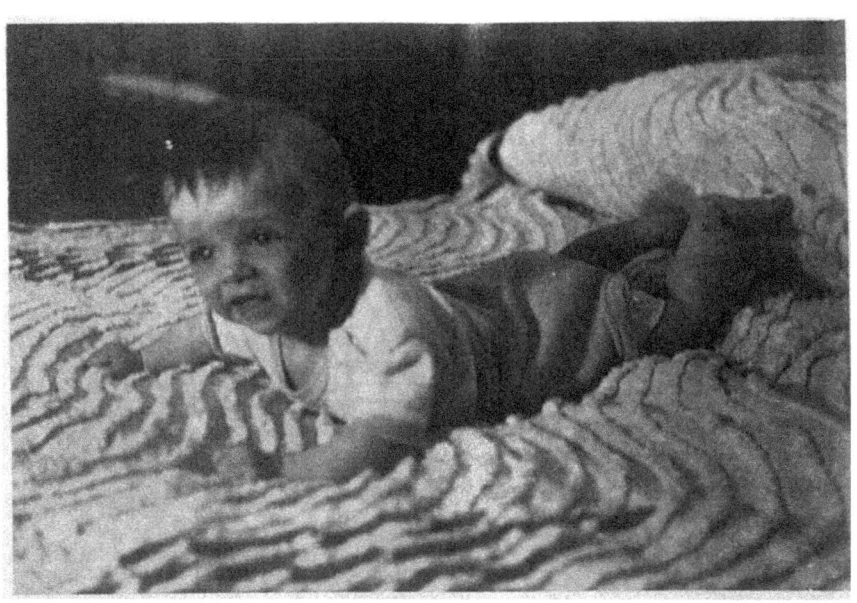

Chapter One

AN AUSPICIOUS BEGINNING (?)

It's Friday, January 17th, 1941, and the population of Bay Ridge increases by one new bright and shiny, blue eyed baby boy, namely, Robert Lane II.

His parents, Robbie, a New York City fireman, (Badge No. 4011) and the former Helen Mary McCloskey took the newborn back to Ovington Avenue, where he'd spend the next thirteen and a half years of his life.

Memories of the first four years or so have faded into the distant mists of time and are unavailable to this day.

One forgotten, painfully sad memory from those years pertains to the death of my Dad, in the line of duty, in 1943 at the age of 32.

The story, as it has been related to me over the years, is as follows: My Father was officially assigned to Hook and Ladder 105 on Pacific Street near the Long Island Railroad terminal at Flatbush and Atlantic Avenue. He was filling in for another fireman on Engine Co. 219, when the company responded to a false alarm.

While making the run, the engine collided with a trolley car at Flatbush and Parkside Avenues.

Dad usually liked to ride in the back of the fire truck on the neatly stacked hoses. In the collision, he was thrown from the truck and severely injured.

Taken to Kings County Hospital, he remained there for the next two weeks for treatment.

He was about to be released on April 9th, when he suddenly died, supposedly from "Generalized Peritonitis, due to a ruptured Ilium".

I've always believed that someone really screwed up in the hospital and cost me my Father.

But evidently, back then, no one pursued the issue.

My Mother, as it turned out, had given birth to my sister, Elizabeth Mary, five days prior to dad's death.

After that, my mother pretty much raised us by herself.

She, of course, had help from members of the Lane family and from her sister, my Aunt, Nora Campbell (nee McCloskey).

Aunt Nora's husband, Charles Campbell, was away fighting World War II as a member of the Navy Seabees 30th Construction Battalion. However, "fighting" may not be the proper term to describe his participation in the war since most of the time he was stationed in Port of Spain, Trinidad.

Once the Germans surrendered in May 1945, uncle Charlie and his mates were sent to the Pacific to fight the Japanese.

The 30th got as far as the Philippines when the war ended in September with the Japanese surrender in Tokyo Bay aboard the battleship USS Missouri.

(One interesting aside: Years later I worked with a man named Carl Ravioli who was scheduled to be in the first assault wave as a heavy machine gunner in the invasion of the Japanese home land. The dropping of the two Atomic Bombs on Hiroshima and Nagasaki in August and the subsequent surrender undoubtedly saved his life.)

Getting back to my Aunt and Uncle, they had married in early November 1941 and had honeymooned in Washington D.C. Three weeks later, the Japanese bombed Pearl Harbor and my Uncle was gone for four years.

My Aunt took a furnished room on Senator Street, about three blocks from our apartment and both she and my mother worked.

The Lane family took care of my sister and I, while Mom worked making beds at three or four fire houses around Brooklyn. Finally, the firemen told her to stay home and raise her family, but they made sure she still got paid.

I'm pretty sure the money came directly from the firemen's own pockets, but that's typical of the way they took care of their own in those days.

This arrangement continued until my sister and I started school and Mom went back to work as a secretary. (I believe she had gone to St. Joseph's Commercial High School before she married my Father.)

My Dad was an iron worker before he became a fireman. He had always wanted to be a fireman and hung around the local firehouse in his off hours.

Rumor has it that he would go on runs with the firemen even before he was a member of the Department. There are even stories that he helped rescue some people from a burning building during that time.

Dad was also a fine baseball player. He was a power hitting center-fielder for a number of "semi-pro" teams in the area, including the "Visitations" and the Fire Departments own squad.

The Cleveland Indians actually invited him to spring training one year. Unfortunately, the Indians trained in Arizona and he would have had to pay his own way out west. The depression was still going on and there was no way he could afford to go. But you can't help but wonder; WHAT IF?

As a fireman, Dad was one of the very, very best.

He was the recipient (posthumously) of the Hugh Bonner Award, at the time the third highest honor given to a member of the Fire Department.

He had rescued a lady named Rose McGowan from a burning building in danger of collapse by swinging on a rope to pluck her from a window and onto a ladder to safety.

This was just one of a number of other medals, including one for bravery given to my Dad. He must have been something!

I wish I had been allowed to know him, but I have no memories of him at all.

What a terrible loss. I can't even begin to think how different my life would have been, had he survived.

Other memories from those early years include those of my Grandmother, Elizabeth McCloskey (nee Hyland), climbing the five flights of stairs up to our fifth-floor apartment (B-51).

The stairwells of our section were constructed with an air space in the middle so you could look down and see visitors wending their way up each step of the way.

I can still see Grandma McCloskey coming up those stairs, step by step, floor by floor, in her good hat with the pink flower on it. (How she ever did it, I'll never know.)

She would always bring a box of hard candy as a gift. I never liked those candies, but I would never, never let her know how I felt.

It qualifies as one of my earliest remembrances since Grandma died in July 1945, and I was only four and a half years old at the time.

Because our building only rose five stories, it did not qualify to have elevators in those days. Our building contained seventy-five apartments spread over four sections, (A-B-C and D) but no elevators.

Our apartment house, however, DID have "dumb waiters" in which to place our garbage. It was actually a manually operated elevator system for trash.

You would open a cabinet door in the kitchen, which would expose a shaft containing a pull rope and a two-tiered storage area. You would haul on the rope until it reached the opening for your apartment, place your garbage inside and lower it to the basement. The superintendent would then remove the contents at some point in time.

Naturally, there were times when the dumb waiter was full and you would just have to wait until it was emptied.

It wasn't that bad a system, all things being considered. It certainly beat carrying your garbage down five flights of stairs and coming back up again.

Then some genius decided that the system was unsanitary and they nailed the doors shut. As a result, we did wind up bringing our garbage down the five flights after all.

Another set of memories from that period was the ending of World War II.

The first of these was the death of President Franklin Roosevelt in early April, 1945.

It was as if God had died.

He was, for all practical purposes, our king.

The whole nation was stunned.

It was followed a few weeks later by the suicide of Adolf Hitler.

(I'm not sure though that the news of Hitler's death was released right away.)

A week or so after that, everybody took to the streets banging pots and pans over the news that Nazi Germany had surrendered, ending the war in Europe.

A few months after that, we took to the streets again when the Japanese surrendered, finally ending World War II.

One other vivid memory I have from that era is of the little rectangular banners in the windows of each family that had men/boys in the service.

These flags were white with a red border and contained a blue star in the middle for every family member away on active duty.

When a star was changed to gold, it meant their husband, father or son had been killed and the whole neighborhood mourned him as one of their own.

After the war, Uncle Charlie returned home and he and Aunt Nora lived in a small furnished room on Senator Street and then moved to an apartment in Astoria while they waited for their new house to be built on 194th Street in Flushing. But there was a time Uncle Charlie took up residence at our place.

(I don't remember if Aunt Nora stayed with us too.)

If he or they did, it must have been very crowded. Ours was only a three room, one-bedroom layout. (I'm pretty sure Uncle Charlie slept on a cot in our living room.)

The reason for this arrangement was that both my sister and I had caught Pneumonia.

Our doctor was Dr. ISAAC KUGELMAS who had a practice on the upper west side of Park Avenue. I went there regularly for cold shots (injections with blue glass needles). They must have worked. I got a lot of colds!

Doctor Kugelmas' nurse's name was Miss Smith, and I recall that she was a very pretty lady with a very pleasant voice.

Later on, she was replaced by another nurse. I was very disappointed. The Doctor's office waiting room was always very warm and stuffy. I didn't like spending time there.

The Doctor was listed in "Who's Who", but the copy of the book he kept in the waiting room had had the page with his biographical data ripped out.

Doctor Kugelmas wore his dark hair in a sort of bun. He always reminded me of The Lone Ranger's "faithful Indian companion", Tonto. We usually would go up to his office by subway. We'd take the BMT to the

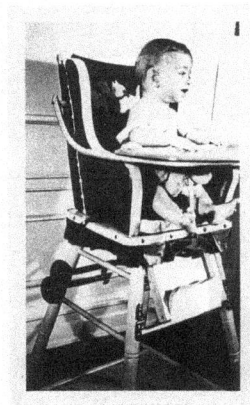 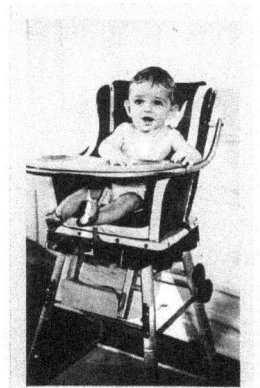 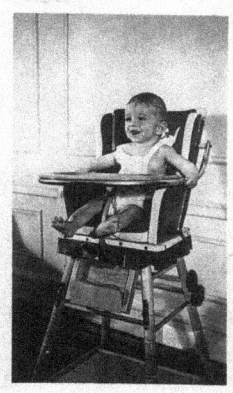

14th Street-Union Square station in Manhattan and change for the IRT Lexington Avenue train to the 86th Street station.

The 14th street station platform on the IRT was curved to accommodate the long cars which ran on the IRT at that time. They had to use sliding

metal ramps to reach the train doors. Those doors were at either end of the cars and could not be reached from the curved platform. A man on the platform would operate a lever which would slide the ramps outward towards the car doors. Passengers would enter and/or leave the trains via these ramps. I was scared to death of those ramps.

After the office visits, my mom, sister and I would go to "Woolworth's" on 86th Street for lunch. I invariably had an egg salad sandwich on toast and a chocolate malted. (yum yum!)

We would then go back to downtown Brooklyn and catch a movie at either the Brooklyn Paramount or the Brooklyn Fox.

I remember that the Fox, in addition to the main features, ran the two "SUPERMAN" serials. in 1948 and 1950.

Once, when I was sick, Frank Mulligan, (John Cuff's uncle) drove us up to Dr. Kugelmas' office in his new green Nash automobile. We went by way of the Grand Central Station ramp onto Park Avenue and up to the office.

I repaid his generosity by throwing up in the back seat of his car. (both directions, I think)

I used to throw up a lot in cars and on buses. Ask my Uncle Charlie. I think I "Christened" every car he ever owned.

Dr. Kugelmas made "house-calls" in his chauffeured limousine at all hours of the day and night and would charge an extra five dollars for the effort.

When my sister and I got very sick in 1946, he walked into our bedroom and from the doorway, took one look, and diagnosed us with Pneumonia.

He wanted to put us into the hospital since we both needed "shots" every four hours morning, noon, and night. But my Uncle said "NO!". He insisted, and I do mean insisted, the nurse show him how to give the shots, (in the rump) and he did it for the duration of our illness.

When we finally got better, around Christmas I think, he went out and got drunk. (Or so he says.) He was quite a guy!

Once, I fell on my head doing somersaults on the awning supports of the apartment house up the street at 267 Ovington. I walked home, but felt nauseous and dizzy. I laid down in bed and began to throw up.

My mother called Dr. Kugelmas and, as usual, he came by limo and told her that I had a hemorrhage of the brain. He said if it had been any worse, I'd have had to go to the hospital, but treated me with medicine instead.

It worked fine and I had no lasting effects. There are those, however, who, over the years, have voiced their doubts.

Back when I had Pneumonia my mother used to make some sort of chocolate shake or malted. There may have been medicine in them, but they were the best tasting shakes I ever had.

We usually drank them off a collapsible easel/chalkboard which folded out and could be used as a tray.

On the top of this easel/chalkboard was a scroll of bright illustrations of the alphabet, trains, planes, buses, ships etc. to use as models for drawing on the chalkboard or pieces of paper. I really loved that easel/chalkboard.

Chapter Two

SCHOOL DAYS

O ur Lady of Angels School was/is located on 74th Street between 3rd and 4th Avenues in Bay Ridge. The church is next door and faces 4th Avenue between 73rd and 74th Streets.

The school was run by The Sisters of Charity of Halifax, Nova Scotia, but most of the nuns seemed to have come from the Boston area.

SCTV once did a quick promo for a fictitious series called "Baa Bah Black and White Sheep Squadron" about a group of flying nuns in World War II.

They showed all the cast members, flying in formation, dressed in nun's habits, preparing to roar into battle.

Rotund John Candy portrayed one of the "Aero Nuns" swooping down on the enemy with a lit, stubby cigar clenched in his teeth.

The possibility seemed all too real to those of us who had gone to a "Catholic School" in their youth.

Any squadron so comprised would be more than a match for any enemy on land, at sea or in the air. God help those poor devils.

The nuns we had were all powerful. They routinely controlled and instructed anywhere from 50 to 65 students in the four "Rs" and all other subjects.

The extra "R", of course, was "Religion".

Every so often, one of those other subjects would be "Music".

They taught us all about "G" clefts and beats to a measure as well as the history of our grade composer and his works.

We would learn about Schubert, Beethoven, Brahms, Liszt and Chopin, but we never heard a note of their actual music.

The only time we produced music ourselves, was in the 5th grade when Sister Elizabeth Marie tried to teach us to play the harmonica. Some in the class actually became pretty good at it. (I did not) Vic Raimo, who went on to high school with me at La Salle Academy, was about the best, as I remember.

The first real exposure I had to classical music was not from school, but from "The Lone Ranger" radio show.

In later years, I learned what most of the pieces used on the show were.

I was not too surprised that they were the works of our class composers, whose music we had never heard.

Talk about missing the spirit of the exercise!

Those cues, as well as the music from the movie serials "Flash Gordon Conquers the Universe" and "Don Winslow of the Navy", helped give me an appreciation for classical music that I still have to this day.

One reason that we never heard any of the music was that there was only one "Victrola" (not phonograph, hi-fi or stereo) in the whole school.

It was a piece of curved reddish-brown wood cabinetry on wheels that stood about four feet high and was passed around from class to class.

It had a rounded lid that covered the turn table which had to be cranked, by hand, to allow the records to play.

Years later, I saw one of those monstrosities in the Northport, Long Island Town Museum. It was in great shape, and I couldn't help but wonder if it was the same machine.

In 1946, my very first day of school ever, was a momentous one, to say the least.

I had never been to kindergarten, so everything was brand new to me. The sights, the sounds, the smells, the other children, the nuns and the classrooms were all new and exciting sensory experiences.

I mentioned the "smells" because, to this day I can recall the aromas of the books, pencils, ink, and crayons, as well as the disinfectant used by the custodians. I even remember the freshly scrubbed, starched scents of the nuns themselves, providing a heady and lasting impression.

I don't think I had ever even seen a nun before and didn't quite know what to make of them. (Penguins?)

I had never seen women (I was pretty sure they were women) dressed like that in all my five years and eight months of existence. They were clothed in black from head to toe with large rigid white bibs covering most of their fronts above their midsections.
On their heads they wore a black head dress with a veil that hung down their backs to below their waists.
These head dresses were slighted peaked in the back and were trimmed with more of that same rigid material framing their faces.
Their collars were about two inches high and made of the same substance.
Around the waist, they were a large pair of rosary beads, which reached down almost to their knees.
Winter, Summer, Spring and Fall, they wore these outfits no matter what the temperature.
All this, plus the fact that, as I later learned, they all were subject to "woman trouble" every month, surely added to their discomfort In retrospect, no wonder they tended to be a trifle cranky at times.
They were very strange creatures, indeed!
On that fateful first day, I had settled in pretty well for the morning's activities.
Seat assignment, distribution of school supplies, use of the cloak-room, as well as arrival and dismissal routines all went well.
At twelve o'clock I went home for lunch.
After lunch, I returned to my brand-new school and lined up in the boy's schoolyard, with my new classmates, to go back to class.
I sat down in my previously assigned seat and prepared to partake in the afternoon's academic rituals.
All at once, the teacher said "Why are you here? You don't belong in this classroom, get out of here and go across the hall to the other class."
I started to explain that I had been here in the morning, but this nun wouldn't listen.
"Don't you talk back to me, mister. You belong across the hall."
I tried once again to tell "Sister" that I had been there before lunch, but got nowhere.
I spent the next fifteen minutes shuttling back and forth between the two first grade classrooms, trying to convince somebody where I belonged.
They eventually checked the class lists and found I was right all along.

I remember thinking that if this is what it's like on the first day, this is going to be a long haul indeed!

Needless to say, nobody ever apologized.

The only other thing I remember about first grade was that every day at two o'clock sharp, the McGarry twins, a boy and a girl, would, without fail, simultaneously wet their pants.

The next eight years spent at OLA were both pleasant and not so pleasant.

The lessons I learned, the friends I made, the nuns themselves and my growing up in a very nurturing environment were parts of the good times.

But sometimes the harsh realities of life would intrude.

One day after school, my friend, TOMMY NACINOVICH, offered me a ride home on his bicycle.

Tommy lived on Narrows Avenue, one block away from Shore Road and the Belt Parkway. It was over three quarters of a mile away from school, and at the very northwestern-most geographical edge of the parish.

Remember, these were the days before busing, so Tommy would ride back and forth to school on occasion, rather than walk.

Only Joan Petrino lived further away, on the corner of Shore Road and 69th Street. (Only non-Bay Ridgers called it Bay Ridge Avenue.) (I used to wonder how she got to school?)

I lived a lot closer to OLA and could walk home every day.

For whatever reason, I turned down Tommy's offer.

It was very fortunate that I did.

On his way home, Tommy was hit by a taxi cab at the corner of Ridge Boulevard and 73rd Street.

Tommy's thumb got caught in one of the door handles of the cab and it was almost ripped off his hand.

Luckily, they were able to re-attach Tommy's finger and he eventually recovered about 90 percent of its usage. It could have been a lot worse.

I've often wondered what would have happened had I accepted Tommy's ride?

Would we still have been hit by the cab or would we have missed the taxi completely, because of the extra weight and the slower pace?

One more note about Tommy and another of his bicycles.

We went to Woolworth's "5 and 10" on Fifth Avenue one day and bought some school supplies and other stuff.
When we came back outside, his bike had been stolen.
We searched the neighborhood, but had no luck.

Some of the nuns themselves made lasting impressions on me over the years.
Three of those who spring to mind were Sister Cresentia, Sister Miriam Agnes and Sister Mary Arthur.
Sister Cresentia was a very elderly woman who taught one of the two first grade classes from the beginning of time, or so it seemed.
For her 50th anniversary as a nun, the whole student body turned out for an outdoor assembly in the girl's schoolyard to honor her.
There were some short speeches by Monsignor Edmund O'Reilly, our pastor and a staunch Yankee fan, as well as other members of the school staff.
The highlight, in my opinion, was the song made up by one of the younger nuns to commemorate the occasion.
The song went like this:

> Sister Crecentia, we greet thee today
> On this occasion all hearts are gay
> Fifty long years in the service of God
> Sister of Charity!

I only heard that song once, but it's remained in my memory all these years.
The second nun to make an impression on me was Sister Miriam Agnes.
She too was an older woman and once told us of an exciting time in her life.
It seems Sister was teaching at another school, when a fire broke out.
The fire spread rapidly and threatened to trap some of the students on the second floor.

The stairwell was engulfed in flames and in danger of collapse.
According to the legend, Sister Miriam somehow managed to hold up the stairs while the children ran down and escaped.
(Some of the wise guys in our class decided that the true story was that she held up the burning children while the stairs ran down.)

I remember Sister Miriam Agnes for one other significant event in my life.

One day, I must have done something wrong and Sister Miriam hauled off and belted me right across the face. I had never been hit like that by any-one before in my life. It wouldn't be the last.

People always talk about nuns hitting people across the hands with a ruler, or with a pointer, twisting ears, or even pulling a girl's hair.

These things may have happened, but I never saw them.

I only saw students (both boys and girls) being smacked right in the chops.

Most of the time, we probably deserved it. (Most of the time)

To this day, on cold winter nights, the imprint of Sister Miriam Agnes' right hand still magically manifests itself on my left cheek. Only kidding!

I can remember having stepped out of line the day before a Parent Teacher's Conference.

I had paid the price and knew that my mom would get a bad report.

I also knew I would have to pay again.

I hid myself across the street from our apartment house on the steps of a two family brownstone house, awaiting my mother's return.

My mom came walking down the street with what seemed to be a weird, strange looking smile on her face. I thought she had snapped.

Thought I to myself: "I am gonna die!"

I finally summoned up enough courage to cross the street and face the music.

To my amazement my mom said that my teacher had told her that I was doing very well, was well behaved, and was a pleasure to have in class.

This came from a woman who, the previous day, had assured me, after giving me a healthy whack, that I was to doomed to eternal damnation plus two weeks.

Go figure.

The third teacher who made a great impression on me was Sister Mary Arthur.

She was our teacher for our entire eighth grade year.

Usually we would have two different teachers for any given year.

We would have one nun starting in September and a different one when we returned from Inter-Term Recess in February.

(The classes would be identified as 7A and 7B, for example.)

It was only in the eighth grade that a teacher would keep a class for the whole year.

Sister Mary Arthur was a great teacher, but not a woman to trifle with. She was a firm disciplinarian, and proved it on more than one occasion. I was always intrigued by the fact that, every so often, a wisp of blond hair would creep out from under her head dress and onto her forehead.

I guess I never considered the fact that nuns had hair too.

With that blond hair, she somehow reminded me of Richie Ashburn, the great centerfielder of the Philadelphia Phillies in the 1950's.

They had one thing very much in common. They both could really hit. The difference was that while Ashburn was a "Punch and Judy" singles hitter, Sister Mary Arthur was pure power.

To her credit and to my mother's eternal gratitude, she managed to extract a 90 average at graduation from Mrs. Lane's little boy.

Believe me, it wasn't easy.

I was a bit of a day dreamer and had an aversion to doing homework. Sister did her level best to cure me of these maladies with what is now called "tough love".

There was one occasion I remember that I thought was finally going to be the end of me at Sister Mary Arthur's hands.

To this day, I owe my life to Margaret McCormack.

One day, as we were preparing to go home for lunch, Sister told us to bring crayons back to school to work on a project of some sort.

This directive, of course, completely slipped my mind.

When I returned to class, I was the only one out of sixty kids to have forgotten his crayons. Sister Mary Arthur was not happy.

When she asked me why I didn't have my crayons, I did the only thing I could think of to save my soul; I lied.

I told her that I didn't have any crayons of my own and that I tried to borrow my sister's box, but she wouldn't let me use them.

Mary Arthur, who knew I wasn't telling the truth, decided to send for my sister, Betty, who was two years behind me in school.

Margaret McCormack was the girl Sister selected to fetch my sister and seal my fate.

A few minutes later, Margaret and my sister returned.

These were undoubtedly my last moments on earth.

When Sister asked Betty what had happened, she told exactly the same hairy fairy tale as I had.

Now, Sister knew it was another lie; Margaret knew it was a lie; my sister knew it was a lie; I knew it was a lie, and even the other 58 kids in the class knew it was a lie, but what could Sister do?

I didn't care.

All I knew was that, by some miracle, my life had been spared.

It seemed that Margaret had a crush on me and had told my sister what to say and that my very existence was at stake.

I am eternally grateful to Margaret to this day.

As for Sister Mary Arthur, she eventually moved on and wound up in the Boston area as the head of some Sisters of Charity Organization. Tommy Nacinovich keeps in touch with her and at last report, she was in good health and doing well.

As for Richie Ashburn, he finally made it to the Baseball Hall of Fame in 1995. It was long overdue.

He was truly one of the finest ballplayers of his time.

Three reasons it took so long were the other great centerfielders of that that era who were lucky enough to have played in New York as opposed to Philadelphia. They were, of course, Willie, Mickey and the Duke.

If there is a Hall of Fame for nuns, Sister Mary Arthur deserves to be elected to it on the first ballot.

This was a great lady. Thank you, Sister.

Believe it or not, we never had a gym class in all my years at OLA.

And for that matter, I never had one when I went to high school at La Salle Academy at 44 East 2nd Street Manhattan either.

We did venture up to the gym on the top floor of OLA on a couple of occasions, but not to play basketball or do exercises or any strenuous physical activity, instead we learned to dance the "Shebelgar".

I have no idea where this God forsaken folk dance came from, but one of the nuns decided that it was an absolutely necessary part of our education.

One enjoyable activity associated with OLA was the "Cub Scouts" and later the "Boy Scouts.

We belonged to Den 2 of troop 277 and Mrs. Val Nacinovich, Tommy's Mom, was our "Den Mother" and we would meet regularly down at Tommy's house for our "den meetings".

Tommy really got into the spirit of "scouting", and advanced through all the levels of, "Wolf", "Bear", "Lion" and "Webloes".

He also earned the "Ad Altare Dei" medal, the highest honor given to Catholic Boy Scouts.

Tom subsequently went to "Regis" high school, M.I.T, and studied in Europe for a number of years, eventually winding up working for IBM.

Me, I'm still a "Wolf".

As part of our endeavors we would periodically put on "skits" for the parents "Troop Night", which were held downstairs in OLA's basement in an area referred to as the "Pine Room"

I think the "Holy Name Society" used to hold their meetings there too. One of the skits we put on I think was something called "The Lighthouse Keepers Daughter".

Nobody in our den wanted to play the daughter.

But Mrs. Nacinovich seemed to have her heart set on doing the skit.

Finally, reluctantly, I was convinced to tackle the part, because otherwise we couldn't do it.

"Big Val", as my Mom used to call her, made a wig out of bright yellow yarn woven into "pigtails" as part of the costume.

I don't remember much about the plot, but in it I had to run up and down the light house staircase several times to, I guess, warn my "father" about one thing or another.

The way we did this was to have me run around in a circle to simulate the trips up and down the stairs while the narrator, Val, related the story.

I looked absolutely adorable in my wig, long skirt and blouse.

The only other time I appeared "on stage" at OLA was in a production of Charles Dickens', "A Christmas Carol".

Naturally, I played "Tiny Tim" because I was the fourth smallest kid in the class and two of them were girls.

I only had one line: "God bless us, everyone!"

There were just two performances and I must have been lousy, because somebody else took my place in the second show.

I said that that was the only other time I appeared on stage at OLA.

I was wrong.

My friend, AL LIPARI, and I decided to put on our version of "Flash Gordon".

Somehow, we convinced the powers that be to let us go ahead, sight unseen, with our epic.

We thought we were just going to do it in our classroom, but as fate would have it, our teacher (Nun) thought it would be nice to use the auditorium and invite the whole school.

It was a disaster.

Tommy Nacinovich, as "Ming the Merciless", giggled uncontrollably throughout the whole gig, and Charlie Byrne forgot all his lines.

We shot the wrong guy in the big action scene, so we closed the curtain and did a "do over".

After the show, my teacher, on the verge of apoplexy, hissed at me: "Don't you EVER do anything like that again!!!!"

I never have.

Al Lipari was responsible for at least one other significant moment in my young life.

My Mother, during those early years, was a terrible cook.

Val Nacinovich eventually taught her how to cook and she became pretty good at it.

But up until then, it was tough sledding.

I never understood why anyone liked chicken, spaghetti and meat-balls or even hamburgers.

Chicken was boiled and the skin would hang off, while hamburgers were always overcooked to the point where ketchup was the only way to introduce any moisture into the equation.

Spaghetti was more of the same.

It consisted of "Muller's" egg noodles, a can of tomatoes, some sort of "Borden's" or "Kraft" grated cheese and salt and pepper.

The meatballs were smaller, rounder versions of the all too familiar hamburgers which I had come to know and loathe.

When I took, Gail, my wife to be, to meet Aunt Nora and Uncle Charlie for the first time, my Aunt served, you guessed it, the spa-ghetti and meatballs for which my Mom was famous/infamous.

When my Aunt left the room for a moment, I told Gail, "This is what I was talking about".

She now understood.
I can only surmise that this gourmet delight must have been a very old family recipe that hopefully died when the two sisters passed away.
Rest in peace and good riddance.

Getting back to Al Lipari.
We were rehearsing our "Flash Gordon" saga in the basement of his house one afternoon, when supper time rolled around.
I was getting ready to leave when Al invited me to stay for dinner.
He mentioned that they were having SPAGHETTI AND MEATBALLS!!!
I broke into a cold sweat.
Anything but that, I thought.
Inasmuch as we had not quite finished what we were doing, I reluctantly accepted his invitation.
We sat down at the dining room table and his mom gave me a very large serving of the dreaded substance.
I gingerly took a fork full of the pasta and could not believe the taste.
What is this, I wondered?
Surely this can't be spaghetti.
I then tried a piece of the meatballs.
They were even better!
I briefly considered asking the Lipari's to adopt me, but I thought that it might not sit too well with my Mom.
There would undoubtedly be a lot of paper work involved and I didn't want to put her through that.
Such was my first experience with "honest to God" Italian food.
Thanks, Al!

I spoke about our Grade Composers earlier in this chapter, well, in addition we also had a "Patron Saint" every year.
As I think back, there are only two that come to mind.

The first was Saint Isaac Jogues who was tortured and finally killed by the Iroquois Indians in New York about 1646.
The other was a man with the incredible name, "Saint Polycarp of Smyrna".
I remembered nothing about this gentleman, but never forgot that moniker.
I also didn't have the faintest idea what or where Smyrna was.

Many years later, I happened to mention his name to my wife who was praying to Saint Joseph with a request.

She thought I had made him up, but I assured her he really existed.

In fact, I suggested she pray to him instead of Saint Joseph.

I reasoned that Saint Joseph surely had millions of people praying to him, while old Polycarp most likely had a much smaller clientele.

"One Saint, no waiting!" was the way I put it.

Wifey gave Polycarp a try and I think her prayer was answered.

She tried again on a number of occasions, but came up empty.

I think she thought he only had that one effort in him.

I looked up Polycarp in the Encyclopedia and learned that he was a disciple of Saint Paul and was the Bishop of Smyrna, Turkey.

He lived to the age of 95 when he was martyred.

I thought:

"If they had just waited a little longer, he probably would have keeled over on his own." "Why go to all the effort?"

I still wanted to know if there was more to learn about the man, so I went to our local "Religious" store up the road in East Northport.

I hoped I might even find a picture of the old gent.

I entered the store, approached the lady at the counter and told her the purpose of my visit.

She looked at me strangely and said she would have to check with her boss.

A few moments later, they both returned from the back of the store and her boss asked me if I were pulling their leg.

He had never heard of Saint Polycarp either.

I assured him I was not and related the story of my past contact with the good gentleman in question.

He took out a book with the names of all the known Saints in Christendom.

Sure enough, there in the index was the listing for Saint Polycarp of Smyrna on page 763.

I thought to myself: "Vindication at last!!"

We turned to the back of the book.

It only went up to page 760.

Chapter Three

P.S. 102

A lthough I attended Our Lady of Angels School, a great deal of my childhood was spent at our local Public School, P.S. 102.
It was/is located on Ridge Boulevard between 71st and 72nd streets.
When we played ball, we never went up to OLA and seldom went down to the Shore Road "diamonds" to play baseball.
This was due to the fact that OLA had very small schoolyards and Shore Road was, as I said before, a bit of a trek.
The Girl's Yard was bigger than the Boy's, but neither was really big enough in which to play softball and there were no backboards for basketball.
As a result, I naturally migrated to the closer P.S. 102 to play ball.
Our neighborhood summer games were softball, stickball and punch ball, all of which were played in the concrete schoolyard at 102.
I didn't start playing softball on grass/dirt until about 1961 with Remington Rand-Univac on Randall's Island in upper Manhattan.
The schoolyard gates were always locked on the weekends so it was necessary to climb a fence and duck under the strands of barbed wire at the top.
The best punch ball hitter was a kid named Cameron who, along with others, would carry a glove in his pocket that he would wear on his punching hand.
I'm not sure whether the glove was cloth or leather. (I seem to remember it being cloth) I'm also not sure whether "Cameron" was his first or last name. Such things were not important when we played.
Cameron dressed rather shabbily, but I suppose we all did back then.

Who cared?

ROLF LANDE, who lived in my apartment house, (apartment C-41, I think) was also. pretty good. Me, I was so-so.

Getting back to softball, I played on 102's Summer Center under 5-foot team.

This is the way they differentiated among the players, under 5 foot and over.

My friends, TERRY HATCH and JIMMY "Wiggles" DONNELLY, were both tall as kids, so they played on the over 5-foot team The players on my team included Robbie Weissfield (2b), Bobby Lento (p), Stevie Marks (1b), and Bobby Campbell (of).

These last three referred to themselves as "The 3 Comets".

I was pretty fast myself and was a little insulted not to be included.

I eventually raced Stevie down at the Shore Road diamonds and beat him.

Stevie insisted on having a relatively long race, from the infield of one of the diamonds to the path bordering the hill on the Shore Road side of the ballfields.

It doesn't look all that far now, but when you're 12 years old and under 5 feet, it's a long way.

I initially played 3rd base, sort of.

I was just learning the game and somebody told me to charge everything.

It led to some interesting plays, errors and bruises.

When Stevie outgrew the team, I switched to 1st base and in the process eliminated a great number of exciting throws that used to emanate from the vicinity of 3rd.

Later on, I started playing centerfield, just like my dad, and since Duke Snider was my favorite Dodger, I liked that just fine.

Besides playing for the Summer Center team, we'd play whenever we could.

Sometimes, we would play as many as three or four games a day.

To quench our thirst during the games, we would buy bottles of soda from a candy store called "Scherrin's" on 71st Street off 3rd avenue. You usually only had to buy one soda early in the day. You would get other ones by collecting the empty bottles left by the older kids and returning

them to the candy store for their two-cent deposit.

The older kids were too cool to return the bottles themselves.

Sodas only cost a dime so, with just a few bottles, you could drink all day.

It should be noted that we shared the bottles we drank from, only wiping the mouth of the bottle with the palm of your hand before drinking and passing it on to the next guy.

So much for sanitary health concerns!

The sodas we drank were: "Mission" Orange and Lemon-Lime, as well as "Hires"

Root Beer, and "Pepsi Cola". They came in 12-ounce bottles, while "Coca Cola" only had 7-ounce bottles.

"Mission" is long gone and "Pepsi" had, as I remember, a different taste back in those days.

"Pepsi" was the best whenever you would shake it up for use in "Fizz Fights".

It was so big and had so much gas, you couldn't lose!

As for the schoolyard itself, there were two fields you could play on.

The "official" field for our team had home plate next to the auditorium and the left field fence along 71st Street.

When we played on that field, the right field fence reminded me of Ebbets Field in that the bottom eight feet was made of wood on top of a three-foot concrete wall. It was backed by the normal cyclone fencing, which continued up for another 12 feet or so.

Bobby Lento's house was just to the right of this right field fence, so that long foul balls hit down the line would sometimes break his windows.

Bobby later married Ann McCormack, Margaret's younger sister and a friend of my sister, Betty.

They still live in that same house, after all these years.

The other field was used by everybody else.

Home plate was by the right field fence (near Lento's house) and had a curiously located basketball pole and backboard (no hoop) right by the pitcher's mound.

A pitcher would have to avoid this pole as he went through his motion.

Right field also had a pole with a backboard but no rim either.

I never saw either of these poles used for basketball and often wondered why they never took the damn things down.

When I took my son, Bobby, back to the neighborhood in 1987, they were gone.

Left field on this diamond had one other notable quirk.

The left field fence was too close for the men who played there, but there was another smaller school yard beyond that fence, which extended back for an additional 100 feet or so.

This forced teams to use an "over the fence" outfielder to cover that area.

They still played with nine men because anything hit over the now very short right field fence was an out.

When we weren't playing, I would sometimes go and watch the men play.

Some of the men used to play with cigars stuck in the corner of their mouths.

The guy (I think his name was "Al") who made the biggest impression on me played shortstop with one of those cigars in his mouth and a New York Giants hat on his bald head.

My perception of Giants fans ever since has been of tough, cigar chomping ballplayers who seemed to be made out of leather.

Years later, I played with Lee Mazzilli's uncle, John, who did nothing to dispel that feeling formed in childhood.

Believe it or not, I actually got into one of those men's games back then.

I was sitting on the concrete wall, watching their game, when one of the players got hurt and couldn't continue.

That left one team with only eight players.

To finish the game, they needed somebody to play the field.

I don't know if someone had seen me play before or if they had seen me having a catch on the sidelines.

At any rate, they asked me if I would like to play. Of course, I said yes. Maybe they were having some fun at my expense. I didn't mind in the least.

I believe the score of the game was pretty lopsided, so I probably couldn't have affected the outcome, no matter what.

They put me at first base and I actually caught a couple of throws for putouts on ground balls hit to short.

One of the throws was bad and I had to stretch low and far to my left to make the play and save an error. (Pretty heady stuff for a 12-year old!) I think I even got an at bat, but I'm not sure.

If I did, nothing noteworthy must have happened because I would have surely remembered that too.

Such was life in the school yard.

Margaret McCormack and I once got in a lot of trouble at 102.
Somebody broke into the school one weekend and after a while,
when the police didn't show up, my curiosity got the best of me.
I went inside to see what a public-school classroom looked like.
I was amazed at all the supplies and equipment they had.
They had a wood working shop and lots of clay for modeling as well as
tons of new textbooks, notebooks, crayons, pens, pencils and chalk.
We had nothing like that in Catholic school.
In fact, some of the textbooks I had were used four or five times
before I got them.
I knew this because on the inside front covers of these books was a
paper label with all the names of the people who had these books
in the past.
I even recognized some of the names.
After a few minutes, I went back outside and went home.
That Monday we were called into the Principal's office in OLA and
accused of being the ones to actually have broken into 102.
Margaret got very upset, as I remember. She was crying hysterically
and gasping for breath at the same time.
They threatened to expel us, but we both steadfastly proclaimed our
innocence and maintained that we had done nothing wrong.
After a while, they let us go, left us alone and we never heard any
more about it.
It turned out that two other kids named Bobby Gartner and Harold
Gottlieb were supposed to have broken into the school and blamed
us to save themselves.
Recently I heard that Margaret's older brother, John, may have been
involved too.
I never found out for sure.

There were other denizens of the school yard who made lasting
impressions on me.
One was Ray Hodget who, because of the similarity of his name to
Gil Hodges of the Brooklyn Dodgers, (whose middle name was Ray)
would pattern himself after the Dodgers' fine first baseman.
Ray himself played shortstop, as I recall.

He would never swing at the first pitch and would go to great lengths to announce his intentions in that situation.

Every time Gil hit a home run for the Dodgers, Ray would treat it as a personal triumph.

Another individual was Roy Thompson, who I seldom actually saw play. It always seemed that Roy was being groomed by his father, or coach, for bigger and better things.

I recollect being amazed, as a kid, with Roy's long and sinewy, vein emblazoned arms.

Speaking of Roy's arms, he once demonstrated his throwing ability by launching a ball from the court yard of John Johnson's four-story Ridge Boulevard apartment house, over the roof and into the street on the other side of the building.

It was, at the time, very impressive.

A year or so later, I found I could duplicate the feat.

Donny Craig was a kid a few years older than I, who became a really good "windmill" pitcher.

He always wore a red baseball cap whenever he pitched. Most of us never wore any head covering at all.

I ran into Donny in our local ice cream parlor, (Hormann's on 3rd Avenue between 69th Street and Ovington) and he told me he used to chew two packs of "Dentyne" gum, whenever he took the mound. Donny considered it his trademark.

Tried it once myself; almost burned out my mouth!

I played with Donny many years later by which time his waist line had expanded sufficiently to justify his nickname of "Buddah".

But even then, he was one tough pitcher.

In fact, I considered him to be one of the two, if lesser, of the local neighborhood "Living Legends".

The other was Georgie Aamand (sic), "The Reindeer".

More about him later.

There was one other player who made a truly profound and lasting impression on me back then.

I only saw him play once and I believe his name was also "Roy", but I could be mistaken.

Roy, if that was his name, had lost an arm playing on top of the old freight cars on the spur line to the Brooklyn Army Base.

That was the legend, at any rate.

At one time, long before I was born, it was called the Bay Ridge Branch of the Long Island Railroad.

As I remember it, he had a bad temper and was somewhat bitter. Can't say I'd blame him.

The way he would compensate for his lost arm was to flip the ball into the air, tuck his glove under his stump, catch the ball and throw it a la Pete Gray of the St. Louis Browns.

When he went to bat, Roy would hold the bat in his remaining hand and HIT THE HELL out of the ball. He was incredibly strong.

Roy was a little on the chunky side though, (a few too many beers?) unlike Gray, who was thin as a rail.

But whatever he looked like, he was somethin'.

The first over the fence home run I ever hit in softball was a lazy fly ball to left field at 102 that must have soared all of 140 feet.

I can still see Bobby Campbell, the left fielder, leaping against the fence, trying to catch the ball, which at this time must have been traveling straight down. A classic "scrape the paint off the back of the fence" blast.

Other things come to mind when I think of 102, that had nothing to do with playing ball.

The first was how, on the last day of school before Summer Vacation, the students would come out of the building throwing their books in the air destroying them.

If anybody had attempted to do that at OLA, they would have been immediately struck by lightning and condemned to Hell.

Since OLA had finished up a few days earlier, (We obviously hadn't had any time off for the Jewish holidays) I would go and wait for my friends to begin the summer.

The second was 102's School Custodian who had a red blotchy birthmark on his face. I never did know his name, but he was a nasty guy.

As you can see, I spent many days playing ball in that school yard.

It was time well invested and it kept us out of trouble.

It's funny though that whenever the people across 71st would complain about our playing stickball, the police would come and force us to stop and get out of the school yard.

Then they would take our stickball bats (broom handles "appropriated" from unsuspecting neighbors) and drop them down a manhole cover. Another crime wave nipped in the bud!

A truly heinous offense, that stickball.

Nevertheless, JOHN CUFF, a good friend who lived in my apartment house, and I would play stickball whenever we got the chance.

It was John who taught me the basic concepts of baseball.

He would be the Yankees and I would be the Dodgers.

I think John won most of the games, but ultimately that didn't matter, it was the fun we had that counted.

John later became a priest and was eventually assigned to the Vatican for a long time.

He left the priesthood after many years, married and raised a family.

That kind of surprised me because, even as a kid and an altar boy, John seemed destined for the priesthood.

For Christmas and for his birthday, he would often receive a Sunday "Missal" or some other religious book or artifact as his presents.

I, of course, chose to stick with gun and holster sets, hockey sticks, baseball equipment, and trains. (Does that make me a bad person?)

Coincidently, John's altar boy partner, Jim Hewitt, got married to Eileen Tubman, who was one of our 1954 classmates, even though he had graduated with John the year before in '53.

It should be noted that sometimes when we played at the summer center, they would insist we use Board of Education bats and balls.

The bats were clubs, fit for a Neanderthal, and the balls were one of two very different types; sponges and cannonballs.

The "sponge balls" would be o.k. for about 2 innings, and then they'd become egg shaped.

All line drives became wobbly knuckleballs and grounders would bounce in 4 different directions before reaching the infielders.

The "cannon balls" were my first experience with guided missiles.

They hurt when you threw them, they hurt when you hit them and they hurt when you caught them.

But they hurt most of all when they hit you!

The reason they gave for using these Board of Education balls was that they were rubber covered and obviously much safer. B.S.!!!

The best thing you could do when one of these projectiles was launched in your direction was to leave town.

The real ball of choice was the "Clincher" which, at the time, cost less than a dollar.

We'd all chip in and buy a ball and use it until the cover came off, sometimes, longer than that.
The money to buy that ball very often came from those empty soda bottle deposits that the big guys were too cool to redeem.

Chapter Four

BASEBALL AND BASEBALL CARDS

One of the prime activities of the summer was the collecting, trading, "flipping" and "pitching" of baseball cards.

I assure you it wasn't the money grubbing, dog eat dog, materialistic, high finance, frenzied industry it became in the 1980's.

It was just the fun activity of striving to get a complete set of cards containing pictures of the ballplayers you heard on the radio, saw on television or at the ballpark.

As I mentioned before, we in Bay Ridge had the added thrill of having many of our own Brooklyn Dodgers living among us.

I really didn't become aware of baseball until 1952, and that was the year most of us in the neighborhood starting collecting.

That year there were two main sets of cards available, a 252 card "Bowman" set and the fabled 407 card "Topps" set.

In the beginning, most of the kids favored the Bowman set due, at least in part, to the fact that the cards were smaller and easier to handle.

There was always a good natured, and sometimes not so good natured, rivalry between John Cuff and I to see who would get the complete set of Bowman's cards.

I can still remember the day John called up to me from the center court yard of our apartment house to tell me he had done it.

There were no (zero) phones in in the entire building, except for one on a table downstairs in the lobby.

Can you imagine? Only one phone for SEVENTY-FIVE families!

It wasn't even a pay phone and, as I remember, it didn't have a dial on it.

If you wanted to make a call, you would pick it up and ask the operator for the desired number.

When there was an incoming call, whoever was passing by the table would pick up the phone, walk out to the vestibule and ring your bell.

They would next walk into the center courtyard and yell up to you. You would then run down the 5 flights of stairs, walk across the lobby to the phone and answer your call.

Hopefully, the person on the other end hadn't died of old age.

This situation only lasted a few months before people started getting their own phones.

I guess the phone company hadn't gotten around to wiring our building.

Getting back to John and the Bowman set.

For weeks he had been close to completing his collection, but I was only a few behind in the hunt.

Finally, it came down to one card: Number 67.

While John was stuck needing just that one, I was creeping closer and closer until I lacked merely three for my set.

We both needed Number 67 and neither of us had any idea who that might be.

By following the pattern of teams within the set, we were fairly sure that the player in question was a Chicago White Sox.

John thought it might be pitcher Sandalio Consuegra or somebody else whose name I can't recall.

Then on that fateful day, John called up to my window from the inner court-yard and uttered the depressing words, "I've got the set!" My heart sank, but I recovered enough to inquire, "Who is it?"

John told me it was "Jim Busby" an outfielder for, as we suspected, the Chicago White Sox.

I made up my mind, right then and there, that I would do everything in my power to complete my Topps set first.

As fate would have it, once again, it came down to one card.

John told me he was going to trade cards with a kid named Richard Addio who lived on Ovington, but on the other side of Third Avenue. Since it was a block away, I had no reason to know him even though we all went to OLA albeit a year apart.

We went to Richard's apartment house and John began to trade with him.

In the midst of John's looking through Richard's cards, I noticed a card that didn't look familiar, but I wasn't sure.

Because it was John's trade, I felt it was only courtesy to wait until he had finished his dealings. (That was not always the case with some of my other friends when positions were reversed.)

When John indicated that the trading session was over, I asked to see the card in question once again.

Sure enough, it was the card I needed for the set; "Jim Wilson", a pitcher for the Boston Braves. (The Braves didn't move to Milwaukee until 1953)

I completed my trade and bided my time until John and I got back down-stairs and then it was my turn to say, "That gives me the set!"

John was surprised and told me that he had a number of "Jim Wilson's" and would have gladly let me have one, had he known.

He was a good friend.

Now, I should point out one thing about the Topps set.

The "set", as we knew it, consisted of 310 cards and was widely dis-tributed early in the summer.

This was the "set" I had completed.

But, one day in late September, I happened to stop in "Otten's" ice cream parlor on Third Avenue between 68th and 69th streets.

A friend and classmate, Kevin Farrell, used to hang out there and I might have gone to meet him.

Kevin wasn't there and, for no particular reason, I bought five cent pack of Topps and opened it up.

Staring back at me was "Glenn 'Rocky' Nelson" of the Dodgers. blinked twice and turned the card over.

It was No. 390; A new set!

These were the "High" numbers that are so valuable today.

They included the cards of future Hall of Famers Roy Campanella, Jackie Robinson, "Pee Wee" Reese and, of course. the "Holy Grail" of Topps baseball cards, Mickey Mantle.

This new set ended with card No. 407, still another Hall of Famer, Eddie Mathews.

I quickly realized it would be in my best interest not to say anything about my discovery, at least until I completed this new set.

I didn't have the money to buy the whole box and probably never even considered it. Not very bright, was I?

Eventually, of course, the secret got out, but to my knowledge, that was the only store in our neighborhood that had those high numbers. I never did complete that new set, but I'm pretty sure I had more than one of those "Mickey Mantle's". If I only knew!

The legendary reason for the scarcity of this last set was that Topps didn't think they would sell at that late date and dumped them into Bay Ridge Harbor. ("The Narrows") If THEY only knew!!

There is one more thing to be said about my experience with baseball cards in 1952.

There were two ways to win cards from other kids; "flipping" and "pitching".

"Flipping" entailed matching your opponent's card tosses.

It could involve anywhere from one to two or more cards.

You would hold a card lengthwise in your hand, swing your arm underhand, releasing it and spinning it down to the ground.

If you did it right and were consistent with your motion, you could make the cards land either heads or tails up, more often than not.

If you held a card in the fingers and palm of your hand and flipped it correctly, you should be successful.

When you looked at the card in your hand and saw "heads", it should land "tails" up and vice versa. Try it sometime.

I could hold my own "flipping", but "pitching" was my undoing. It was similar to "pitching pennies", but involved cards instead.

The idea was to get your card closer to the wall than your opponent. You could also win by getting a "leaner" against the wall or by landing on top of your buddy's card.

Billy Royall was another good friend and classmate of mine, but he must have won over $34,000,000 from me, at today's prices, pitching cards.

My style, if it could be called that, was more flinging than pitching. But Billy could really pitch.

No matter how good a shot I made, Billy would, routinely and effortlessly, beat me good.

To be able to use his style, you had to have fingernails and good-sized hands. I had neither.

I finally mastered "pitching" at the age of 49, so if Billy is still out there, I'm ready for him…I think.

Chapter Five

THE BROOKLYN DODGERS

As I've mentioned before, quite a few of the Dodgers lived in Bay Ridge during the baseball season.

Duke Snider lived at 176 Marine Avenue.

Pee Wee Reese lived in Barwell Terrace, a few steps above 97th Street.

Carl Erskine lived on Lafayette walk, off of 94th Street.

The others I was aware of, "Preacher" Roe, Bobby Morgan, "Rube" Walker, and Russ Meyer were all adopted sons of Bay Ridge in the '50's.

Bill Antonello, of course, required no adoption proceedings, he was a born and bred Bay Ridger.

I know there were others, such as Clem Labine and Ben Wade, but I never found out where they lived.

It's too bad since Clem Labine, in particular, was a personal favorite. I managed to run into Clem, in later years, at card signings that I attended with my son, and he was as nice as I could have hoped for.

But, all the Dodgers of that era were very friendly and accommodating. That was not the case with the Yankees.

John Cuff's dad took me to a couple of games up at Yankee Stadium during the 1953 season.

It seemed to me that the Yanks went out of their way to avoid signing autographs outside the Stadium after the games.

The players would, almost to a man, exit the clubhouse carrying something in both arms and brush through the small crowd awaiting them.

I really didn't care too much since I was a Dodgers' fan, but I felt kind of sorry for those kids who did.

I found out later that most of the Yankee players actually lived in NEW JERSEY!!! That must have explained it.

The first "Dodgers" memory I can recall came in October of 1947.

When my Uncle Charlie returned from the service, he and my Aunt decided to build a house out in the wilds of Flushing. (Actually in "Fresh Meadows".)

I remember driving out to their new home in my Uncle's new "Dodge" on the day "Cookie" Lavagetto broke up Bill Bevan's no-hitter in the 4th game of the World Series that year.

My Mother and my Uncle were listening to something on the car radio.

Suddenly my Mom started screaming: "Cookie, Cookie, Cookie!" when the big moment arrived. I had no idea what was going on.

(I'm fairly certain we were just passing the settlement of "Quonset" huts that had been erected for the returning veterans and their new families next to the Belt Parkway, across from "Plum Beach".)

I'm sure I didn't know or care a thing about baseball at the time.

I just remember my Mom going crazy.

Me, I threw up!

The next memory occurred a few years later in 1951.

I was at my friend RICHIE GIUSTRA's house on 77th Street, between Ridge Boulevard and 3rd Avenue, reading comic books.

His two older brothers, Frank and Peter, were downstairs listening to the radio.

Richie's father, Frank, was a Doctor and they lived in a BIG house.

Doctor Giustra had his office on the left side of the house, off a main hallway, on the first floor. (The office had its own entrance.)

There was a narrow, curving, back stairway which led from the kitchen up to the second floor.

I guess it was supposed to have been used by servants, back when the house was built.

(I don't remember the Giustra's having any servants of their own)

Richie and I spent most of our time either up on the third floor or down in the basement.

It seems that Richie and his family had gone out to dinner the night before to the "Hamilton House" on 4th Avenue and 100th street.

They ran into the Dodgers' left-hand pitcher "Preacher Roe", who gave

NATIONAL LEAGUE CHAMPIONS

Kingpins of the National League for the second straight year, the Brooklyn Dodgers won the flag in one of the most dramatic pennant finishes of all time. Manager Walt Alston relied on his "old pros" to gain the coveted final victory. But two men, Don Newcombe and Sal Maglie, were mainly responsible for the Dodgers emerging winners as they hurled clutch triumphs time and time again.

Here are the champs of the senior circuit:

In the front row (l. to r.): Sandy Amoros, coach Joe Becker, coach Billy Herman, coach Jake Pitler, manager Walt Alston, Pee Wee Reese, Clem Labine, Carl Erskine, Dixie Howell, Gil Hodges, Carl Furillo.

In the second row (l. to r.): traveling secretary Lee Scott, Duke Snider, Sandy Koufax, Chico Fernandez, Char-

Le Neal, Gino Cimoli, Ken Lehman, Randy Jackson, Jackie Robinson, Dale Mitchell, trainer Harold Wendler.

In the third row (l. to r.): clubhouse custodian John Griffin, Rube Walker, Ed Roebuck, Don Drysdale, Roger Craig, Don Newcombe, Junior Gilliam, Sal Maglie, Don Bessent and Roy Campanella.

In back of 1956 sign, batboy Charlie Di Giovanna.

them all an autograph.

Now, at the time, I still didn't know baseball from a hole in the wall, so I'm sure "Preacher Roe" was just a name to me.

The following day, while Richie and I were upstairs reading comics, I was vaguely aware of a radio playing somewhere in the house.

His two brothers were listening to the Dodgers' game and they were both asking out loud, "Why don't they bring in Preacher?"

As it turned out, Roe was injured and two other pitchers were warming up in the bullpen, whatever that was.

A few minutes passed while Richie and I went about our business, not at all aware of the progress of the game.

Suddenly, we heard blood curdling screams coming from the room where the radio was still playing.

We ran down to see what in God's name was going on.

We thought that someone had been killed or at least badly injured.

As we entered the room, we saw both brothers standing there in tears. When we asked them what had happened, they sobbed uncontrollably, "BOBBY THOMPSON, RALPH BRANCA, HOME RUN, GAME OVER, DODGERS LOST!!!" I had no idea what they were talking about.

The following year, 1952, was the first one in which I began to take an interest in baseball myself.

I learned the rules of the game from John Cuff, began to collect baseball cards and started to watch games on television.

In the beginning, I'm afraid I was more intrigued by the opening of the telecasts rather than by the games themselves.

WOR Channel 9 (Dodgers) and WPIX Channel 11 (Giants and Yankees) would introduce their games with some clever animated clips showing the home team's caricatures preparing for the arrival of the visitors, whoever they might be.

For the Dodgers, "Quartsy" Schaefer, (The Dodgers' sponsor was Schaefer Beer.) would swing a bat and hit a ball back at the camera. The name of the next opponent would then be displayed on the ball. Channel 11 was even more imaginative.

The "pin headed" Giant's mascot, (as drawn by the greatest of all sports cartoonists, Willard Mullin) would be shown awaiting his next adversary.

In the case of the Dodgers, Mullen's "Brooklyn Bum" would be greeted by the Giant as the "Hobo" crossed the Brooklyn Bridge.

The distinguished "Yankee", (again drawn by Mullin) would greet the out of towners, such as the Washington Senators, who were depicted as classic carpetbagging Southern Politicians.

One of the earliest baseball superstitions I ever developed was the firm belief that, if I watched the game, my team would lose.

I use the term "my team" because, although I was a Dodgers fan, I also watched, appreciated and rooted for the Giants.

It was tough to root against the Giants when they played the Dodgers. I liked them both.

There were places in Brooklyn where such an admission could be extremely dangerous, if not fatal.

The first game I ever attended was with the choir of OLA in May 1952. As fate would have it, the Dodgers played the Giants.

If you had good attendance at daily practice and at Sunday's 10 o'clock Mass, one of the priests of the parish, usually Father McKenna or Father Eckert, would take us to a Dodgers game as a reward.

We usually sat in the upper deck of the left field stands in Ebbets Field.

There was fence in the stands at about the foul pole which prevented fans from migrating to the better seats closer to the infield.

In the game, the Dodgers' starting pitcher was a gigantic lefty by the name of Chris Van Cuyk.

He didn't pitch all that well and was knocked out of the game early.

When the new Dodgers' relief pitcher entered the game, I was shocked to hear the Dodgers fans boo him.

It was Ralph Branca.

The same Ralph Branca who served up Bobby Thomson's pennant winning home run the previous year. The fans had neither forgotten nor forgiven.

Later in the game, Carl Furillo hit a line drive home run that looked like it was coming right at me, but eventually landed in the lower deck.

However, most of the games I went to were with the P.S. 102 Summer Session.

If you saved ten (I think) "Borden's" ice cream pop wrappers, you got a free ticket to the game with the school group.

As usual, we sat in the upper deck of the left field stands.

One of those games was the first game of a Dodgers/Phillies double-header on May 8th, 1953.

The great Phillies pitcher, Robin Roberts, had the Dodgers beaten, going to the ninth inning.

But in the ninth, Dodgers' catcher, Roy Campanella, hit a home run into the lower deck in center field to win the game in dramatic fashion.

I can still see Richie Ashburn racing back to the wall and leaping in vain to try and save the game for the Phillies.

We had a good view from the upper deck since the center field wall angled out towards right field after it joined the left field wall.

As it turned out, the Dodgers used the picture of Campanella nearing the home plate reception of his teammates for the inside front piece photo of their 1954 Yearbook.

In the shot, you can see the dejected losing pitcher, Roberts, crossing the third base line behind Campanella, on his way to the visitor's dugout.

That, however, is not the end of the story In 1990 an acquaintance of mine, Mark Trost, who now works for David Letterman, produced two videos called "Baseball Classics".

Volume I contained the 1952 and 1953 World Series highlight films with Dodgers playing the New York Yankees, as usual.

Volume II featured the 1954 New York Giants and Cleveland Indians World Series.

Since it was a short series with the Giants sweeping the Indians in four games, it was necessary to fill out the tape with additional footage. The extra material consisted of some interviews with players of the era.

The first was Ralph Kiner, the great home run hitter of the Pittsburgh Pirates, a future Hall of Famer and longtime broadcaster for the Mets. The second was conducted by one of the Dodgers' play by play announcers, Connie Desmond. (The other two announcers were, of course, "Red" Barber and a very young Vince Scully.)

The subject of this second interview was Roy Campanella, who would also become a well-deserved Hall of Famer.

In the course of the conversation, they showed a clip of "Campy" hitting a home run into the center field stands in Ebbets Field, in the bottom of the ninth inning, off Robin Roberts, to win the game for the Dodgers.

You guessed it!

It was the same game I went to, way back on May 8th, 1953.
Taken from the home plate area, the clip even shows Richie Ashburn racing back to the wall and turning away as he realizes the ball is gone. What a thrill it was seeing it all again after so many years!

I recall going to a Dodgers/St. Louis Cardinals game with Tommy Nacinovich and his dad, and Tommy insisting we try to get seats in the upper deck on the third base side of home plate.
Tommy reasoned that, since the Cardinals had a lot of lefty swingers, they were likely to foul off a lot of pitches in our direction, and we would undoubtedly catch one. It didn't work.

The first night game I ever went to was a Dodgers/Chicago Cubs contest, and I remember being awed by the dazzling, fairy tale and "Disney"-like colors of the field under the dazzling arc lights.
As I walked up the narrow ramp to our seats on the third base side in the lower deck, the vibrant green of the grass, the blackness of the sky, the whiteness of the Dodgers' uniforms and the rainbow of colors of the advertisements on the outfield walls, are sights I've never forgotten.
The winning pitcher in the game was the Cubs' Warren Hacker, who came in in relief and struck out my favorite player, Duke Snider, to nail down the victory for the Cubbies.
My soon-to-be step father, Joe Hilbert, who took my Mom and I to the game, teased me for a long time about "Duke Schneider" (sic) being bested by Hacker.
In a later game, the Dodgers blasted Hacker, who I actually liked, and the "Duke" launched two monster home runs in the general direction of London, England, to cap the evening's festivities. End of discussion!

The most famous game I ever went to was a Dodgers/Milwaukee Braves game on July 31st, 1954.
By this time, my Mother had married Joe and we had moved to 2115 Ave "O" in the Kings Highway area of Flatbush.
One of our new neighbors, Mr. Lou Fiddler, gave me two third base box seats, four rows from the field.

For some reason, Joe couldn't go, so I called John Cuff back in Bay Ridge and asked him to hop on the subway and meet me at the ballpark.

Travelling by subway, in those days was not the potentially terrifying experience we know today.

In fact, it was the fastest and most convenient way to get around the city.

Prior to the game, during the "visitor's" batting practice, John and I got autographs from Johnny Logan, the Braves' shortstop, and coach Johnny Cooney.

The only other autograph I ever got inside Ebbets Field was from Pittsburgh Pirates catcher named Jack Shepard.

I've since misplaced that one, but I still have the other two.

Once the game started, it quickly became apparent it was not to be the Dodgers' day.

John and I were immediately able to steal third base coach and Dodgers' manager Walt Alston's signals and I'm pretty sure the Braves were too.

The fact that Alston was coaching third was somewhat strange, since that job was usually handled by coach Billy Herman. (Maybe he was sick.)

Johnny Podres started the game for Brooklyn and I remember him standing on the mound, cap over his heart, showing a nice head of sandy blond hair and facing the flag above the right field scoreboard for the National Anthem.

He wasn't around much longer than that.

Dodgers' pitchers came and went as the Braves' hitters wore a rut in the infield dirt, circling the bases.

Milwaukee and Dodgers' home runs flew out of the park like migrating geese.

Eddie Mathews hit two and Andy Pafko hit one for the Braves, while Gil Hodges, Rube Walker and Don Hoak each hit one for the Dodgers. Hoak almost had a second one, but had it taken away on a great leaping catch by the Braves' centerfielder, Billy Bruton.

But the biggest hitting story of the day was supplied by the Braves' big first baseman, Joe Adcock.

Adcock clouted a Major League Record tying FOUR home runs and a 3rd inning double, giving him a Major League Record total of 18 bases in a nine-inning game.

As a matter of fact, he almost had a FIFTH homer.

The double he launched, hit three quarters of the way up the eight-foot left field wall, just missing another round tripper.

Not a bad afternoon's work!

That record stood for almost 50 years, longer than both Babe Ruth's and Roger Maris' season home run records, and until the "steroid" era.

The story has an interesting Post Script.

The following day, on his first trip to the plate, Adcock doubled off Dodgers' righthander, Billy Loes.

On his next at bat, Adcock was beaned, good and proper, by Clem Labine.

as if to say, "Stop it, Joe, you're not that good!"

I mentioned that a number of the Dodgers lived in our neighborhood. It was relatively easy to journey to their homes, ring their doorbell, or knock on their door and spend a few moments talking to them after getting their autograph.

They were always very cordial.

"SPORT" magazine ran a great color picture of Duke Snider in their September 1954 issue taken by "Ozzie Sweet", undoubtedly the best sports photographer of his era.

I was a subscriber to the magazine and when I received my copy in the mail in late July, I practically flew down to the "Duke's" house on Marine Avenue to ask him to sign the photo.

When I got there, a couple of young girls were presenting him with a cake on the sidewalk in front of his house.

I thought it might be Duke's birthday but I wasn't sure.

At any rate, "Duke" signed the picture and chatted with all of us for a few moments, saying that he had not seen the picture before.

After I left "Duke's" house, I walked a few blocks east to "Pee Wee" Reese's home in Barwell Terrace, a few steps above 97th Street.

I knocked on "Pee Wee's" door and after a few moments he came to the door, licking chicken off his fingers.

As with the "Duke", "Pee Wee" couldn't have been more gracious.

He signed his picture that I had gotten from a previous issue of SPORT and spoke with me for a short time before returning to his meal.

My next stop was at Carl Erskine's house on Lafayette walk off 94th Street.

As I approached, Carl was leaving his house carrying his son, Danny, in his arms.

I told Carl that I would come back some other time for his autograph, but he said it would be no trouble and he would be happy to sign now.

He signed his "SPORT" photo and asked if he could see the other color pictures that I had removed from earlier issues and placed in an album.

He thumbed through the portraits until he came to one of the great St. Louis Cardinal slugger Stan "The Man" Musial.

At that point he exclaimed, "Oh, that guy!" and closed the book.

I ran into Carl many years later at an autograph session at Hofstra University and related the story to him.

He told me that, surprisingly, he had a very good lifetime won and lost record against the Cardinals. (Something like 14 wins against 6 losses) I said to him, "You pitched Musial that well?"

He said, "Nope, I pitched "Red" Schoendienst and Enos Slaughter that well and avoided Stan Musial like the plague!"

In the course of the conversation, Carl told me that, in the 1950 game in which Gil Hodges hit four Home Runs against the Braves, he also got four hits.

He described the hits as follows.

The first was a sacrifice bunt that died on the foul line, the second was a broken bat single over first base, the third was a bloop that barely reached the outfield grass and the fourth was a routine ground ball to third that hit a rock and went over third baseman Bob Elliott's head.

Carl had written about this in his book, "Tales from the Dodger Dugout". What wasn't in the book was the story of his fifth at bat.

It seems Carl hit a vicious line drive to left center and Sid Gordon, who was not a particularly good fielder, made a great running catch on the blast.

The only time he got good wood on the ball, Carl came up empty. There ain't no justice!

There's one other story about my going to a player's house for an autograph.

A friend and I, (I think it was Tommy Nacinovich) went to the house of Bill Antonello, a reserve outfielder on the 1953 pennant winning team.

Bill's dad was the superintendent of an apartment house on Ovington Avenue, a few blocks from where I lived.

We rang the bell on Bill's apartment door and his mom answered.

We asked if Bill was home and if we might get a couple of autographs.

Mrs. Antonello said that Bill had gone to the park with his daughter and would be back in a little while.

Seeing that we were disappointed, she invited us in to wait for his return.

We were given milk and cookies and listened to her stories about Bill when he played for Mobile in the Minor Leagues.

Bill never did return, and after a while, we thanked Mrs. Antonello and left.

What a nice lady!

Can you imagine anything like that happening these days?

There is one more baseball memory I recall, which has nothing to do with our beloved Dodgers.

Mr. Fiddler, who had given me the tickets to the "Adcock" game, also gave me a couple of "freebies" to an exhibition game at the Polo Grounds, between the Giants and the Boston Red Sox.

I believe it was held to promote the "Fresh Air Fund" charity of the Daily Mirror newspaper.

I don't remember much about the game itself other than the fact that the Giants won and that Paul Giel (The former University of Minnesota quarterback) pitched 4 or 5 innings and got credit for the win.

After he finished his work for the night, Giel made his way to the distant centerfield clubhouse by following the first base stands and right field wall on his way to the showers.

All along his route, the Giant fans gave him a nice little round of applause for his efforts as he passed.

But the most vivid memory of all happened before the game itself.

Prior to the game the teams competed in a home run hitting contest.

Each team would have 5 batters who would get 5 fair balls each to see who could hit the most homers.

The Giants who participated were Willie Mays, Bobby Thomson, Henry Thompson, Monte Irvin and Dusty Rhodes.

The Red Sox included the immortal "Splendid Splinter", Ted Williams and 4 other guys I don't recall at all.

Ted had recently returned from his 2nd tour of duty as a Marine Corps pilot and was making what would be his only appearance in the home of the Giants.

Mays hit one, Monte Irvin hit two and nobody else on either team hit any until "Number 9" stepped into the batter's box.

On the first pitch, Ted hit the ball into the upper deck in right field.

On the second pitch, Williams blasted the ball over the right field roof.

The third pitch landed in the upper deck in right center.

The fourth offering cleared the roof in right field once again.

Then, something really strange happened on the fifth pitch of the at bat.

Ted actually hit a FOUL BALL, yes, a FOUL BALL into the seats in right field.

Mr. Williams was not happy!!

On the sixth pitch, Ted took out his revenge on the little white base-ball, hit it over the roof in right center and sat down.

The Giant fans roared their approval for one of the sport's all-time greats.

Williams had often expressed his desire to be perceived as the greatest hitter to ever play the game.

He made a believer of me that night.

Chapter Six

LA SALLE ACADEMY

During the eighth grade, we at OLA began to apply to the various High Schools in the area.

The area, however, included all of Brooklyn, Manhattan, some of Queens and even Staten Island.

Today, application is made via a consolidated test and the marks forwarded to the schools of your choice.

In our day you had to travel to the individual schools and take their own personal entrance exam.

This necessitated availing ourselves of the wonders of the New York City Rapid Transit System; i.e. the Subways.

I must have gone to about 15 different schools.

Fortunately, I gained acceptance to all of them, so I had my choice.

About the 11th school I went to, was a rinky-dink little building on the lower east side of Manhattan, more precisely, the Bowery.

Don't ask me why, but as soon as I walked into La Salle Academy at 44 East 2nd Street, I knew that this was the place I wanted to go.

I've talked to any number of my Fellow Alumni over the years and they, almost to a man, said they felt exactly the same way.

There was just something about the place.

The other schools I applied to included, Power Memorial, St. John's Prep, St. Francis Prep, which at the time was located in the Williamsburg section of Brooklyn, St. Ann's, which would later become Malloy and relocate to Queens as did St. Francis, St. Agnes and Xavier, the military school.

I even think I went up to Mount St. Michael in the wilds of the Bronx, but I'm not sure.

St. Peter's was located on Staten Island and I had to take the old 69th Street Ferry to get there.

On most of these excursions, I would travel with a couple of my class-mates who were going to take the entrance exam with me.
On rare occasions, I would be the only one headed for a given school.
This was the way I learned to navigate around the city.

Our Subway line in Bay Ridge was the 4th Avenue local which began at 95th Street and traveled into Manhattan via the tunnel under the East River.
There were two express lines to which you could transfer at the 59th Street and 36th Street stations respectively and get to the city faster via the Manhattan Bridge.
They were called the Sea Beach and West End and both originated or perhaps terminated, depending on your point of view, at Stillwell Avenue in Coney Island.

Getting back to La Salle...
As I mentioned in a previous chapter, about a dozen of my OLA class-mates wound up at 44 East 2nd Street along with me.
These included Kevin Farrell, Matty Monahan, Brian Flaherty, Tommy Convey, Ed Phelan (who later became a Christian Brother), John Malloy, John Keenan, Bill Donovan, Vic Raimo, John McCann and Jimmy Hass.

Once at La Salle I joined the school's Track Team.
Fortunately for me, the Catholic High School Athletic Association (CHSAA) had made accommodations for smaller participants.
They divided runners into three weight divisions; Sub-Midget, (under 100 lbs) Midget, (under 110 lbs) and Junior (under 120 lbs).
The rest of the runners competed with one another regardless of weight.
Since I tipped the scales at about 95 lbs as a Freshman, I qualified as a Sub Midget.
Our Sub-Midget relay team was pretty good, but Rice, Cardinal Hayes, All Hallows. St. Francis and Loughlin had teams that were as good if not better.

My relay mates were usually Gene Corcoran, Henry Cahill, and Phil Kelly.

The first medal we ever won was up at Fordham University in the Bronx, Manhattan and Westchester Meet. (The BMW's)

This meet was held on a banked indoor wooden track, outdoors.

We managed to finish in third place, winning a bronze medal.

Ed Kelly, one of our teammates, took a Polaroid (Remember them?) picture of me breaking the tape at the finish line, winning our heat.

Based on our time, we earned the bronze besting all but two of the other teams in the other heats.

That medal was the first of five we won that year.

Our Freshman team as a whole was truly a great one.

The 880 Relay team was the best in the city.

Don Durdaller, Jim Savage, Dave Futrell and Jack Waring made up that stellar quartet.

There were times when each of them would compete as individuals if we had a chance to win a Championship.

In the CHSAA Indoor Championship held in February, we did just that! Don won the 50-yard dash, Jack won the 100, but the star of the meet was Dave Futrell. Dave won the Shot Put and the High Jump and ran the third leg on the gold medal winning 880-relay.

I first met Dave outside the Field House of the East River Drive Track after La Salle's Freshman Field Day back in September.

Dave, who was black, had run against my classmate John Callaghan in the meet.

Dave was seated on a park bench with his back to the East River Drive when I exited the Field House. I had to wait for one of my friends who was slow showering, so I sat down next to Dave and we began to talk.

Brennan crosses the finish line.

Warming up before the big race.

La Salle

Track

1958

First Row: D. Coluccio, R. Bell, A. Fontaine, H. Cahill, D. Durdaller, W. Zayas, E. Blake, E. Chanda. Second Row: J. Waring, M. Supple, B. Austin, M. Kozoriz, N. Singleton, B. Stader-
man, W. McKeown, B. Lane. Third Row: J. Ramirez, J. Cor-
dova, D. McEntee, B. Brennan, D. Futrell, W. Faustino, J.
Raimo. Fourth Row: R. Stalzer, R. Santangelo, , Chimenti,
J. Collins, P. Walsh, Lamoreaux, E. DiBiasi, P. Maloney.

I didn't realize it at the time, but our class was one of the first in the
school's history to be integrated.
Dave and I became good friends, (He used to call me "Smedley")
and years later I was one of the few white people at Dave's wedding.

Dave and Charlie Alias were our pioneers and both good guys.
Unbeknownst to any one, Charlie, who played on the basketball
team, was a world class drummer/percussionist as well.

Charlie professionally went by the name "Don" and toured with Eartha Kitt and others as well as playing at the Newport Jazz Festival while still in his teens.

Some of the notable artists with whom Charlie/Don (His middle name) performed and/or recorded with were Miles Davis, Herbie Hancock, Nina Simone, Roberta Flack and Joni Mitchell.

When he passed away in 2006, Drummerworld Magazine gave him a glowing Tribute as one of the greats.

In my Sophomore year, I still weighed under 100 lbs. and as such still ran as a Sub-Midget.

We had some new guys on the relay team and didn't fare as well.

Luckily, I was able to garner a couple more medals in the 50-yard dash and the high jump.

I finished second in the indoor BMW's 50 (Held outdoors again) and second in the High Jump in the CHSAA's held in June.

The High Jump medal involved A bit of "chicanery" on my part.

The official who was keeping the record of the jumpers, lost track of the heights cleared by each contestant.

He then made the mistake of asking me if I had cleared a certain height.

The height in question was one I had never cleared in my whole life, so naturally I answered, "Yes".

The result turned out to be: Second Place!

CROSS COUNTRY TEAM—Mr. J. Marone, B. Lane, J. O'Donnell, H. Cahill, W. Brennan, R. Stalzer, D. Coluccio.

They're off and running at V.C.

On your mark!

It wasn't until the following Monday that Brother Anthony, one of our Track Moderators, caught up to me in our 3rd floor hallway and told me I had "won" a medal.

As it turned out, the meet directors had lost the medal in question, so I had to go down to Dieges and Clust Jewelers on Fulton Street to collect my ill-gotten hardware.

Indoor and Outdoor Track were run in the Winter and Spring.
Prior to that, in the Fall, it was Cross Country up at Van Cortlandt
Park in Riverdale.
I didn't run X-Country in my Freshman year, I don't know why,
but I didn't.
Come Sophomore year I started to run the 2 ½ mile Varsity course
over hill and dale.
In the Manhattan meet I actually finished 10th in a field of over
a hundred.
In many of the meets, however, the number of runners was signifi-
cantly larger.
The top five finishers on each team were counted and used to deter-
mine the meet's champions.
The first to cross the finish line was awarded 1 point, the second 2
points, the third 3 points and so on.
Total low score determined the winning team.

Most of the time I was the 4th point scorer for our team in our
Senior year.
Henry Cahill, Bill Brennan and Danny Collucio were usually the
first three.
The others making up the team included Karl Stalzer, John Cerino,
Danny Moloney, John O'Donnell and John Crowley at one time
or another.
Our sprinters didn't care for X-country at all.
I enjoyed it.
One thing I could never get through my thick skull was that to post
a really good time you had to run hard across the opening, flat, first
500 yards before getting into the various hills.
Call me stubborn.

Once in the hills, I would consistently pass runners, but without
being in the front of the pack entering those hills, I couldn't make
up enough lost ground to register a better time. (Hind sight is 20/20)

We actually won the 1958 Manhattan meet as Henry and Bill finished
first and second respectively.
Bill was very intense (and a little crazy) so it was a source of irritation
to him that he could never beat Henry.

Henry eventually became a Christian Brother, but left the Order after about 10 years to become a teacher up in Nyack, New York.

We still get together at our class Reunions and remain friends to this day.

SUB-MIDGETS FOREVER!!

After Sophomore year, I would occasionally get lucky and win a medal from time to time.

I won my last medal in my Senior year running the 120-yard low hurdles.

As it turned out, I had brought a lovely young lady to the meet with me. I made sure I got into a heat I knew I could win, never thinking about the possibility of a medal.

Sure enough, things went as planned and I breezed through my heat in fine fashion.

The young lady was witness to my triumph, having stayed with my friend and teammate, ED CHANDA, while I was down on the track.

It started to rain after I had showered and changed and we were getting ready to leave when Brother Peter, our Track Moderator came up to us and told me I had indeed collected some hardware.

No one was more surprised than I, but I played it cool asking Brother Peter to please bring the medal to school on Monday, since the young lady and I were both getting wet and couldn't wait around to get the award.

Outdoor Track — 1958

K. Stalzer

D. McEntee

J. Waring

D. Maloney

D. Durdaller

B. Lane

Rounding the crucial turn

On your mark, Get set* ——

Relay Team

Austin passes to Fontaine.

The long reach—so short, yet so far.

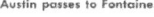

D. MALONEY   N. SINGLETON   W. BRENNAN   D. FUTRELL

I was trying to give the impression that winning a medal was no big deal and almost a weekly occurrence. Yeah, right!

Speaking of "Brothers", there were a few who stand out in my mind.

Brother Cormac (Godfrey) was a fine teacher, one of the school's assistant basketball coaches and as tough as nails.

Whenever a foolhardy individual would incur Cormac's wrath, he would lob a piece of chalk across the classroom at the offender.

The recipient would then have to return the chalk to the front of the class where Cormac was waiting.

While the victim was making the trip, Cormac turned into JAMES CAGNEY, complete with all the twitches and gestures of Cagney's screen persona.

Next, Cormac would remove his watch and place it gingerly on his desk.

He would then begin to speak softly to the offending scholar while periodically smacking him across the chops to help emphasize the error of his ways.

Many referred to this as "Cormac's Hit Parade", a list on which you did not want your name to appear.

When the message had been conveyed, Cormac would resume teaching and the newest member of the "Parade" would return to his seat all the wiser for the experience.

I first ran into Cormac in Sophomore year when he was my Latin teacher.

At the time, I was having trouble at home with my Step-Father and would often not go home after the day's track practice, but would rather hang around the school until late at night and then take the Subway home.

The Brothers would leave the lights on in the gym for me although they would sometimes say to me, "Go home, Lane, it's past your bedtime."

Occasionally, one of them would venture down to the gym and play some basketball with me. (I wasn't very good)

One day, Brother Cormac said he would give some extra points to anyone who could correctly translate a passage from "Julius Caesar's Gallic Wars".

I was a pretty good Latin student and got it right.

The deal was that I could either have 10 points on the Monthly report card or 5 points on the Quarterly one.

I opted for the 10 points.

Cormac told me, "You do realize that 5 points on the Quarterly are worth more than 10 on the Monthly, don't you?"
I told him I was aware of that fact, but I needed the 10 on the Monthly.
"What do you mean you need them?" he asked.
I explained that my Step-Father insisted I maintained a 90 average or I could not continue to run on the Track team.
"Oh, really", replied Cormac.

A week or so later La Salle held its Parent Teachers Night.
When Cormac met my parents, he asked them if it were true that I had to, in fact, carry a 90 average to remain on the team.
They said yes, that was the case.
Cormac then said, "Get off his back, he's doing just fine."
My mother commented, "I don't like you very much."
"I don't care if you like me or not, get off his back." was his reply.
End of conference.

Brother Cormac was an ardent Yankee fan, so when the 1955 World Series came down to the 7th and final game, he assured us in no uncertain terms that the Bronx Bombers would emerge triumphant.
"These are the Yankees were talking about, they just don't ever lose to that team from Brooklyn!"
Quite a few of our school's population, however, came from Brooklyn and in spite of history, they hoped for once he would be proven wrong.

The Dodgers had faced the Yanks 5 times in the World Series over the decades and had lost them all.
They fell to the Yankees in 1941, 1947, 1949, 1952 and 1953.

The next day, after Johnny Podres had shut out the Yankees 2-0 to finally bring the Championship home to Brooklyn, Brother Cormac was not in a cordial frame of mind.
Someone had taped the back page of the Daily News with Willard Mullin's depiction of the "Brooklyn Bum" mascot saying "Who's a Bum?" to the door of our classroom.
Brother Cormac was not amused.
"Take that down... now" he whispered, pointing to the drawing.
It was immediately removed.

Another Brother who made a lasting impression on me was Brother Conrad, the Vice-Principal during my Freshman year.

Brother was a very slim, almost frail, soft spoken and bespectacled individual.

He would make the afternoon announcements over the P.A. system prior to dismissal in a very quiet voice.

He was also one of the Brothers who would come down to the gym while I was killing time in the evening before heading home.

I had noticed that Conrad didn't wear sneakers, but rather high top, black leather shoes, which I took to be Referee's footwear.

One afternoon one of the students in my class named Roach, was giving a new young teacher a lot of grief.

Roach stormed out of the classroom to the lockers which lined the walls outside in the hallway.

Through the glass panel in our classroom door, we could see Brother Conrad approaching Roach.

Suddenly, we heard a tremendous uproar, but it was out of our sight.

Something or someone had crashed into the line of lockers.

We all thought Roach had killed Brother Conrad.

The door opened and the next thing we saw was Brother Conrad dragging Roach along the floor by the scruff of his neck back into the classroom.

"Take your books and desk down to the Custodian and have him throw them in the furnace, you're out of here!" hissed Conrad through clenched teeth.

It turned out that he was, at one time, the Lightweight Boxing Champion of Buffalo, New York, hence the black shoes.

Brother Conrad is still alive out in California and good buddy, Bob Conner, keeps in touch with him.

The other Brother of note was more a legend than a teacher.

Brother Cajetan Rock was a rather an eccentric individual.

Whenever he would fill in for an absent faculty member, chaos would ensue.

Brother Cajetan possessed a paralyzed pinky finger on his right hand. When he "disciplined" you, he would use both hands on either side of your head.

In doing so, the paralyzed digit would invariably wind up in your left ear.

It became a "Rite of Passage" in La Salle to "Take two, Phony Gom!" from the "Cat Man".

To this day, I haven't the faintest idea what "Phony Gom" means. Nobody else does either.

One day, Cajetan was subbing as a Math Teacher and having a difficult time with one of our guys. (I think it was Patrick Henry)

In frustration, Cajetan exclaimed, "Henry, you're so stupid, you can't even count" and continued "How many fingers am I holding up?"

Henry, who was a VERY bright guy, immediately responded, "Four and a half, Brother."

"Come here, friend" replied Cajetan and promptly initiated Henry into his fraternity.

Believe it or not, the school still sells T-shirts with Brother Cajetan's picture on them. He was loved.

The years I spent at La Salle were four of the best in my life.

Being a member of the Track Team afforded me a certain identity within the student-body.

Not that I was that good, but it allowed me to belong to a special group of guys that truly represented La Salle in the finest sense.

It was an honor, a privilege and my pleasure.

I'll always be a La Salle "Cardinal".

Chapter Seven

SUMMER VACATIONS

E very year, or just about, my Mom would manage to take us on
a vacation.

Nothing spectacular, mind you, just a few weeks away from the heat
of the city in July or August.

Our apartment was on the top floor of our building, and as such we
were right under the black tar paper roof that capped our three-
room abode.

In the summer, that roof would soak up and absorb all the heat of
the summer sun, and I do mean ALL of it.

It wasn't too bad in the early evening because most of our time was
spent outside, either downstairs in the street or up on the roof itself.

Needless to say, there were no such things as "Air Conditioners" to
alleviate the discomfort.

On the roof there might be a stray breeze or two to cool you off, at
least somewhat, but that was it.

The only two places in the neighborhood that were blessed with A/C
were the "Loew's Bay Ridge" theater and "Lowen's" drug store on
the corner of 69th Street and 3rd Avenue.

A large number of our neighbors spent many an evening at the movies.

Sooner or later, however, you had to go home and try to sleep, and
I do mean try.

The windows of our bedroom faced north, but most of the winds all
seemed to want to come from the south, east, or west.

As a result, we sweltered.

Don't forget folks, these were the days before fitted sheets.

So, as you tossed and turned in your bed, the sheets would stick to your sweaty body and wrap themselves around you.

Years later, I realized for all our uncomfortable nights in that apartment, we never even entertained the thought of buying a God-damned fan!

I know money must have been tight back then, but how much could a fan have possibly cost in those days?

The first recollections I have of our summer vacations were of those spent at "Canaan Lake" in Patchogue on Long Island.

There were pictures of my mother, sister and I, taken when I was about two years old, but they don't ring a bell.

That would make it the summer immediately after my father had died. The pictures are there, but the memories are not.

The Lane Family had been going to Canaan Lake for a number of years, but my memories don't kick in until about 1945.

Even then, the only clear remembrance that survives is that of my Mom and I going to a carnival and riding the Merry-Go-Round.

While we were riding, they played the song "The Merry Go Round Broke Down", and it did just that.

After getting off the incapacitated ride, we went and had our picture taken.

It was a black and white photo, but they tinted it by hand to give the illusion of color.

I saw that picture many times over the years and it always brought back fond memories.

I think the last time I saw the photo was in the '50s at my Aunt Nora and Uncle Charlie's house.

When they passed away, I had hoped to recover it from their belongings, but no luck, it was gone.

I asked Uncle Charlie's niece, Stella, who had been given what few personal possession's my uncle had kept, if she had seen the picture, but she had not.

My Uncle did leave me a couple of things I had asked for prior to his death in 1995. (Aunt Nora had passed away in 1985.)

He left me his two "Seabees" yearbooks from 1944 and 1945 as well as a nice picture of him and his Navy buddies, marching in a parade after the war, somewhere in Queens, I think.

His niece told me that Uncle Charlie was "The throwing out-est person"

JULY 25 1943

CANAAN LAKE
PATCHOGUE
N Y 4 4 9 U

she ever knew, so there wasn't much left.
She also told me that he had given her strict instructions to make absolutely sure I got those two yearbooks. Thanks, Uncle Charlie!

My cousin, PATSY HOWLEY, told my wife, Gail, of a couple of stories which are real testaments to my well-documented stubbornness that occurred during those years at Canaan Lake.
It seemed something had been a source of annoyance to me one morning.
I promptly walked up to the family "outhouse", some distance away, and proceeded to hunker down for an extended stay.
Patsy, who always looked out for me, God bless her, became increasingly distraught as the day wore on.
She finally went to my Mother and voiced her mounting concern.
"He'll come back when he gets hungry" my Mom told her, "Don't worry."
But she still did and eventually I did too.
There was one other manifestation of my "thickness" that Patsy recalled.
One of our other cousins, Barbara, was very bossy.
She had decided on a choice of activities with which I didn't agree.
After some time, Barbara finally pleaded her case to Patsy.
"We're older than he is", she reasoned, "He has to do what we say."
"Forget it, Barbara", Patsy told her, "If he doesn't want to do it, he's just not going to do it. Haven't you learned that by now?"

The next vacations I recall were those taken in a place called "Yulan" in 1947 and 1948.
I refer to Yulan as a "place" because there was no town, just a Post Office, a store called "Times Square", and an "ESSO" gas station about a mile down the road from where we stayed. That was it!
The closest "town", if you wanted to call it that, was named "Eldred" and was about a mile east of the Yulan Post Office.
This bustling metropolis had a supermarket, several stores and even boasted its own fire house. WOW!
The place we stayed at was called "The Yulan Hotel". (How original!)
It was situated on the west side of "Washington Lake", which was about a mile long and about half a mile wide at its widest.
It was a real nice little lake.

For years I mistakenly thought its name was "Highland Lake" and it wasn't until 1986, when Gail and I went back for a look-see, that I saw the light and found out the correct name.

We went to the lake with my Mother's friends from 237 Ovington, Mr. and Mrs. George and Jean Casey.

They were very nice people, and Mrs. Casey was a very pretty lady.

Mrs. Casey was a diabetic and had to take Insulin injections a couple of times a day. (John Cuff also became a diabetic several years later.)

The Yulan Hotel was a pretty neat place from a six or seven-year old's point of view.

The hotel had three or four buildings that made up the place.

There was the long, two story main building, which also contained the dining room and kitchen, and a separate three story "big' building, a few dozen yards north.

The third structure was the brick "Bar and Grill", which is now a private home.

That "big" building was still there when we returned in '86, but it was listing badly and had been condemned and posted as dangerous.

The rest of the buildings had all burned down over the years.

The lake itself was a great place to swim, row, or canoe.

It had a rectangular, multi-level dock enclosing the kid's swimming area and a small beach bordered by a grassy lawn containing several "Adirondack" chairs.

To this day, I don't know how anyone can sit in those chairs.

They are the most uncomfortable things in the world and, once you're in them, are almost impossible to get out of.

Most of the time you were left to your own devices for amusement, with the obvious exception of the water activities of course.

Aside from that, you were pretty much on your own.

One of the almost daily rituals was walking down to "Times Square" for newspapers, comic books, souvenirs etc.

It was about a two-mile door to door to door journey, and provided a leisurely stroll for anyone so inclined.

One incident that was not so pleasant, was when a kid named "Brandon" (I think) tried to drown me by pushing me off the dock.

I don't remember having anything too much to do with this guy, but for some reason he didn't like me one bit.

A group of six or seven people were sitting and standing on the dock, when this curly blond-haired little troll decided to give me a shove into the water.

At the time, I hadn't yet learned how to swim, so I went straight to the bottom, probably only six or seven feet down.

I didn't seem to panic at all until I saw a snapping turtle swim right in front of me.

Forget about the fear of drowning, I was afraid of that turtle.

I looked up to the surface of the water and saw a pair of feet dangling down from the pier.

I managed to push off the bottom and grab one of those feet.

It all happened so fast that no one, including my Mom who was a real good swimmer, had had a chance to react.

It turned out that the guy whose foot I grabbed, couldn't swim either.

After they hauled me out, I was pretty upset once I realized the full impact of what had just transpired.

When I finally calmed down and had changed into dry clothes, I decided to go looking for this little cherub.

After all, right was on my side and I knew that "Justice" must prevail. WRONG!

I came back from that little confrontation with the most beautiful and glorious black eye you ever saw.

So much for the idea of "Justice Triumphant".

It had not been a good day.

The following year, 1949, we took a place in Rockaway, Queens, a block or so from the "Rockaway Playland" amusement park.

We shared a second-floor apartment with a childhood friend of my Mom, Narda Bianchi, and two of her children, David and Diane.

She and her husband, Mario, had two other kids, twins Bobby and Johnny.

The twins were a couple of years older than all of the rest of us, so they didn't spend the summer with us.

The Bianchi's lived on the corner of Troy Avenue and Cortelyou Road, in the "Little Flower" (St. Therese of Lisieux) parish area of Brooklyn and across from Holy Cross Cemetery.

We used to have to take two or three buses to get to their house, and I've already detailed my love for motorized transportation.

It wasn't the most pleasant of journeys.

Mario used to play ball with my Father in "Red Hook" and was a pretty good second baseman.

Mario had lost a leg when I knew him, and there were rumors that he hung around with a nasty crowd and had paid the price for some questionable activities.

I heard, in later years, that he had lost his other leg too.

For a number of years, before and after '49, we would meet up with Narda, David and Diane and go to "Riis Park" for a day at the beach.

This was a journey of epic proportions.

We would get on the 69th Street bus, take it to Avenue "U" and 86th Street, transfer to the Avenue "U" bus and ride it to the last stop, Flatbush Avenue.

We would then wait and try to get on the "Green Line" bus for the trip over the Marine Park Bridge, (now the "Gil Hodges" Bridge), to Riis Park.

Getting on that bus was always a challenge, since it was usually packed.

If things worked out right, we would wind up on the same bus as the Bianchi's, but that didn't happen too often.

They had boarded the bus at its starting point, Flatbush and Nostrand Avenues, where there were men in charge of loading the buses.

No such luck at Avenue "U", where you might have to wait for a couple of buses to go by before you could finally squeeze on.

I don't remember too much about the summer of '49 except for sneaking into the amusement park, lighting all the "Votive" candles in the local Catholic church, St. Camillus, getting sunburned at the beach and being introduced to "Quaker Puffed Wheat" and "Quaker Puffed Rice".

I've never forgotten the scent of those two breakfast cereals.

(It was also the first time I ever encountered green pistachio ice cream)

Another aroma that I'll always remember is the odor of the city dump that ran from Avenue "U" to the bridge.

Thankfully, the bus drivers would drive at a truly terrifying velocity along this horribly scented stretch of road, whenever they could.

I'm sure they didn't like the overwhelming stench either.

Most of the time it was clear sailing, but every once and a while, there was the inevitable traffic jam.

There is nothing quite like being stopped dead on that odorous strip of road on a blazing hot summer afternoon.

It was then that I came to the conclusion that Hell must smell like this, only better. It was brutal!

The dump is closed now and it became the "Marine Park Golf Course".

I played there once and it still stinks, but for a different reason.

The wind that blows off Jamaica Bay allows you to hit mammoth drives in one direction and propels your shots right back in your face in the other.

It was a terrible place to play.

The vacations of 1950 and 1951 were THREE of the best I've ever had. They were spent at "Camp St. Joseph's Villa" outside of Hackettstown, New Jersey.

I say "three" vacations because I went back to the camp twice during that second year.

Tommy Nacinovich had gone by himself the previous summer, and Val, his Mom, asked my Mom if she thought I would be interested in going with Tommy in 1950.

My Mom said she was sure I would, and one July day we got on a bus on East 33rd street in NYC at the Church of the Sacred Heart, run by Msgr.

Joseph Congedo, and headed for the wilds of New Jersey.

I don't think I had ever been outside of New York State in my life, so a trip to New Jersey was akin to going to the moon for me.

The camp was run by the Xaverian Brothers and proved to be a very exciting, enjoyable experience.

The camp got its milk, and I suppose it's vegetables, from a farm directly across the road from the main entrance.

You could usually tell where the farmer's cows had spent their time grazing the day before.

Whether it was by the strawberries or the scallions, the taste of the milk would reflect the appropriate location.

The "Mess Hall" was a large, two story, octagon shaped building in the center of the complex.

It was big enough to seat all the campers at once for every meal.

It was also occasionally used for some other night time activities, such as the camp "Talent Show".

I actually won one year with a very animated version of the "Disney" song, "Bib-a-Dee, Bob-a-Dee, Boo".

I really hammed it up!

I initially wasn't going to take part in the contest, but at the last minute I got up and figured, "What the heck, give it a shot!"

THE SLEEPING QUARTERS AND JUNIOR PLAY GROUND,
CAMP ST. JOSEPH'S VILLA, HACKETTSTOWN, NEW JERSEY.

MESS HALL, ST. JOSEPH'S VILLA, HACKETTSTOWN, N. J.

I even surprised myself that I would "chew up the scenery" like that.

The cabins where we bunked were very long and contained two separate sleeping areas, one on either side of a common entrance. They were broken down so that everyone in the cabin was about the same size and age.
Bunk beds lined both sides of each "dorm", with a wide aisle in the middle where the "Brother" in charge would dole out milk, straight from the farmers can, and cookies at bed time.
The only kids who didn't get any milk were those "Midnight Sailors" who were prone to wetting their beds.
An ounce of prevention...
If you happened to get a top bunk, the easiest, and most dangerous, way to get down was to grasp the wooden side rails and somersault out of your bed onto the floor below.
It was a little scary the first time you tried it, but after that it was no big deal.
Of course, we never told our Moms about this acrobatic dismount. I'm sure they would have been horrified.
In a center area between the two wings was a "wash up" area that you would use to brush your teeth and wash your face.
This atrium had no roof over it and the floor was made up of small white stones that crunched under your feet when you walked on them.
In the middle of this outdoor latrine were several wash stations with a square row of pipes containing eye-high faucets that would only accommodate about eight campers at a time.
You would fill up individual metal wash basins with the cold water, use the bars of soap provided and proceed to wash and brush.
When you were finished, you would dump the soapy water onto the drain table, which was below the faucets, rinse out the pans and place them on top of the pipes, upside down, for the next person to use.

As I remember, there were only two toilets, one for each wing, and one shower.
Primitive indoor/outdoor living at its best!

The camp swimming pool was located about a quarter of a mile down The road from the main camp grounds.

It was a beautiful pool with a shallow wading area at one end and a deeper part, with diving boards, at the other.

You could get certified as a "Red Cross" swimmer if you passed a basic test which entailed crossing the width of the pool and turning around to come back to the starting point.

I wasn't interested in, and perhaps a little afraid of, taking the test.

Tommy, however, did try and succeeded in passing the test.

His approach and style were bit peculiar, to say the least.

Tommy didn't use the Australian crawl, the side stroke, or even the breast stroke; he used the dog paddle.

I can still see young Mr. Nacinovich flailing his way across the water, clumsily traversing the pool, but give him credit, he made it.

If you left the pool early enough, there would be a table set up back at the main campus area that would dole out bread and jelly to all of the returning swimmers.

I didn't like to leave too early, so I seldom got any.

Now that I think of it, it seemed as though we spent a lot of time unescorted in our daily activities.

So, it was not unusual for the campers to walk back from the pool either alone or with just a friend or two, but no staff.

There were no periodic formations to take "nose counts" of the campers, but I don't remember losing anybody either.

The camp boasted its own outdoor "Amphitheater", where, weather permitting, they would show movies, once or twice a week.

Dormitories, St. Joseph's Villa, Hackettstown, N. J.

NEW CHAPEL AT CAMP ST. JOSEPH'S VILLA, HACKETTSTOWN, NEW JERSEY

If the weather was bad, they would use the "Rec" hall instead.

Some of the feature films were interesting, but it was the "Republic Studios" serial chapters that were the best part of the show.

I had seen any number of serials on television back home, but they were either those made by "Mascot" pictures or by "Universal" studios.

The New York stations, all seven of them, had never televised the "Republic" cliffhangers.

As a result, I didn't know anything about the "Republic" productions.

The first "Republic" chapters I saw were from "Dick Tracy's G-Men", including the final chapter where Tracy finally captures the villainous super spy, Zarnoff.

But even better things lay ahead.

One rainy night we had to go into the "Rec" hall to watch the movies.

I almost didn't bother to go since I was not feeling too well.

As the projector began to count down to the beginning of the film, I noticed a frame that said the name of the picture was "The Adventures of Captain Marvel".

Sure enough, when the credits began to roll it was, in fact, Republic's version of the great "Fawcett" comics super hero.

I couldn't believe my eyes.

To this day "Captain Marvel" is almost universally considered the finest chapter play ever produced.

Captain Marvel himself was portrayed by cowboy star Tom Tyler.

What a perfect choice!

Tyler was fully capable of doing the heavy lifting required by the role, and was doubled in the flying sequences by probably the greatest stunt man of his era, Dave Sharpe.

Sharpe went on to double such major stars as Douglas Fairbanks Jr., Tony Curtis and Efrem Zimbalist Jr., in movies and on television.

For my money, he was the best

While I was in camp, I saw the first five or six chapters of "Captain Marvel", but I didn't get to see the rest of the serial for many years.

By far, the single most bizarre activity at the camp was a game called "Smugglers and Revenuers".

I'm not quite sure what the rules were, but it seemed to be an insane version of "Capture the Flag".

The campers and staff would be divided into two teams, one stationed at our "Indian village" near the swimming pool and the other in the main camping area.

Beer cans, with point values painted on them, would be smuggled into the enemy's camp and, at the end of the day, the team that had planted the most contraband in the other's territory, won. I think.

There were also points awarded for the capture of the opposing force's personnel, who were identified by either blue or red arm bands, head bands or whatever.

Cheating was rampant and some of the captures were not so peaceful. The game went on from breakfast to dark, and sometimes longer.

The ultimate prize, of course, was to grab the opposition's battle flag located in the very center of each combatant's stronghold, and very well-guarded.

The craziest attempt I ever saw was when one of the Brothers commandeered a horse from a local farmer and galloped into the Indian village to affect a capture.

I don't think he was successful.

One of the campers was up in a tree as the rider streaked by and I thought for a moment he was going to jump down and try to knock the Brother off his mount.

People, and even groups of people, would get lost for hours hiding from the enemy.

I once ducked into a grove of small trees to avoid being captured and found about a dozen other staff and campers already there.

They had no idea where they were, and neither did I.

How we ever found our way back to camp, I'll never know.

As I said, it was the wildest game ever.

I believe it was eventually banned by the Geneva Convention.

Too bad, it was a lot of fun!

The next two years, 1952 and 1953, were spent in Sound Beach, L.I., with the Nacinovich's.

Sound Beach is located a few miles east of Port Jefferson on Long Island's north shore.

Tom's Mom and his younger sister, "Little Val", along with my Mom and sister, had rented a bungalow from a family named "Di Viglio", while Tommy and I were at St. Joseph's Villa for the two prior years.

The bungalow had two bedrooms, a living room, a small kitchen, one bathroom and an enclosed screened-in porch.

We were about three blocks from the bluffs overlooking the Long Island Sound.

To use the beach, you had to wear a tag signifying that you were a legitimate resident of Sound Beach, if only for the summer.

At the top of the bluff was a canteen where you could buy sodas and ice cream as well as an attached, roofed, family picnic area, complete with a wooden floor, tables and benches.

The long stairway down to the beach was right next to the canteen.

There were about 55 steps going down to the water, and about 817 going back up, or so it seemed.

That whole canteen/picnic complex was swept out to sea, in one night, by Hurricane Gloria in 1985.

The beach itself was typical of Long Island's north shore, not sand, but pebbles.

Once you entered the water, the footing became more treacherous to even the most tough skinned and agile bathers.

Again, not much sand, but a lot of rocks.

Thankfully, the water was, as a rule, clean, fairly calm and easy to swim in.

Yes, by now I had learned how to do the Australian crawl, but Tommy was still doing that dog paddle.

One day we decided to see if we could swim a distance of a mile.

The beach's swimming area was defined by three nylon ropes with plastic or wooden floats attached to them.

We figured that each lap across the waves was equal to about one city block, so twenty laps would constitute a mile.

I don't remember how long it took, but I do remember being very dizzy when I finished.

Putting your face in the water and snapping it to the side every few strokes to breathe over the course of a mile tends to do that.

That's my story, and I'm sticking to it!

If you recall, I mentioned the Dodger's lefty hurler, Preacher Roe, a while back.

Now, ol' Preach was a fine pitcher, but not a good hitter, in point of fact, he was horrible!

One July afternoon in 1953, I was sitting on my bed listening to the Dodgers radio broadcast from Pittsburgh, when Tommy came into the room and sat down.

Roe came to bat, and Tommy said that he thought it would be better if they always made Preacher an "automatic" out.

It would speed up the game a little, Tommy reasoned, and eliminate the possibility of him hitting into a double or even triple play.

"Fat chance", I thought.

The words had no sooner left Tommy's lips when Roe swung and proceeded to hit the only home run of his Major League career over the left field wall in Forbes Field.

The radio announcers went wild, I fell off my bed laughing and wise guy Tommy almost fainted.

After Preacher crossed home plate, completing his one and only home run trot around the bases, his Dodger's teammates paved his way back to their dugout with a plush carpet of white towels.

When they returned home to Ebbets Field the following week, all the Dodger's sluggers, Duke Snider, Gil Hodges, Carl Furillo, and Roy Campanella, presented Roe with a huge bat that they alleged he used to bludgeon his mighty blow.

This was the last vacation our family took before my Mother remarried in the summer of 1954

She married Joe Hilbert, also a fireman, whom she had met through my sister, Betty.

Joe's nephew, Billy(?), was Betty's classmate in OLA.

They had waited until I graduated grammar school before telling anyone, except my sister and I, of course, about their plans.

When they went on their honeymoon, Aunt Nora and Uncle Charlie took the two of us on our own vacation; back up to Yulan.

A number of years had passed, and although we had originally planned on staying at the Yulan Hotel, it didn't work out that way.

The intervening period of time had not been kind to the old place, and my Uncle decided not to stay there.

But this was Yulan and not the Poconos or the Jersey Shore.

We drove up the road a few hundred yards to the only other lodging on the lake, the "Highland Cottage", and checked in.

The cottage was a three-story affair with a porch that fully surrounded the building on three sides.

At the time, I thought the dining room was quite roomy, but when my wife and I visited in 1986, it wasn't large at all.

The cottage rested high on the crest of a hill, with a wide lawn sloping down about 50 yards or so to the water's edge.
(Wifey couldn't resist wiggling her toes in the cold, clear water of good old Washington Lake on the oppressively hot day of our visit.)
The food at the cottage was always terrific and I especially remember the wonderful aroma of the freshly baked rolls at breakfast.
But you had to get to the dining room early since these delicious rolls went quickly, and when they were gone, they were gone.
While we were there, we went to see a couple of movies at the "Riviera" theatre in Barryville, a few miles of west of Yulan on the banks of the "Delaware Water Gap".
Two of the pictures we saw were, "Magnificent Obsession", with Jane Wyman and Rock Hudson, and "The Black Shield of Falworth", with Janet Leigh and Tony Curtis, doubled, of course, by Dave Sharpe! What a treat!

This really was the last of our "Family" vacations.
The places we went and the people we met will always live in my memory and make me wish I could revisit them all over again.
I can't complain though, these vacations were a lot of fun and I'm very, very lucky and grateful to have had them as a wonderful part of my life.
Thanks, EVERYBODY! (Except "Brandon"!!)

Chapter Eight

CAMP GRANT

The two best summer vacations I had in the late 1950's, were spent as a camp counsellor at Camp Grant in Calverton on Long Island. I was CHIEF BOB, first as a Counsellor in Training (C.I.T.) in 1957 and in my second year, 1958, as a full-fledged "Chief".

The Camp was run by the Rotary Club International Organization for under privileged kids from the New York City area.

The Camp was a gift from Jeannie L. Grant to the Rotary club with the stipulation that it was ALWAYS to be used as a boy's camp.

More about that later.

After my Junior year at La Salle, my Mom, who worked for the Kings Highway Savings Bank, made an arrangement with one of the bank's officers to have me work at the Camp.

The camp was located on a bluff overlooking Long Island Sound just east of Baiting Hollow.

The grounds contained cabins for the campers, a mess hall which doubled as a "rec" hall, a main quadrangle, an archery/air rifle range, a ball field, a basketball court, a shower/latrine building and an infirmary.

The counselling staff was made up of high school "jocks" from the greater New York City area and Westchester.

The kitchen staff were all college students from Tuskegee Institute.

The full-fledged counsellors each were responsible for up to eight campers in their own ten-foot square cabin.

The kids slept on removable and washable canvas slings attached to double deck metal racks on both sides of the cabin, while the

"Chiefs" had their own single spring mattress bed in the middle of the sleeping area.
The cabin themselves had large shutters on the front and back of the structure.

These shutters could be propped up or closed, depending on the weather.
Large full screens covered the area inside the shutters allowing some cool ventilation into the cabin.

The swimming area was accessible by a couple of long flights of stairs behind the mess hall which led down to the shore of the Long Island Sound.
For those of you not familiar with the North Shore of Long Island, the beaches are composed mainly of large pebbles, not sand.
The area itself was roped off and divided into three skill determined sections, beginner, intermediate and advanced.
Each section was patrolled by camp staffers (life guards) stationed on eight-foot square rafts at the deepest end of each skill area.
Each area was about 10 yards in length.
The further out you went, the deeper the water and the more proficient the swimmers.
Proficiency was determined by testing and not by age or size.
One of the best swimmers in camp was an eleven-year old named Timmy who swam for the New York Athletic Club.

One afternoon I was assigned to the third raft.
I swam thru the first two areas on my way to my post without stopping.
By the time I approached the final raft, I was fairly tired.
I was about four feet from the raft when Timmy decided to jump off the raft and onto my shoulders.
Timmy caught me between breaths and pushed me about a foot under the top of the water.
I struggled to get Timmy off me and get back to the surface.
I could see the blue sky through the clear water above me, but couldn't reach it with Timmy hanging onto me.
I guess he thought it was a game and not a deadly serious situation.
Finally, a couple of the staffers on duty at the raft jumped in and got Timmy off me.

By the time I pulled myself onto the raft, I was exhausted, but happy to be alive.

I wanted to strangle Timmy, but there were too many witnesses and I was way too tired to strangle anybody.

One of the activities available to the campers was archery.

Surprisingly, I was the only one who knew how to use a bow and arrow.

I have no idea where I learned this skill.

Perhaps it was during my two summers at Camp St. Joseph's Villa or in a previous life time.

At any rate, I became the "de facto" expert/instructor for the camper's archery classes.

Once the class was over, the kids like to watch me shoot at the target to see how many bulls-eyes I could make in a row.

In addition to this I would, on occasion, do some really stupid things For example, I would try to catch an arrow in flight before it hit the target.

To do this I made sure that one of the other counsellors who had become pretty good shots were doing the shooting and that they had no desire to kill me.

There was one other incredibly dumb thing that I did.

A kid named Lester was a real pain in the ass.

No matter what you asked him to do he would disobey and not co-operate.

One day I was in a particularly foul mood and had no desire to put up with Lester's nonsense.

Lester had wandered a short distance away from the archery range and refused to come back.

I warned him that if he didn't return, I was going to shoot him with my bow and arrow.

All the other campers and their counsellors had already left the area so it was just me, Lester and my little bow and arrow.

I let fly with my arrow purposely shooting wide of Lester.

The arrow missed him by a good margin, but skipped along the ground and sailed up through the screen of the Arts and Crafts cabin. The Arts and Crafts teacher, Tony Avila, came running out of the cabin clutching my errant arrow and screaming what an idiot I was.

I must admit, I had to agree with him.
Funny thing though, no mention was ever made of the incident and Lester
never gave me any more trouble.

There were other kids that gave some of the other counsellor's fits.
John Muzzullo had a little camper named Jonathan who took off and ran into the woods next to the camp.
John caught up with Jonathan after a merry woodland chase of about half an hour or so.
The next day John was covered from head to toe with Poison Ivy while little Jonathan was clean as a whistle.

When kids acted up, my C.I.T., Johnny Schroeder and I would threaten our nine/ten-year-old campers with the ultimate punishment: "Face Connecticut".
The offending camper would have to bend over in our cabin and we would swat him on the butt with the flat straw part of a broom.
Nobody ever got hurt, the other kids enjoyed it and the message to behave had been transmitted.

One of the campers I liked best was a 10-year-old boy named Arnie Stevens.
He was a good kid and a natural leader.
I never had to worry when my campers went to an activity without me since Arnie would take charge and keep them in line.
If a kid had a problem of which Johnny and I were not aware, Arnie would tell me and we would do our best to correct it.

Once, a camper named Bobby was new to the Camp and didn't know how to take care of himself.
Arnie came to me and said that Bobby stinks and all his dirty clothes were buried in his duffle bag.
I spoke to Bobby and showed him how to take his clothes over to the Camp's washing machine and then took him into the shower and showed him how to wash himself.
It was his first time away from home and he was very shy and a little scared.
From that point on, nobody had more fun than Bobby.

He really came out of his shell and the rest of the kids came to accept him as one of their own.

Years later I was going out with a girl who lived in the Bronx.
Somehow, at about four o'clock in the morning, I managed to get on the wrong train trying to get home.
I may have fallen asleep and missed my connection.
I realized my mistake and tried to retrace my steps.
I got off at a station somewhere in the Bronx and waited for a train going in the other direction.
I was the only person on the platform, or so I thought.
All of a sudden, a large black man started walking towards me.
I thought for sure I was in big trouble.
When the guy got about ten feet away from me, he said, "Chief Bob?"
It was ARNIE STEVENS who was now a plain clothes policeman!
We spoke for about twenty minutes until my train finally showed up.
I was very proud of that young man.

Three of the guys I became friends with at camp were BILLY MONAHAN, GARRY SPIEGEL and GERRY GERBER.

All of them went to James Monroe High School up in the Bronx.

After the Camp closed for the season, I hung out with Billy for a while, but the trip up to the Bronx from Brooklyn became too much.
Garry was the manager of the Football Team while Gerry was the starting quarterback and Billy was a defensive free safety.

Billy was also a bit of a trouble maker.
Once on his night off, Billy got into a scrap over a girl at a local night spot.
The natives swore they would come up to the camp bent on payback.
Foolishly, I let Billy talk me into hiding out in the woods with him the following night armed with bows and arrows.
Thankfully, the "Townies" never showed up.

Another staff member I hung out with was LOUIE NUNEZ from Saunders Commerce High School up in Westchester.
I was fast, having run on the track team at La Salle for four years, but Louie was BLAZING FAST!
One night, one of the guys had way too much to drink and began to run around the compound in his birthday suit.
I took off after him hoping to catch him before any of the Camp Directors saw him.
I was gaining on the inebriated individual when Louie passed me as if I was standing still.
Louie tackled the streaker and we dragged him back to the showers to try and sober him up.
Boy, that water was cold!!

One of the little traditions of the camp was to help awaken any of the staff who might have over slept and missed the morning formation/head count.
These formations were held every hour or so to find out if any of the campers had gone AWOL and not afford them too much of a head start.

If a staffer didn't fall out for the morning muster, the other "Big Chiefs" (Senior Counsellors) would creep into the cabin of the "Sleeping Beauty" and set off a small cannon under his bed to awaken him.
(The cannon was normally used to signal the beginning of the day after the playing of "Reveille" over the PA system.)

The cannon itself used a shotgun shell to achieve the desired effect. It was LOUD!

One of the drawbacks to this method of rousing a tardy somnambulist was that the cannon blast would, on occasion, set fire to the staffer's mattress.

C'est la guerre!

One of the duties the counsellors had was night time "Guard Duty".

Once a week, one counsellor from each of the cabin areas, Midgets, Juniors and Seniors, would stay on duty until 11 o'clock or so to make sure all the campers were safely bedded down for the night.

We called it "Fire Watch", but it never came to that.

As it turned out, it was a great time to sit on the steps of your cabin and just look up at the moon and stars and enjoy the peace and quiet of a cool summer's evening and dream.

Sometimes, one of the other counsellors, usually Billy, would stop by and we would quietly shoot the breeze to pass the time.

We talked of many things, school, girls, sports, girls, home, girls, our ambitions for the future, girls...well, you get the idea.

It was one of my favorite memories of Camp Grant.

Once during every two-week-cycle the camp would put on a talent show.

The counsellors and their campers would sing songs, do comedy skits and generally make fools of themselves.

Some of the kids had real talent.

One of the "Senior" campers was a nasty kid named Paul.

He was always getting into trouble.

During one of the shows, Paul stunned everyone with his fine singing voice as he sang the Rock and Roll ballad "The Treasure of Love".

This from an individual whose vocabulary consisted primarily of four-letter words and whose facial expressions were limited to a sneer.

Speaking of singing, JOHNNY SCHROEDER, my C.I.T., belonged to a Rock and Roll group called the "Vocal Kings" Schroeder, whose real last name was "Palmieri" (His mother had re-married) and I had been C.I.T.s together the year before and were good buddies.

Since he was a year younger than I, John had remained a C.I.T. and continued to work in the kitchen with the cooks.

When I was asked who I would like to have as my aide, I jumped at the chance to have Schroeder as my cabin mate.

John had told me that once he and his group had been in a Rock and Roll contest over in Staten Island.

They sang a song they had written and did well in the show, but did not win.

Another group approached them and offered to help them with their material.

Schroeder said the other group had stolen their song and recorded it. He said that he and his friends were in the process of suing the other group.

I took what John said with a grain of salt.

One day we were listening to music on the radio, when Schroeder exclaimed, "THAT'S THE SONG!!"

About that time, an announcement blared over the P.A. system saying, "Johnny Schroeder please report to the Camp office, you have a phone call from Alan Freed" For those of you that don't know, Alan Freed was and is universally considered to be "The Father of Rock and Roll".

At that time, he was at the peak of his popularity and power.

Unfortunately, Alan told Schroeder that there was nothing he could do to help.

By the way, the song in question was the all-time classic, "LITTLE STAR".

There came a time at Camp when I found it necessary to adopt a secret identity.

When evil doers would plot to undermine the peace and serenity of camp life, a masked figure wearing a crimson cape with powers far above and beyond those of normal counsellors, would spring into action.

His true persona was cloaked in mystery and known to only a few.

He was the mighty SUPER CAMPER!!!!!

During one of the talent(?) shows, my buddies and I put on a little adventure skit featuring gun shots, a flying sequence or two and a battle royal.

We had designed a special costume for the occasion.

It consisted mainly of a white T-shirt with a multi-colored crest and the red letters "SC" on a white background surrounded by a circle of blue.

It seemed that some merchandise was missing from the Camp's Canteen/Store and it was up to SUPER CAMPER to find the perpetrators. (Oops, alleged perps) I changed into my SUPER CAMPER outfit and sprang into action.

The villains were dividing up their loot at their hideout when SUPER CAMPER swooped down and caught them red handed.

(We had stacked a couple of the mess hall tables on top of each other and I had climbed on top of them, out of sight of the audience, and leaped off into a fight with the four criminals.)

They fired their (empty) BB guns at our hero to no avail.

He then broke their weapons in half, threw them away and proceeded to pummel the crooks into submission.

The melee featured some rope swinging, jaw breaking punches and judo flips.

When his job was done, SUPER CAMPER turned to the onlookers and reminded them: "Crime does not pay and Justice will always triumph!!"

Having delivered his message, SUPER CAMPER sped out the mess hall door and disappeared into the night.

There was no doubt in anyone's mind, however, that should he ever be needed again, SUPER CAMPER would return!!

Sadly, Camp Grant no longer exists.

It met its demise back in the late sixties, due to some legal sleight of hand.

As I mentioned earlier, the intention of Jeannie L. Grant was to have the land used as a camp for boys forever, a truly noble sentiment.

One year, however, the grounds were used for some other purpose and the courts decided that Ms. Grant's will had been violated and as such was null and void.

Camp Grant was eventually plowed under and an upscale semi-private community of luxury homes now inhabit the former camp grounds. Can you imagine what these homes are worth today?

Ms. Grant must still be rolling over in her grave.

I'm sure that a goodly number of fine upstanding citizens made a ton of money swindling their way through the fruits of their legal skullduggery.

Summing it all up, Camp Grant was a wonderful place for underprivileged boys to escape the summer heat and humidity of the city and perhaps gain a few pleasant memories to last them a lifetime.

It's unfortunate indeed that the needy city kids of today will never have the chance to spend a couple of weeks in the country at Camp Grant overlooking the Long Island Sound and seeing a different side of life.

If only SUPER CAMPER could somehow turn back the clock.

)

Chapter Nine

SUMMERS IN THE CITY

The vast majority of our summer vacation time, of course, was spent in good old Brooklyn, U.S.A.

Before and after our annual vacation journeys to distant lands, we had no trouble finding plenty of things to keep us pleasantly occupied.

Truly, adventure lay around every corner, on every roof top and in every apartment basement and alley way.

One problem, however, was that Terry Hatch's parents insisted on taking him up to someplace called "Maine" every year.

Now what could they possibly find up in "Maine" to rival the wonders of Bay Ridge?

Terry and I spent a lot of time during the school year exhausting ourselves in just about every way imaginable.

Although Terry went to P.S. 102, we had plenty of time after school and on weekends to get in a lot of "daring do".

Whether it was playing softball, hockey, football, or guns, (We never called it "Cowboys and Indians") we always had something to keep us busy until the street lights went on.

That was the universal signal to call it a day and go home for supper.

There were so many things to do that the summer would seem to fly by, and before you knew it, it was Labor Day and time to go back to school.

Summer would always start slowly, as if you had forgotten what to do with all that free time on your hands.

But then you would hit your stride and go swimming, go to a ball-game, catch a movie, play box ball, or "Johnny on a Pony" (We called

it "Buck Buck"), or stickball, or punch ball, or "ring-a leave-ee-o", or
tag, or stoop ball, or marbles, or roller skate, or…
Well, you get the idea.
If you wanted to go for a swim, you had a number of choices.

The first, most exotic and convenient was to go to "Flagg Court" and
splash around in it's private, "Residents Only", outdoor pool.
Flagg Court is a very large apartment complex on the west side of
Ridge Boulevard that takes up the whole block from 72nd Street to
73rd Street and stretches half way down the hill to Colonial Road.
It was THE PRESTIGE APARTMENT HOUSE in all of Bay Ridge.
As a matter of fact, two of my classmates in OLA, Billy Elias and Jean
Shay, lived in Flagg Court.
I don't know what the waiting list for potential residents was, but
I'm sure it was quite lengthy.
In the middle of the structure was a beautiful jewel-like body of aqua
colored, crystal clear water that was restricted to the use of the ten-
ants and their families.
Luckily, the daughter of one of my Mom's friends had a boyfriend
who worked as a lifeguard at the pool.
So, for a brief period of two summers, we were able to rub under-
water elbows with the elite.
All good things, however, must come to an end and in the case of
Flagg Court's pool, a tragic one.
One night, some guy, I can only assume he was drunk, decided to take
a swan dive off the roof of one of the buildings, aiming for the pool.
History does not record if he made it or not, but the result was the
same in any event.
The pool was eventually closed down and filled in to a make a lovely
garden that remains to this day.
I can only wonder how many of the current residents even know
what they're missing?
The second aquatic choice was to go to the "Sunset Park" pool.
Sunset Park sits on the crest of a hill that rises from 5th Avenue to
7th Avenue between 41st and 44th Streets.

There is no better view of New York Harbor, (including the "Statue of
Liberty) than the one from the top of the hill in "Sunset Park".
The pool, however, could be a problem.

The swimming area itself was a typical New York City "Municipal" affair, and, as such, was all you could ask for.
There was a large main pool and a separate smaller one for diving.
My Father and his three brothers, Jack, Jimmy and Billy, had played baseball there for a team named the "Cubs", back in the '30s.
At some point in time, a decision was made to plow the ballfield under and construct a swimming pool.
The same thing happened in "Red Hook" and in other parts of the city.
My best guess is that they were all "W.P.A." projects.
I only went to the Sunset Park pool a couple of times, probably with the Lane/Howley kids, since they lived only a few blocks away.
My Mom didn't think it was a safe place to go, so we didn't go often.

The third choice was to walk down to Shore Road, get on the 69th Street Ferry and sail across the "Narrows" to the "St. George Pool" in the "Cromwell Center", on Staten Island.
On beastly hot evenings, we thought nothing of making this trip to gain temporary relief from the heat and humidity.
You would pay the nickel fare, get on the boat and within a 100-yards of shore, the temperature would drop 20 degrees.
In fact, it became somewhat chilly.
The trip across would take about 20 minutes, depending on which boat you caught.
The "Hudson" was the slowest as I remember and the "Gotham" the fastest.
Could it be that "Batman" and/or "Robin" was at the helm, or perhaps it was "Catwoman" herself?
You know how women drivers are.
In any event, after a refreshing cruise, you would get to within a 100 yards of the Staten Island shore, and a wall of thermal fury would smack you right in the kisser.
A jolt back to reality, indeed!
After getting off the boat, it was a fairly short stroll to the pool.
You could walk along "Bay Terrace", or if you were feeling particularly stupid, you could save some time by venturing through the underground tunnel of the "Staten Island Rapid Transit" subway.
The tunnel and tracks of the "SIRT" were about 50 feet lower than Bay Terrace and were a more direct route to the "Center".

In fact, the "Center" was the first stop on the rail line after the Staten Island "Ferry Terminal" starting point.

Terry and I only got caught in the tunnel once when a train came through, and we had to hug the wall to avoid being hit.

There were body sized indentations in the tunnel wall that were put there for the track worker's safety and we were quick to use them.

And, of course, we thought nothing of the danger of the "Third Rail", we were too smart.

Wisely, if a little slowly, we came to the decision to never try that idiocy again.

As with the other Municipal pools, there were a couple of areas in which to submerge your overheated body.

The result was that there was plenty of room for one and all.

After a pleasant evening at this delightful public pool, we would reverse our steps and hop on the ferry for the voyage back home.

Funny, but no one seemed to be overly concerned about us traveling around alone after 10 pm, and miles away from home.

It was a different time back then.

Back on land, we would somehow, almost magically, decide what any given day's activities would be.

But no matter the eventual choice, there was one item that was almost indispensable to kids of our generation; the "Spaldeen".

Whether it be stickball, punch ball, stoopball, or any of a dozen other street games, the one constant was this little pink ball.

Although the official name stamped on the sphere was "Spalding", (the manufacturer's logo), everyone in Brooklyn, and I'm sure in the rest of the city's five boroughs, called it by its "Nom de Guerre".

It cost 15 cents back in those days, and supplied many, many hours of outdoor enjoyment to boys and girls alike.

Indoors, I would play "hockey goalie" on our small fifth floor landing. I would shoot the ball against the outside wall of our apartment and then try to make the "save" before it got past me and dropped into the stairwell, all the way down to the first floor.

If it did, I would have to go down, retrieve it, come back up and continue to play.

It could get very tiring, but I loved it.

There were other brands of balls available, such as the "Pennsylvania Pinkie", but none of them could bounce as well or last as long as the "Spaldeen". It was tough!

Even when it finally split in half, we would still try to play stick ball with it, but not too successfully.

Some kids would press the remaining half into the open palm of their hand, or on their forearm, creating a suction and leaving a tell-tale circular imprint when it finally let go.

You couldn't ask for a better piece of athletic equipment.

Why they stopped making them, I'll never know.

One of the unique things about city summers was the way they cleaned the streets.

Normally, during the rest of the year, a sanitation worker would walk down the street with a big push broom and shovel, which he used to sweep and scoop any debris he encountered.

The shovel was mainly used to pick up any horse manure left by the carts that delivered fresh vegetables, blocks of ice and other products throughout the neighborhood.

Everything he found would then be dumped into a wheeled garbage can that he pushed along his route.

These guys did a great job and took great pride in their work.

God forbid we should utilize this method today to give jobs to those who need work or who are on the "public dole".

In the summer, however, there was an additional method employed to "sanitize" the streets.

Every so often, a big tank truck would drive down the middle of the street and unleash powerful sprays of water to flush and clean both sides of the pavement at once.

On a hot summer day, you would always be faced with a great dilemma.

Should I avoid the spray and continue to bake or should I run along side the truck and get completely soaked to cool off, if only for a short period of time?

I usually opted for the latter.

TERRY HATCH and I spent a lot of time together, both summer and winter.

We had a lot of similar interests and got along well.

Terry was a year younger than I, but a lot taller.

Whether it was "Guns", or roller hockey or football or just hanging out, we seemed to understand each other.

Terry's uncle worked for "Marx" toys and gave him a lot of their stuff.

I didn't much care for those toys, I thought they were kind of cheesy.

His "Gun Belts" were a different story.

I'm not sure where he got them, but he had a couple of the best-looking gun belts and holsters you ever saw.

Normally I would get some "Texan Jr," cap guns for Christmas, along with a belt and holster set.

Some of these sets were good and some were not so good.

As a result, I would borrow one of Terry's rigs whenever we decided to do our part in the winning of the west.

He being the bigger of us, would be "John Wayne", while I was "Bob Steele".

Many years later, I had the thrill of sharing lunch with "Bob" in the old "Peabody Hotel" in Memphis while attending a "Western Film Festival".

I walked into the hotel's restaurant and saw Bob sitting in a booth by himself.

I figured this was a once in a lifetime opportunity, so I walked over and asked if I might join him.

To my delight he said, "Sure, sit down".

We spent the next hour or so discussing everything under the sun, and only stopped when a couple of the "Festival" hosts came by to present Bob with an honorary "Kentucky Colonel" scroll.

I took my leave but had a picture taken with Bob before I left.

Unfortunately, it turned out to be a double exposure and it is barely recognizable.

Perhaps with the great strides they've made in photography in the past 50 years, there's still a chance to correct the image.

However it turns out, I'll always remember having lunch with the greatest cowboy star, "pound for pound and inch for inch", of them all: BOB STEELE!

Terry Hatch was responsible for another of my cowboy memories.

One day I accompanied Terry to his church on Ridge Boulevard and 73rd St.

Terry was not Catholic and going into a Protestant Church was somewhat daunting to me.

But we were on our way to somewhere and he had to drop off a note to the pastor, so I figured I'd chance it.

When we got inside the church's small auditorium, they were showing a "western" with a cowboy I had never seen before.

It should be noted that our family had perhaps the first television in our area, and since "westerns" were a staple of the early days of "TV", I thought I had seen just about every cowboy that ever was.

Therefore, I concluded that this guy must be the official "Protestant Cowboy".

I found out years later that he was "Bob Baker" whose films, to my knowledge, were never shown on any of the New York TV stations, all SEVEN of them!

Chapter Ten

HOCKEY

W inter time in Bay Ridge consisted largely of trying to keep warm. My Mom would bundle us up and send us off to school during the week, just like millions of other kids.

The weekends were filled with touch football games and when the weather turned nasty, snow ball fights, the building of snow forts and sleigh riding.

Then one night in the winter of 1952 things changed.

I was watching our 12-inch RCA set and in the midst of zipping around the channels, I stumbled on to a curious telecast.

It was some sort of sporting event with which I was not familiar.

The players seemed to be moving around on a surface of white, holding on to some type of sticks and chasing a little black disk.

There appeared to be some sort of cage at either end of the playing surface with a strangely equipped player standing in front of it.

I watched for a few minutes, not really understanding what was going on before my eyes.

Suddenly the announcer, Bud Palmer, shouted "GOAL" and all the players on the team that had just put that little disk in the other team's cage raised their sticks in celebration.

It was ICE HOCKEY and I was immediately hooked!

I found out the home team was the New York Rangers of the National Hockey League and that they played their games at Madison Square Garden on 49th Street and 8th Avenue in Manhattan, or as we called it, THE CITY.

I had learned about the rudiments of BASKETBALL during my summers at St. Joseph's Villa and was aware that they played at MSG.

But I had never even heard of HOCKEY.

The few times I had gone to "The Garden" was to see the Ringling Brother's Barnum and Bailey Circus or the World Championship Rodeo.

The first two times I attended the Rodeo, Gene Autry was the star attraction.

I had only heard Gene on his "Melody Ranch" radio show and read his comic books so it was a thrill to see him in person at last.

I take that back. It was not the first time I had seen Gene.

Although none of the theaters in our area, to my knowledge, showed his films and his westerns had not made the jump to television as yet, Gene had pioneered with his own TV series about 1950.

The "Lone Ranger" starring Clayton Moore and Jay Silverheels was the only one to pre-date him on the new medium.

As much as I enjoyed Gene, I really wanted to see Roy Rogers.

I finally got the chance in the early 1950's.

I couldn't believe I actually was in the same building with Roy, his Golden Palomino, Trigger and Dale Evans plus Bob Nolan and the "Sons of the Pioneers" singing group. (They were the best!)

But, let's get back to HOCKEY.

The next day after the game I watched on TV, I ran up to my local hardware store and asked them if they sold hockey sticks.

The owner said they did and that they cost $1.00 (Can you imagine?)

I bought one, went back home, put on my roller skates and using a "SPALDEEN", began to imitate what I had seen the night before, on the street in front of my apartment house.

Within days, all the kids on our block had purchased sticks and we began to play.

The "SPALDEEN" was quickly replaced by a roll of electrical tape which became our "puck".

(A real puck just did not slide on the black pavement very well)

Soon we all learned the names of the Ranger players and gravitated towards our favorites.

Names like Max Bentley, "Bones" Raleigh, "Gump" Worsley, (the goalie), Ivan "The Terrible" Irwin, Danny Lewicki, Wally Hergersheimer, Andy Bathgate and Dean Prentice became our heroes.

My personal favorite was a player named Bob Chrystal.

He was a "defenseman" that the team tried to make a "forward".

His claim to fame was that he had scored the Calder Cup winning goal for the Cleveland Barons of the AHL the year before.

Many years later, I took my son, Bobby, to a New Jersey Devil's game at the Meadowlands Arena.

In between periods, we ran into Fred Shero the former coach of the 1974 and 1975 Stanley Cup Champions Philadelphia Flyers and later the coach of the New York Rangers.

Fred at the time was doing color commentary on the Devil's radio broadcasts and had just returned from a trip to the Men's room.

We talked with Fred for a couple of minutes and turned to go when I said to him, "Fred, you played with Bob Chrystal, didn't you?"

Fred replied, "Bobby Chrystal, I haven't seen him in years!"

He then told us that Bob had trouble with his wind and often couldn't finish his shift.

He said that they could probably fix that with medication today.

Fred also said that the last he heard of Bob was that he was working for Molson Breweries in Canada.

We finished our conversation and Fred went back to the radio booth.

I played hockey for many years, both roller hockey and later ice hockey. Over the years, I collected my share of bumps, bruises, cuts and stitches.

In addition, or is it subtraction, I managed to lose a pretty good number of chicklets (teeth) along the way.

Those things happened to hockey players of our generation.

Remember, we played without helmets or masks in those days of yore.

The teeth I have now are the best I've ever had, and just think, I don't have to go to the dentist anymore.

The first bit of needle work I got was when a defenseman lost control of a puck in his own zone and I poked it past him on the way to a breakaway goal, or so I thought.

He spun around as I went past him and his stick caught me across the bridge of my nose and left eyebrow.

For a moment I only thought of scoring the goal, but then the blood started to flow down my face.

I fell to the ice and started blinking to make sure I could still see.

Fortunately, I could.

I went to the local emergency room, told them I was a Policeman, using "OFFICIAL" cop lingo.

"I'm on the Job, I work at the Eight-Two (82nd Precinct) and my partner is outside in the car with my "Tin" (badge) and my "Piece" (weapon)."

They took me right away and sewed me up (15 stitches) quickly enough for me to get back to the game for the third period, bent on revenge.

The referees, however, would not let me back in the game since I had a bandage that completely covered my left eye.

While I was pleading my case to the officials, I felt someone tapping on my shoulder from behind.

It was the defenseman who had opened me up.

He was a big young kid and he had tears running down his checks as he apologized for what had happened.

It was his first game in the league and he had evidently panicked.

I told him it was o.k. and that I understood.

When I got home, my wife just about fainted when she saw my bloodstained jersey and eye patch.

The incident which initially altered my bridgework happened as follows.

I stupidly went down to block a slapshot, missed and got kicked in the mouth by the shooter's skate as he followed through.

It cost me five teeth.

Needless to say, when I got home, my wife almost fainted again.

One time we were played a team from the Bronx when one of their players ran over our goalie, Jackie Nocera.

I was the player closest to the incident so it was my job to grab that guy and go (fight) if necessary.

As we tussled, I told him in no uncertain (profane) terms not to ever do that again.

Nothing really much came of it just a lot of pushing, shoving, grabbing and holding in addition to the above-mentioned conversation.

I'm not the toughest guy in the world so I was glad that the other player seemed reluctant to dance (fight), but I had done my job and maybe intimidated him.

The next week we had the late game and I arrived early and caught the end of the first contest.

The guy I had grabbed the week before had beaten the living crap out of three of the other team's toughest players.

This was one tough dude and I had escaped with my life.

Thank you, God!

Later that same season, we were playing that same team from the Bronx, (I think they were called the Shamrocks) when a huge brawl broke out.

I paired off with the Shamrock jersey nearest me and when I looked up saw that the player I was holding onto had very Irish flaming red hair.

I thought to myself: "This is not going to end well!"

As we vigorously tugged at each other I gave him my most viciously ferocious glare and warned him, "Don't even think about it."

As the tussle subsided, I violently shoved "Red" away as if to say, "You got off easy this time." (Yeah, right!)

Years later, my team, (The Tomahawks) was playing in a tournament against a team called the Flyers.

The Philadelphia Flyers of the NHL were known back then as "The Broad Street Bullies" so you can imagine what the mind set of this team was.

While we were skating in the warmups, at the other end of the ice there was one nut job who was hitting his own teammates in practice.

When we lined up for the opening face-off to start the game, guess who is standing next to yours truly?

I asked the referee for time, skated back to our bench, took my teeth out and put them in a cup behind our coach.

When I got back to center ice, I turned to "looney tunes" and did my best imitation of a spastic psychopath while flashing my remaining two-canine fangs in a bizarre smile.

"Llllet's haave a nnnice gggame, O.K.?" I stuttered.

His jaw dropped, his eyes almost popped out of his head and I didn't see him for the whole game.

An ounce of prevention...

There was one other noteworthy incident which deserves mentioning.
One evening I was to have a date with a charming young lady.
Note: I ALWAYS dated charming young ladies!
Unfortunately, the morning prior to the date in question we had a game.
Half way through the third period I skated by a player who was in the midst of taking a slap shot.
As he finished the follow through of his swing, the blade of his stick caught me flush on my left ear.
I wasn't cut, but my ear immediately swelled to twice it's normal size and turned a gloriously vivid shade of dark purple.
Needless to say, that evening it was very difficult to be cool and suave with one swollen ear the color of a ripened eggplant.
I don't think that even Cary Grant could have pulled that one off!

Eventually, I became a pretty good goal scorer.
I didn't have the greatest shot in the world, but I was very accurate and had a quick release.
I also made a conscious effort to get to "good" ice (shooting angles) as often as possible to maximize scoring opportunities.
When I shot the puck, the goalie would have to make a save since I seldom missed the net.
Another thing I did fairly consistently was to skate my position well.
I usually played left wing and my centers knew where to find me when they passed the puck.

The three players whose styles best fit mine over the years were FRANKIE LUZIA, JIMMY DOMINIQUE and JOEY BUONACORE.
The first time I skated with each of these three gentlemen, the chemistry between us was instantaneous.
They made me a goal scorer.
Thanks, fellas!

On the last shift of the last game I ever played, I scored what was to be my final goal at the age of 50.
What was unusual was that my shot went through the legs of a defenseman named JOHN KAISER.

I played with and against John for years and EVERY time I would take a shot against him, John would manage to block it with his feet or legs.

It was the ONLY time my shot EVER got through John and it beat the other team's goalie, low to the glove side.

I still have that puck from my last goal on one of my basement book-case shelves in a place of honor.

Both my son, Bobby III, and his son, Bobby IV, are playing now.

My son has this dream that the three of us will play a shift together some day.

I seriously doubt it, but you never can tell.

(Don't tell my wife)

Chapter Eleven

AUNT NORA AND UNCLE CHARLIE

Whenever big occasions or holidays would roll around, Christmas, New Years, Thanksgiving or birthdays, my Aunt and Uncle would be there.

It didn't matter if we went to their house, or they came to ours, that's how it worked.

They never had any children of their own, so we became their primary niece and nephew.

Uncle Charlie had nieces and nephews from his side of the family, but I don't think I ever met them until my Aunt's funeral in 1980.

We had broken off contact with the "Lane" side of the family in 1948. I believe it was because of a matter of finances.

As I understand it, the "City" had finally awarded my Mom some money for my Father's death, and some of the Lanes thought it would be a good idea for her to let them have the cash so that they could buy a house.

They had been renting any number of houses over the years, and saw this as a chance to break the cycle and have a place of their own.

My Mom told them that since she was a single mom raising two small kids, she needed every cent she could lay her hands on.

This was no fortune we are talking about, perhaps $5000, five years after my Dad's death.

Evidently a heated argument took place and we had no contact with the Lanes for the next thirty-nine years.

My uncle Jack informed me, after my Mom's death, that she had told him if he had been the one who made the request, she would have loaned him the money.

But the person who asked and the way it was asked, caused the rift.
Uncle Charlie was the closest thing I had to a father figure.
He was smart, good looking, a nice dresser, and seemingly very calm.
I don't think I ever saw him lose his temper.

But he was tough, make no mistake about it.
To me he projected authority in the finest sense of the word.
Years later, our family went to visit him in his "Tom's River" retirement community, and they were incredibly amused by the way I deferred to his wishes.
I do have a reputation for being a trifle stubborn, so when my uncle would give me driving instructions and directions, my wife and the two kiddies thought it was hysterical when all I would say was, "Yes, Uncle Charlie, yes, Uncle Charlie, yes, Uncle Charlie..."
I thought all three of them were going to wet their pants in the back seat of our car, trying not to laugh out loud.
He taught me many things I value to this day, not because they might put money in my pocket, but simply because he thought it was important for me to know them.
He taught me to tell time, how to determine direction, how to tie my shoe laces and necktie, etc.
He also had a little rhyme he taught me that was supposed to keep a person from becoming tongue tied.
It goes like this:

> If a fella,
> To a fella,
> Said a fella,
> Can a fella,
> Tell a fella,
> What a fella means?

So far, it has worked to perfection!

Going out to their home in "Flushing" was always a fun time, and we'd usually stay while.
I used to pal around with a kid named Dennis Cass while we were there.
Dennis had an older brother named "Skeeter", and he would let me use his brother's bike whenever we went anywhere.

To this day, I still don't know "Skeeter's" real name.

I'm afraid, at the time, I was a dreadful rider.

I don't know if the bike was too big for me, or whether not having (and NEVER have had) a two-wheeler of my own, caused my problems.

At any rate, whenever I would come across a patch of sand, especially going around corners, I would crash.

Somehow, I survived, and since the area was just building up, adventure lurked around every corner.

Whether it was climbing through the houses under construction or descending into the "Stygian" depths of the new sewer systems or even getting covered with mud on the right of way for the future "Long Island Expressway", life was good!

One of the things we did was collect bottle caps from the various construction sites in the area.

It may seem strange today, but you could spend a whole day picking up beer and soda caps at the construction sites and not getting any duplicates, so wide was the variety available in those days.

Dennis was also a member of the "Captain Marvel Club", and as such was able to de-code the messages appearing in each issue of "Captain Marvel" Comics.

He even had a "Captain Marvel" sweatshirt, which I thought was fantastic.

"Captain Marvel Comics' were produced by "Fawcett" publications which dropped its comic line in the early 1950's because of a court decision that the "Captain" was a "rip off" of the "Superman" character.

The two, of course, were completely different entities, and when Fawcett gave up the ghost, it's unique style of comic book disappeared forever.

Fawcett had its own following, and rightly so; it was a class act!

The Captain Marvel comic was so popular that, for a while, it would be issued twice a month.

The Captain had a whole family of "Marvels", each with their own comic line.

"Captain Marvel Jr." appeared in the comic bearing his name, as well as in "Master Comics", along with "Tom Mix", "Nyoka" and others. (More about her later, or should I say the real live actress who portrayed her in the Republic movie serial, "Perils of Nyoka". Her name was Kay Aldridge, and she was quite a fascinating character in her own right.)

"Mary Marvel" was the Captain's sister, and had her own title and starred in "Wow Comics" along with "Bulletman" and others.

All three "Marvels" teamed up in the "Marvel Family Comics"

There was even a "Captain Marvel Bunny" for a short period of time.

In addition to the "Marvel" line, Fawcett produced a great roster of "Western"

Comics starring "Rocky" Lane (no relation), Hopalong Cassidy, Tom Mix, "Lash"

Larue, Bob Steele, Rod Cameron, Monte Hale, and even Ken Maynard.

These comics usually had full color photographs of the star on each cover instead of drawings, and were really neat in themselves.

In the spring of 1953, I can remember going up to the candy store closest to my Uncle's house (It was about 4 blocks away on Francis Lewis Boulevard, near St. Kevin's Church), looking for the next issue of "Captain Marvel Jr."

I'm still looking.

My Uncle was a very determined man, to say the least.

While their house was being built, my Aunt and Uncle would make regular trips from Astoria where they lived to check on the progress of the construction.

As I said before, my uncle was in the "Seabees" during the war so there was no way the builder was going to get away with anything.

Once, they visited the site after a rain storm and found a recently partially erected wall connecting their house to the one next door had not been covered to protect it from the elements.

My uncle knocked it down.

He also found out that the street in front of the house was not up to code.

Somehow the "City" heard about it and the contractor was forced to re-do the whole thing.

Did I mention that my uncle worked for the Transit Authority at the time?

The New York CITY Transit Authority, that is!

The contractor eventually tried to buy back their house to get them out of the neighborhood.

That didn't work either.

One other thing: My Uncle Charlie once told me, years later, that his house had "New York City Board of Education" flooring in it, unlike the others on their block. I wonder how that happened?

My uncle once took me horseback riding at a local ranch in the area. Yes, there was, at the time, a working ranch in Queens, a short distance from their house on 194th Street.

(I'm pretty sure it's now the Kissena Park Golf Course)

Well, we got our horses (Mine was named "Lady".) and headed back to the house to show Aunt Nora.

We passed some construction machinery along the way and "Lady" panicked and took off on a dead run.

My uncle chased, caught up to us and reined in "Lady", just like in all the cowboy movies.

We finally got to the house and presented ourselves to Aunt Nora as if nothing had happened.

When it came time to return the horses, my uncle asked me if I'd like to ride back with him to the ranch. I, however, politely declined.

Shopping excursions with my Mom and Aunt were among my least favorite childhood activities, right up there with trips to the dentist. The way it would work is that we would travel by subway to "Fulton Street" in downtown Brooklyn.

In those days, there were a large number of major "Department Stores" within walking distance of each other between "Jay Street" and "Flatbush Avenue".

These included "Abraham and Strauss", "Martin's" "Oppenheimer Collins", "Namm's", "Loeser's", "Browning King" and "Russek's".

It was a major shopping area.

(Years later, my wife, Gail, actually bought her wedding dress at "Martin's".) The trips themselves were incredibly lengthy, tiring and boring.

We would stop in virtually every store, try on innumerable clothes and buy absolutely nothing.

We would then get back on the train, go up to 34th Street in Manhattan, and shop in both "Gimbel's" and "Macy's".

After again buying nothing, either my Mother or Aunt would say something like this, "You know, I kind of liked that jacket we saw on Fulton Street."

So we would get back on the train and head back to Brooklyn.

At least we would be getting closer to home.

Once back downtown, they could either not remember where they had seen the jacket in question, or decided it wasn't that nice after all.

When they finally determined to call it a day, we would board the B-37 bus, on Fulton Street for the ride, along Third Avenue, back to Bay Ridge.

If I was lucky, I didn't throw up.

Uncle Charlie built my "Lionel" train set layout.

Right after the end of the war my Mom, Uncle and Aunt started giving me some electric trains for Christmas presents.

At first it was a very basic set, a locomotive, tender, box car, oil car, flat car and caboose.

There were no switches or accessories, just a plain oval of tracks.

But I thought it was the greatest set ever.

Each year I would get a new car or accessory until one year my uncle mounted the entire set on a painted, four by eight-foot piece of hinged plywood.

He used ultra-strong piano hinges to allow the plywood to fold in the middle for storage purposes. It looked terrific.

He had laid out streets and electric light outlets to add realism to the layout.

About that time, they started to make a line of "Plasticville" build-ings for use with train sets.

These buildings included a firehouse, a police station, a passenger train station, a school and a gas station.

When they were placed over the light outlets, they looked great.

Over the years, my folks added some "Lionel" accessories as well.

They included a coal ramp and loader, an operating milk car which would unload metal milk cans onto a magnetic platform and a rotating beacon.

The layout evolved over the years with the addition of some "switches" to make it more intricate and interesting.

My Uncle would keep the layout stored in his garage for the rest of the year until Christmas time.

He would then take it down, work on the new additions and test it until everything worked perfectly.

It was always an exciting day when the train set arrived at our apartment.

It meant that Christmas was near and the good holiday times were at hand.

I always will be grateful for that wonderful train set.

After we moved out of Bay Ridge in 1954, the train set made fewer and fewer appearances at Christmas time and was eventually relegated to the basement of our house on Avenue "O" in the "Kings Highway" area.

When I got married, the train set remained at my Mom's and step father's until I reclaimed it some eight years later.

It had suffered some moisture damage over the years, but it worked. Some of the tracks had rusted out and needed to be replaced.

The "rolling stock", however, had been kept in one of Uncle Charlie's old suitcases, complete with a "Seabees" sticker on it, and were well preserved in their original orange and blue "Lionel" boxes.

I still have my wonderful train set, and perhaps one day it will roll again.

Chapter Twelve

RADIO, EARLY TELEVISION AND THE MOVIES

Entertainment back in the '40's and '50's came in a number of forms. The most all-encompassing was the ever-present device known as RADIO.

Day or night, seven days a week, radio offered an infinite variety of shows to please just about every taste.

There were soap operas, westerns, comedies, quiz shows, music shows, science fiction shows, adventure shows, detective shows, talk shows, news programs, sports, and religious programs.

In addition, there was a whole gamut of children's fare including Superman, Captain Midnight, Tom Mix, Terry and the Pirates, Tom Corbett-Space Cadet, Space Patrol, Sgt. Preston of the Yukon, Jack Armstrong, Frank Merriwell, Straight Arrow and Let's Pretend.

Sometimes the entire family would sit in their living room and "watch" the often exquisite piece of furniture with the lighted dial which dominated their evenings.

Whether it was Jack Benny, Bob Hope, Bing Crosby, The Lone Ranger, The Shadow, The Green Hornet or Sam Spade, we willingly welcomed them into our homes as old friends for their weekly visits.

Radio was a very warm medium.

It drew you into its universe and created a very personal relationship between the listener and the performers.

Imagination played a vital part in creating this camaraderie.

Everyone knew what The Lone Ranger or The Fat Man or Fibber Magee's closet looked like. No pictures were necessary.

Your mind's eye supplied every detail, especially if you were curled up in bed, listening to one of your favorite shows in your darkened bed room.

In later years, the radios became much smaller and lent themselves to even more intimacy.

Whether it be a baseball game, a detective show or an episode of the Lone Ranger or even the Shadow, the picture came in loud, vivid and clear.

Can you imagine being convinced you could "see" the INVISIBLE Shadow on your RADIO?

Such was the power of this fascinating medium.

President Roosevelt utilized this power to convey his messages to the listening public throughout the Great Depression and World War II. His "Fireside Chats" actually made him one of radio's biggest stars.

Then, about 1947, things began to change.

Slowly, but inexorably, there came a new force to be reckoned with: TELEVISION!

At first, it was just a few flickering images for a couple of hours a day. The rest of the time there was nothing or, at most, an Indian headed "Test Pattern" being broadcast over the airwaves.

There were initially only a very few channels available in the NYC area. The major Radio networks, CBS, NBC and ABC started their own TV stations.

They were WCBS-Channel 2, WNBT-Channel 4 (NBC) and WJZ-Channel 7 (ABC)

There was, however, a 4th network that soon entered the fray.

It was called the Dumont Network and broadcast on Channel 5 in New York under the designation of WABD for its founder, Alan B. Dumont.

These Channels were followed, in time, by WOR-Channel 9, WPIX-Channel 11 and WATV-Channel 13 out of Newark, New Jersey, wherever that was.

Old "B" movies became a staple of early Television broadcasting.

A great percentage of these were westerns.

I'm not talking about the major cowboy stars such as Roy Rogers and Gene Autry, but rather lesser stalwarts like Jack Hoxie, Rex Lease, Reb Russell, Rex Bell and Jack Perrin.

It was a treat when a film of some of the better saddle aces such as Bob Steele, Tom Tyler, Tim McCoy, Buck Jones or Ken Maynard thundered into our living rooms.

It wasn't until several years later that Republic Pictures joined the trend and released some of their product to the television stations. It was then that "Wild Bill" Elliott (as Red Ryder), The Three Mesquiteers, Don "Red" Barry and "Sunset" Carson made it to the small screen.

Channel 13 would start their broadcast day around 4 o'clock with a serial chapter, usually a "Mascot" production, followed by a western and a kiddie show, "Junior Frolics", hosted by "Uncle Fred" Sayles. After dinner, around 7 o'clock, they would rebroadcast the same serial chapter and western, followed by a non-western feature film. They would then sign off for the night.

The network stations didn't call it a night until a few hours later. Channel 4 would feature "Broadway Open House" with Jerry Lester and Channel 2 would run movies on "The Late Show" and even "The Late-Late Show", introduced by Leroy Anderson's recording of "The Syncopated Clock".

We had one of the first televisions in our neighborhood if not all of Brooklyn.

The year was 1947 and we, along with Aunt Nora and Uncle Charlie, bought identical RCA, 12-inch, black and white sets.

Each of them was housed in beautiful wooden Queen Anne Cabinets that stood over 4 feet high and had doors that closed to conceal the TV when not in use.

My Aunt and Uncle's cabinet also housed a separate record player in the top of the cabinet that could be accessed by raising its lid. (Maybe the world's first home entertainment center?)

Since my Aunt and Uncle owned their own home, they could erect an outdoor antenna on their roof. We, of course, could not.

Uncle Charlie approached the owner of our apartment house, a Mr. Bjorn Johnson, and asked if we could put an "outdoor" antenna of our own up on the roof of our building.

Mr. Johnson said "No", reasoning that if he let us put one up, eventually, everyone would want theirs up there too.

This discussion continued, off and on, for a couple of months, always with the same answer, "NO!".

Now, as I've said, Uncle Charlie was not one to take "NO" lying down. He went to the city and had the building cited for inadequate wiring and forced Mr. Johnson to have the whole apartment house re-wired. After all that, we STILL didn't get an outdoor antenna.

The indoor antenna we DID have was an odd contraption, to say the least.

It was not the run-of-the-mill "Rabbit Ears', but rather a unique "T" shaped structure with barbell like discs on the ends of its crossbeam. These discs were about eight inches in diameter and made of silver burnished metal.

I've never seen, or heard of anyone who has ever seen, one of these strange antennas.

As I've said, programming for the fledgling medium was sparse.

Nothing was transmitted on Channel 4 until "Howdy Doody" came on at 5:30 in the afternoon.

Prior to that, all that was to be seen was the ever-present Indian Head Test Pattern".

I sometimes wondered what tests they could be running behind that Indian Head?

My Mom, Aunt, Sister and I once went to the Dumont Studios in "The City" to see a show called "Johnny Olsen's Rumpus Room".

(Note: The people in Brooklyn always referred to "Manhattan" as "The City".)

I've heard that those studios were located in the John Wanamaker building, but I honestly don't remember.

Johnny Olsen later became the announcer on "The Price is Right"

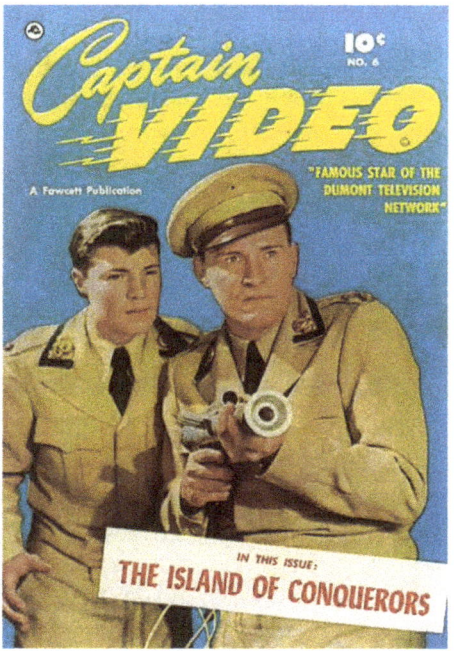

and on any number of other shows.

"The Rumpus Room" was sponsored by "Sauce Arturo" tomato sauce and featured Johnny's wife whom he called his "Million Dollar Penny". There would be prizes for quiz contestants selected from the audience and a parade to select the best-looking kid in attendance.

I surprisingly DID NOT win, but received a very large tin of potato chips for my trouble and humiliation.

The most significant moment in the proceedings was when I happened to look over to a corner of the studio and saw the entire Captain Video "Mountain Laboratory" set disassembled and propped up against a wall.

Talk about shattered illusions!

CAPTAIN VIDEO was the first space hero to hurtle across the early television air waves.

He was first portrayed by Richard Coogan, who left the series after a couple of years to be replaced by Al Hodge, who was the original "Green Hornet" on radio.

The Captain's young assistant, "The Video Ranger" was portrayed by future soap opera stalwart, Don Hastings, whose brother, Bob, was

"Archie Andrews" on the radio, and later a member of the "McHale's Navy" crew on television.

Fred Scott, who passed away a few years ago, was the announcer as well as the stay at home laboratory Ranger, "Rogers".

It was his job to tune into Captain Video's "Secret Agents" around the globe on the laboratory's all-seeing "Scanner" viewing screen, about halfway into the show.

These "Agent's" adventures usually were clips from "B" western movies starring the likes of Jimmy Wakely, Johnny Mack Brown, or "The Trail Blazers"; Ken Maynard, Hoot Gibson and Bob Steele.

These interruptions allowed the magnificent studio sets to be changed for the next exciting scenes.

One of these "sets" was a piece of wall board with imitation bricks that would show up from time to time in London, Paris, Berlin, Budapest and wherever the need would arise.

The cast members would be transitioning from one part of the studio to another, pause in front of that wall to deliver a line or two of dialogue, and move on.

It was also used for the interior of jail or prison cells, merely by placing some bars in front of it.

A significant problem with some of the cheaper sets was that they would wobble noticeably if the action became too spirited.

The Captain also possessed a number of great inventions, such as an "Atomic Rifle", a super jet plane and even a space ship.

But, my favorite invention of all was a sort of X-Ray telescope called the "Opticonscalometer".

For all its fantastic capabilities, the "Opticonscalometer" looked suspiciously like some old plumbing fixtures No matter, even with all its faults, "Captain Video" was still great fun in those early days of television.

The only other TV show I was ever on was "Rootie Kazootie".

"Rootie" was a little hand puppet whose girl-friend puppet was named "Polka Dottie" and his little dog was called "Gala Poochie".

The villain on the show went by the name "Poison Sumac".

The host, who presided over the goings on, was "Big Todd Russell".

"Howdy Doody" and "Buffalo Bob" it was not!

Some of the TV sets themselves, were very interesting in their own right.

There were any number of set manufacturers back in the late forties and early fifties.

Makers like RCA, Motorola, Zenith, Admiral, Crosley, Halicrafters, Dumont, Westinghouse, Philco and Sylvania were all cranking out 12-inch or even 14-inch sets for sale to a now ravenous viewing public. There were round screens, screens surrounded by "Halo-Light" and even fish bowl-like magnifying glass attachments which would make a small screen appear larger.

"TELEVISION" had arrived!

Prior to the coming of television, the only visual entertainment medium available to the public was, of course, the "MOVIES".

We in Bay Ridge had a dozen or so theaters within walking distance of our homes.

There were Loew's Bay Ridge (pronounced "Lowey's" by one and all), Loew's Alpine, the RKO Dyker, the Electra, the Stanley, the Harbor, the Coliseum, the Fortway, the Ritz, the Shore Road, the 46th Street, the Center, the Park, the Berkshire and some I may have forgotten.

The Alpine and the Dyker offered "First Run" pictures while the Bay Ridge was mostly a "Second Run" venue.

If you somehow missed a film at the Alpine or Dyker, you might just catch it a week or so later at the Bay Ridge or the 46th Street.

Back then you could enter the theater when it opened in the morning and stay until it closed about 11pm or even 12am.

On the weekends there would usually two different sets of films shown on a given day.

The early show was "Kid Oriented" fare and would contain a few cartoons, a "Serial" Chapter, a newsreel, perhaps a "short subject" and two full length features, one of which would invariably be a "Western".

This program would be shown twice and then the Admission Price would change from 25 cents to perhaps 75 cents and so would at least one of the films.

The other theaters would feature films from lesser studios and well-worn prints of previous hits.

I saw my first "Three Stooges" short at the Electra along with 40 color cartoons, a "Wild Bill" Elliott western and a "Lash" LaRue oater. Of the 40 cartoons there were a whole bunch of "Heckle and Jeckle's", but not one "Mighty Mouse". BUMMER!!
In fact, after I while, I wasn't sure I hadn't already seen some of the cartoons more than once.
It all became one big blur of color and noise.
As for the "Stooges", I thought they were retarded.
In the one I saw, they were dressed as cavemen and spent a lot of time hitting each other over the head with clubs.
I still have no use for them.

The first Roy Rogers film I ever saw was "On the Old Spanish Trail" at the 46th Street theater.
Jane Frazee (not Dale Evans) was the leading lady and the cast included Tito Guizar plus Bob Nolan and the Sons of the Pioneers. (Whoops! I almost forgot to mention "Trigger", Roy's Golden Palomino.) The version I saw was a beautiful "Trucolor" print, but only a black and white print survives today for television viewing. Pity!

I didn't realize until years later when the better films had been released to television how many I had seen at our local theaters.
When "It's a Wonderful Life" was first telecast, I remember thinking to myself, "I've seen this picture before".
I had no idea what the title was, but I remember being touched by the charming story as a kid.

Our local theater, Loew's Bay Ridge, unlike The Alpine on 5th Avenue and 69th Street, had a balcony.
I think they charged an extra dime(?) to sit up there.
The RKO Dyker on 86th Street and 5th Avenue had one too, but since we didn't go there very often, I don't think I ever sat in that section.

I do remember, however, going to the Dyker with my Mom and sister to see Walt Disney's 1948 film, "Melody Time".
In addition to "Melody Time", they showed the "Coming Attractions trailer for "Return of the Badman" with Randolph Scott.
To this day, I recall being terrified of Robert Ryan's portrayal of "The Sundance Kid" as shown in the trailer even though I didn't see the whole film until many years later.

One other thing I remember about going to the Dyker for was to see the Columbia Pictures serial version of the TV series, "Captain Video" Each week Al Lipari and I would walk up to 86th Street to catch that weeks "chapter".
The theater issued an "Official Captain Video" punch card which, if you attended all of the first eleven episodes, entitled you to see the last chapter free.
Unfortunately, the serial itself was nothing like the TV show.
We stopped going after three or four weeks.
But I digress.

In the back of the Bay Ridge's balcony there was a wide, carpeted corridor which contained an "imbedded in the wall" phone booth and also boasted a paper cup dispenser for the adjacent water fountain.

Each cone shaped cup cost a penny. (Luxury, indeed!)

The last film I saw at the Bay Ridge, before we moved in 1954, was called "A Flight to Tangier" with Jack Palance and Corinne Calvert. About 15 minutes into the picture, the projector broke down or the film tore beyond repair.
They turned on the lights and asked everyone to leave.
In retrospect, it seemed a fitting way to say goodbye to an old friend who had afforded me so many hours of pleasure and whose days were numbered.

Chapter Thirteen

THIS AND THAT

There are some stories which I either just thought of or could not decide the chapter to which they belonged.

In most cases, it's your basic stream of consciousness ramblings.

On Wednesdays at OLA, we would have "Released Time" at 2:00 rather than the normal 2:50 dismissal time.

The reason for this was that the Catholic kids who attended public school would come to OLA for "Confraternity" sessions and "Religious Instruction".

The thing that was strange about those days was that the nuns would insist that we clean out our desks of all our books lest the "Public School" kids steal whatever we were foolish enough to leave behind.

Now, some of my friends, like Jimmy "Wiggles" Donnelly and his sister Denise, attended these classes and I can't believe that they had the slightest interest in our school supplies.

But, in those days, such was the prevailing attitude among the nuns.

I was notorious for losing the key to our apartment, so the only way I could get into our house was to go up to the roof of our building and go down the fire escape and into our bed room window.

Since my Mom worked, I would often not see her from the time I left for school in the morning until the street lights went on in the evening and it was time to go home for supper.

The "fire escape" method was sometimes used to travel down to Rolf Lande's apartment rather than walking down the five flights of our "B" section and up the four flights of Rolf's "C" section to get to his and his sister Janet's apartment.

This seemed highly efficient to all concerned.

One Summer Saturday, I came home from my Aunt and Uncle's and I couldn't find anybody outside in the neighborhood to play with.

This was very strange, since there was always SOMEBODY around on our block.

I started calling my friends to find out where everybody was.

Rolf was the first one I called.

As it turned out, it was Rolf's birthday and everybody was at his apartment for his party.

Since we were away at my Aunt and Uncle's, his folks had no idea when we would return or how to get in touch with me to invite me.

I was kind of embarrassed to interrupt the party and quickly ended the call.

The next thing I knew, I heard the sound of a lot of people running across the roof above my head.

It was all my friends coming over to drag me back to the party.

What a great feeling!

Speaking of roof tops, there was one on which I almost met my doom.

I was at JOHN JOHNSON's apartment on Ridge Boulevard when I somehow wound up on the roof of his building.

I was looking at the view when his superintendent started chasing me.

All the apartment buildings on the block were of the same size, (4 stories) and were separated by three-foot walls back to back.

In my attempt to avoid capture, I would run and jump from one roof to the other.

I had just about lost my pursuer when I came to one of the walls and leaped onto it to cross over to the next building.

Instead of an easy transfer, I found myself looking into a three or four-foot wide air shaft that went straight down to the ground floor.

Luckily, I had built up enough speed and momentum to hurl myself across the yawning chasm and not take the express elevator all the way to the bottom. (Dave Sharpe would have been proud!)

It wasn't till later that evening that it finally dawned on me how close I had come to entering the "Pearly Gates".

To me, at the time, it was just another adventure. (Pretty dumb, huh?)

After Tommy Nacinovich and I got too old for the Cub Scouts, we both joined Troop 550 of the Boy Scouts.
Tommy, as usual, jumped in with both feet, progressing through the various levels of the program while I was content to remain a "Tenderfoot". (the lowest level) Tommy even earned the "Ad Altare Dei" award, the highest honor bestowed on Catholic scouts.
One of the requirements was to make a five-mile hike to the St. James Pro-Cathedral in downtown Brooklyn. (Is there such a thing as an "Amateur" Cathedral?)
Tom didn't want to make the trip alone, so he asked me if I would go along with him.
I said that I would, and we packed bag lunches for the trip.
We had no idea how long the journey would take.
As I remember, it took about two and a half hours and we were pretty tired at the end.
Needless to say, we took the subway back home.
I seemed to recall that we had to get one of the priests at the Church to verify that we had indeed made the effort.
When Tommy finally received this medal at a ceremony conducted at our church (OLA) later that year, I was very happy for him.

Once, "550" went on an overnight trip to Camp Pouch on Staten Island.
It was, as I remember, the weekend after the Kentucky Derby of 1952 in which a horse named "Dark Star" upset the heavily favored "Native Dancer" to win the "Run for the Roses".
None of the newer scouts, including me, had ever done a sleep over.

We were told to bring along 2 blankets to keep us warm through the night and that they would be more than sufficient. WRONG!!!
We slept, or tried to sleep, on the floor of a wooden "lean to" which was open to the elements on one side. (We froze our little butts off!)
At one point, one of the older scouts (I believe his name was Eddie Dahl) threw some gasoline onto the fire in front of our "lean to" to try to supply some degree of warmth to our frigid existence.
It worked...for about 20 seconds.
The next morning, we tried to thaw ourselves out in the open at what passed for breakfast in the great outdoors.

There were some eggs and some coffee, HOT COFFEE!
I have never developed a taste for coffee, but on that morning, I tried mightily to consume some.
No matter how much milk and sugar I added, I still couldn't drink it. But at least it was hot.
I must have gone through 4 or 5 cups that morning, not drinking, just holding them tightly in my hands and close to my face and body, trying to avail myself of their blessed warmth.

St. Michael's, a parish about a mile and a half from OLA, didn't have a "Scouting" program of its own, so DANNY SCHAEFER joined our troop.
Danny was another real good guy and fit right in with our group.
Danny's dad owned the Schaefer Funeral Home across Fourth Avenue from St. Michael's, on the corner of 42nd Street.
Once, when it was Danny's turn to hold our scout meeting, we wound up having it in the basement of the funeral home with coffins all around us.
It was quite an interesting experience.
I last saw Danny about 25 years ago and we had lunch together in his old neighborhood.
I later called him about 15 years ago from a funeral parlor in Queens when my wife's father passed away, just to say hello.

There's nothing like old friends.
No need for, "Why haven't you called in so long?".
Just two old buddies picking up where they left off like it was yesterday.

My Uncle Charlie could do most anything, at least in my mind.
It turns out he could even cook.
Once when my Mother, Aunt and Sister went out shopping, Uncle Charlie cooked supper for just the two of us.
He made breaded pork chops that night and to this day I swear they were the best I've ever had.
Years later, he would occasionally remind me of that meal and recall how much I enjoyed his culinary efforts.
I guess he appreciated my remembering them so fondly.

After graduation, Tommy Nacinovich didn't go to La Salle with me.

He went instead to Regis, THE MOST PRESTIGIOUS Catholic High School in all of New York City. (He was the only one to make it in 1954) (John Cuff had entered there the year before Tommy) Tommy told me, many years later, that Sister Mary Arthur and Sister Gabriel Marie, the other 8th grade teacher, hand-picked the students who would take Regis' entrance exam.

I believe he said there were five or six boys chosen for tutoring.

In those days, you would travel by subway to each individual school and take their test.

If nothing else, you got an education on how to use the New York City Transit System.

(As I said before, I even took the 69th Street Ferry to Staten Island to take the test for St. Peter's.)

Tom also told me, the year before (1953), to "prep" for Regis' exam, the Sisters had bought a few of the old tests on which to practice.

As it turned out, that year's exam was one that they had purchased.

The result was that ALL of the OLA applicants qualified for entry.

Tommy subsequently went to the Massachusetts Institute of Technology and upon graduation, went on to complete his education in Europe.

He then went to work for IBM for the next 30 years.

Pretty smart fellow, eh?

Tommy and I both had "Lionel" train sets.

His was "O-27" gauge, while mine was standard "O".

The difference was that Tom's tracks had a 27-inch circular diameter, while mine required 36 inches to complete a circle.

The wheel base on his engines and rolling stock was also narrower.

I say "engines" because Tommy's layout accommodated TWO sets of trains, one of which was a passenger car rig while the other was freight.

Tom's dad was a professional engineer and designed a really cool layout which could roll under Tommy's bed when not in use.

My layout was strictly "freight" and had a lot more accessories.

I had an elevated coal unloading ramp and accompanying coal loader that used a conveyor belt to dump the coal back into a waiting coal car.

In addition, my set featured an operating milk car that would deliver little magnetized silver cans onto a waiting metal platform.

Uncle Charlie had also rigged up a number of light outlets over which I could place buildings, such as a school house, police station, fire house or even a Cape Cod home. I still have them.

These structures were made by the "Plasticville" company and fit in perfectly with my Uncle's set up.

They initially started their line of buildings with a small freight station and soon added a bigger passenger station.

After that, they would introduce a new product every couple of weeks. Whenever I saw a new one, I would save up my allowance (50 cents a week) and buy the latest one.

I don't think they ever cost much more than a dollar, but they looked just great on my layout.

There was another thing that Tommy and I had in common.

We each had gotten identical "Colson" bicycles when we were about ten.

Actually, they had three wheels, but we never called them tri-cycles. (We were FAR too grown-up to do that!)

To us, they were the Cadillac of wheels.

They were chain driven rather than having their pedals on the front wheel of the bikes.

That was for little kids, not us.

All other "bikes" paled by comparison.

As I've mentioned before, Tommy eventually got an honest to God bicycle, while my Mom thought it was too dangerous, so I never got one. (Bummer!)

There were two special ice cream treats that were something out of the ordinary bill of fare.

The first was a chocolate malted milk flavored concoction called a "Cho-Cho Bar".

What made it unique was the fact that it came in a plastic (?) cup with a "Popsicle" like stick inserted through its lid.

To eat it, you would invert the cup and lift it off the lid, exposing the semi-soft ice cream inside.

As I remember, there was no coating on the ice cream, just smooth eating.

The second was something called a "Melo-Roll".

"Melo-Rolls" came in the normal three flavors; vanilla, chocolate and strawberry.

I think they were made by Borden's, but I'm not sure.

(Perhaps it was "Sealtest".)

They were a two-inch log of ice cream wrapped in paper with tabs on either side to allow you to remove the protective covering.

They even had their own special "cone" to accommodate the cylinder of ice cream It was a standard flat-bottomed affair with a rectangular shaped top to hold the oddly shaped "scoop".

The problem was that you needed three hands to successfully drop the "roll" into the cup.

One hand to stop the cone from tipping over and two to remove the paper covering.

Without the aid of a "NORDEN" bombsight, it was also possible to miss the cone completely!

Our apartment house on Ovington Avenue was directly behind the firehouse which housed Hook & Ladder 109 and Engine 241 back then.

The firehouse was located on the south side of 69th Street (Not Bay Ridge Avenue as non-Bay Ridgers called it) between Bay Ridge Place and Third Avenue to the east.

Whenever the firemen went on a run, we were certainly aware of it. My Mother even taught us a little prayer to say whenever we heard them go.

It went like this: "God protect the firemen on their way".

The firemen would occasionally come out of the back of their quarters and play ball in the Bartlett's family back yard, which was right next door.

I would watch them from the fire escape outside our fifth floor bed room window until the alarm bells would ring and back inside they'd go in a hurry.

I also remember going into the firehouse after they'd gone to a fire and just walking around out of curiosity.

The firemen would leave the main doors wide open so it was no great feat at all to go in and look around. (How times have changed!) I never went up to the second floor where the sleeping quarters were. Because of that, I never got to slide down the brass fire pole the men used to get down to the trucks as fast as possible when the alarms rang.

There was a wooden staircase that went up to the second floor which seemed to have at least a hundred steps, all in one straight flight. It was a little scary for this young man, maybe that's why I never went up there.

One other thing; during World War II, we had a CIVIL DEFENSE helmet and two gas masks in our bedroom closet, one each for Mom and Dad.

Evidently, my sister and I were expendable. (Just kidding, I think.)

In a previous chapter I mentioned the Bianchi family.

Their house was a place my Mother, sister and I would often visit and stay overnight on occasion.

Narda Bianchi (nee Nolan) was a childhood friend of my mother from her Red Hook days and they had maintained their friendship over the years.

Narda's youngest son, David, and I would even refer to ourselves as cousins even though we were not related at all.

One of David's real cousins was named Tommy and the only things I recall about him was that he had blond hair, a raspy voice and was allergic to tomatoes. (Funny what you remember)

One thing I do remember VIVIDLY about their house was the water. It was not "City" water, but rather "Flatbush Well Water" and it tasted truly terrible.

We would often come in from playing outside on a hot summer day dying for a glass of cold water.

No matter how long you ran the faucet, it still tasted like liquid cardboard and was not at all refreshing.

Eventually I heard that the area did switch to city water years after we had lost contact with the Bianchi family.

No one in that neighborhood mourned the loss of that horrible elixir.

Then, a funny thing happened during John Lindsay's term as the Mayor of New York City.

One summer, as it turned out, the city was faced with a severe water shortage and they actually re-activated the Flatbush Well Water system.

The television news media gave great coverage to the event, since our revered Mayor never met a camera he didn't like.

After Lindsay had expounded at length about the wonderful resource the wells would provide, someone suggested he take a drink of this newly found treasure for the cameras.

Instead of downing some of this delightful nectar himself, Lindsay deftly handed his glass to one of his aides (flunky?) and let him do the honors.

(If he dies, he dies!)

When I saw this on the newscast, I couldn't help but wonder if our beloved Mayor had prior knowledge about the vile, flat taste of that accursed liquid.

We'll never know, will we?

One of the universal joys of childhood has always been bouncing on beds.

With or without parental knowledge and/or permission, kids all over the world have, at some time, partaken in this wonderful activity.

In my case, it was somewhat more involved than just jumping up and down.

My Mother, sister and I shared the bedroom of our three-room apartment.

They slept in the big bed in the middle of the room while mine was up against the wall opposite the window.

Therefore, I was farthest away from what little breezes entered the room in the sweltering summer months.

Not that there were many to speak of anyway, (As previously mentioned, we NEVER even bought a God damned fan!)

As I got older, my Mother began to petition the landlord for the next available four room flat.

Somehow, it never happened.

That may be due in part to the fact that I don't remember ANYBODY ever moving out of our building.

As far as the jumping went, it was quite a bit more inventive than just plain old bouncing.

To begin with, I wouldn't get onto the bed in the normal fashion.

What I would do was to enter the room at top speed and hurl myself head first over the bed's foot board landing in its middle.

But that was just the appetizer to the main course!

In addition to the two beds there was a five-foot high chest of drawers off to the left of the big bed and next to the doorway of the room.

First, I would climb up on the chest, leap off the top (feet first) on to the big bed and bounce to the right propelling Little Bobby, head long, like a

mini guided missile toward my smaller, higher bed.

(My bed had both a box spring and mattress, while my Mom's bed had only one mattress on top of a frame-wide supporting spring)

The trick was to avoid crashing into the wall that paralleled my bed.

I wonder what would have happened had the truth of my aerial escapades ever surfaced?

I've mentioned in a previous chapter how people tried to cope with the hot, muggy summer nights in Bay Ridge.

Those attempts took many forms.

Although I never slept on the fire escape outside our bedroom window, I know of a number of people who did on theirs.

Others were even more adventurous in their quest for relief.

Mary Dell'Accio told me that her whole family would journey down to Bliss Park and sleep outdoors on the park's hill during some of those dreadfully steamy nights.

Mary Ann Lento, who lived across from the Colonial Road entrance to the park, confirmed the fact that the Dell'Accio's were certainly not the only ones to avail themselves of that nocturnal luxury convenience.

Chapter Fourteen

BASIC TRAINING

The year is 1963, early fall to be precise and I've had enough of college.

I'm twenty-two, JFK is still alive and Viet Nam has not begun in earnest.

I know it's just a matter of time until Uncle Sam comes knocking.

(The DRAFT is still in force and I'm Classified 1-A)

I figure I'll outsmart the powers that be and join the MARINE CORPS. Outsmart??

I meandered up to the Marine recruiting trailer located in a triangle at the intersection of Avenue J and Flatbush Avenue.

Ironically, it was less than half a block from Dorothy Montuori's apartment building and the store front from which I worked as a newspaper delivery boy for the World Telegram and Sun back in 1957.

I walked up to the door of the recruiting office and was greeted by the following sign: OUT TO LUNCH

BACK IN 15 MINUTES

I thought to myself: "This is a message from GOD!". I never went back.

The next day I got a call from my buddy, JERRY "Harry" HARRINGTON, that his Army National Guard Unit had openings and to come down and join up.

Two days later, I went down to the Armory on Eighth Avenue and Fourteenth Street over in the Park Slope section, ready to sign on the dotted line.

I told the guard/watchman inside the front door why I was there and he told me to go see a Mr. Argo down the corridor to the left.

When I got to the room in question, there were two or three other applicants already there.

Mr. Argo told us he was a Warrant Officer (Whatever that was) and he would handle our preliminary paperwork.
He explained what was involved in being a member of the Guard and had no problem with our fulfilling our military obligation in such a manner.
After listening to his narration, I felt sure that this was the way to go.

Mr. Argo set up an appointment for my "G.I. Physical" to be taken at the Fort Hamilton Army Base right by the Brooklyn side of the Verrazano Bridge.
No sooner had I taken the physical than I received my Army Induction notice from the Selective Service Local Board No. 41 with the reporting date of 9 December 1963. (Official Military Jargon)
I called Mr. Argo in a mild state of panic and told him of the letter.
I was convinced I had blown it.
Mister Argo said not to worry, he would take care of it since I was already in the process of joining the Guard. (Phew!!)
On a letter dated the 14th of November, I received a notification from the Co-Ordinator-in-Chief Clerk of Local Board No. 41, Florence L. Manzione, that my "induction into the armed forces scheduled for 9 December 1963 had been cancelled" (Thank you, God!!)
Note: I still have that letter.
By the way, I should mention that in the midst of all the confusion I had joined the WRONG Guard unit!
Harry's unit was an Artillery outfit and I had joined an Ordnance outfit. I didn't know the difference.
I had merely followed the directions given me by the guard/watchman at the front door of the Armory that first day.

Just one more thing.

Through the guys I became friends with in that Ordnance outfit, I met my wife, Gail, a couple of years later. (Kismet?)

After being sworn in on November 7th, 1963 (Non-Military Jargon), I began to attend weekly Thursday night meetings at the Armory for the next few months.
I was now Pvt. E-1 NG22022330 Lane, Robert NMI (No Middle Initial)

In late January, I received orders to report to Fort Jackson in Columbia, South Carolina for Basic Training starting March 1st, 1964.

Two dozen other recruits and I were instructed to meet in the city at 4am by the 34th Street Armory for transport by bus to La Guardia Airport.
Military Air Transport Service (M.A.T.S.) would then fly us down to Columbia.
The plane they used was and old propeller driven TWA Constellation which had been converted for military use.
This four-engine relic must have been 15 years old at least.
Since it was my first plane ride, I helped the pilot by continuously counting the wings and checking to see that the engines were not on fire.
I'll bet he had no idea that he was in such good hands.

When we arrived at Fort Jackson's Reception Center, we were greeted by a chorus of earlier arrivals chanting, "You'll be sorry!"
We spent the next couple of days getting our G.I. haircuts, taking our aptitude tests and physical exams and being issued our boots and uniforms.
We also had our first Army meals, most notable of which was "Braised Chipped Beef on Toast" more commonly referred to as "S.O.S."
(S—T ON A SHINGLE)
Most of us passed on this culinary delight while a couple of guys couldn't get enough of that dreaded substance.
These few, brave (foolhardy?) souls went back for seconds and even thirds.
On the third day we were marched to our Basic Training Company area on the Tank Hill Area of the Fort.
We were assigned to "Bravo" Company, 4th Battalion, 1st Training Brigade, 3rd Army.
Our battle cry was "BRAVO SIR YOU'VE SEEN THE REST NOW SEE THE BEST" How thrillingly stimulating!

There were four two story Platoon Barracks on Bravo Company's street. Trainees were assigned alphabetically to these barracks, 50 to a barrack.

A thru E – 1st Platoon, F thru L – 2nd Platoon, M thru S – 3rd Platoon and T thru Z, 4th Platoon.

The Company Commander was Captain Louis J. Schiano.
The First Sergeant was Sgt. Toms and the Field NCO was Sgt. Jordan.
The four Platoon Sergeants were Sgt. Todd, Sgt. Lynch, Sgt. Harper and Sgt. Powell and they meant business.
They were there to do a job and were going to turn us into soldiers or kill us in the attempt.
Bravo Company was made up of a mixture of Regular Army Volunteers (RA's), Draftees (US's) and primarily our National Guardsmen (NG's) from Brooklyn.
It was interesting to see relationships develop between guys from so many divergent backgrounds.
The guys from Brooklyn pretty much knew what to expect from each other so that bonding was solidified rather quickly.
It was the others who had to feel their way.
We had trainees from Boston, Chicago and a number of Southerners both black and white.
Eventually though, friendships were established across the spectrum within a couple of weeks.
There was even a case or two where white southerners became good buddies with some of the black guys in our company.
The good guys learned to disregard skin color and accept each other as individuals.
There was one instance where little Luther Jefferson was being picked on by a white kid from Alabama when Joe Johnson, a native of West Virginia and Jim Hudson from North Carolina stepped in to defend Luther.
It was nice to see that.
Outside of my buddies from Brooklyn, I became good friends with Pat Kelly who hailed from Chicago and our Platoon Leader, Stuart Holmes, who had attended Clemson University in South Carolina.
Very early on, I decided not to call Holmes by his given name and always referred to him as "Sherlock".

Holmes really enjoyed his new "Nom de Guerre".
Surprisingly, no one had ever called him that before. Go figure.

Basic training was divided into an eight-week cycle plus a "Zero week".

Week 1 – Drill and Ceremonies, General Orientation and the Care of Weapons
Week 2 – Chemical, Biological, Radiological Training plus Hand to Hand Combat
Week 3 – Rifle Marksmanship and Target Detection
Week 4 – Army Trainfire with "Pop Up" Targets
Week 5 – Bayonet Training, Compass and Map Reading
Week 6 – Infiltration Course and Grenade Usage
Week 7 – Bivouac and Squad Tactics
Week 8 – Physical Training Test, Overall Proficiency Tests and Graduation

There were any number of things that I remember about those couple of months spent at Fort Jackson.
I'll try to recount a few of them.
The things that stand out most were the guys themselves and their different backgrounds.
Aasgeir Korsnes from Brooklyn, who liked to be called "Scotty", was a NYC policeman and eventually became Company Commander of our National Guard outfit and was also a member of the Masons Fraternal Organization.
Pete Gardini from South Ozone Park in Queens was and still is a world class character.
I could write a couple of chapters on his antics both in and out of the Army.
There was nothing Peter wouldn't do.
The sergeants back at the Armory all thought he was nuts.
Maybe so, but he's now a millionaire and still a good friend.

Some of the other guys who spring to mind for one reason or another were Joe Braswell, Jasper Cummings, Jim Green, Pete Parisi, Dom Suarto, Charlie Sacco, Vinnie Bacon, Stu Block, Leon Faulk, Danny Fiano, Wayne Hawthorne, Donald

Kubasak, Carl Martucci, James McNamara, Tony Nigro, Tom Rocco, James Shavers, Jim Hartnett, Glenn Hill, Kenny Tavani and Ronald Costa.

I'll start with Costa.
He evidently came from money and had joined the Army by mistake.
From the very first day he did everything in his power to get out.
No matter what we were doing, Costa would mess it up.
I initially thought he was just plain dumb.
He always had this blank look on his face and seemed to not understand just about anything.
This little routine went on for about three weeks.
Then one day on the rifle range, the guys were making fun of his ineptitude when Costa dropped his façade for a moment and said words to the effect that, "You guys think I'm stupid, but I'm the one who's getting out and all of you are still going to be stuck here".
Realizing what he had said, he morphed back into his other persona, hoping none of the sergeants or officers had overheard him.
The last I heard, Costa was discharged soon after as "Unfit for Military Service".
I sometimes wonder how that affected the rest of his life?

One of the first memorable moments I can recall from my days in Basic happened shortly (no pun intended) after we had received our first G.I. haircut.
We looked pretty silly with our shaven heads and we all now realized we were really in the Army.

While I was sitting on my bunk in the barracks one evening, another recruit approached me and said he thought he recognized me from someplace.
I told him that I was sure we had never met, but he persisted for the next few days trying to identify me.
Finally, he asked me if I had been in the movies.

I laughed and assured him that I had not.
In spite of my denial, he kept belaboring the point.

After I while, I broke down and confided to him that I had indeed been in the movies and the reason he couldn't place me was due to my lack of hair.

He triumphantly commented that he knew he was right all along.

I told him I really didn't want my true identity exposed and just wanted to fit in and be one of the guys.

He then asked me what my "Reel" name was.

After swearing him to secrecy, I confessed to him that I was actually the lovely movie star "VERONICA LAKE", she of the long, luxurious, blonde "peek-a-boo" hairstyle.

He never bothered me again.

There was one other odd thing that happened during those first few days at Fort Jackson.

I was standing on the chow line when a recruit with a pronounced southern drawl quietly asked me if I had in fact come from Brooklyn. When I told him that, "Yes, you're right, I am from Brooklyn", he continued "How many people have y'all killed?"

Not knowing really what to say, I answered, "To tell you the truth, there have been so many, I've lost count."

During the first weeks of Basic, there were a couple of "cadre" assigned to our barracks.

These were men awaiting orders for assignment based on their expertise and they functioned as temporary aides to our Platoon Sergeant. One of these gents was a fellow of Japanese ancestry named Nishyama. Evidently yours truly had fouled up some task during training and Nishyama ordered me to "Drop down and give me ten!" (pushups)

That particular day I wasn't feeling overly well and I questioned the wisdom of his directive by saying, "By the way, who won the war??" Nishyama replied, "Make it twenty!"

One of the curious things about Basic was the proficiency of the National Guardsmen from the New York Area in all areas of training as opposed to trainees from the South.

Whether it was marching, shooting or physical and mental competency, there was a noticeable difference.

One of our platoon buddies, a guy named Hooks, was so poor at marching that whenever we stopped counting cadence, he would immediately get out of step.
Our Platoon Sergeant would then proceed to yell at him to get back in stride.
The offending Hooks would then spend the next few yards skipping down the road in an attempt to rectify the situation.

On the rifle range, the guys from up North would consistently out-shoot our Southern buddies.
Even yours truly, in spite of the fact that I had never fired a rifle prior to arriving at Fort Jackson, somehow managed to fire "Expert".

Let me now address the phenomenon known as PETER L. GARDINI.

Peter was a few years younger than I, but when we first met back at the armory in Brooklyn, we immediately became fast friends.
Peter was always one step ahead of those in charge.
They just couldn't figure him out.
When we arrived at Fort Jackson, Peter continued to befuddle the powers that be, much to their consternation.
No matter how they tried to discipline him, Peter would always manage to outwit them.

No matter what the weather, it was required to traverse a seven-foot high horizontal ladder of about two dozen metal rungs prior to eating our meals.
Everyone would have to negotiate the ladder before entering the mess hall.
Failing to successfully complete the task would necessitate dropping to the ground and doing a dozen pushups.

Peter figured out that if he opted for the pushups, he would be one of the first to get into the mess hall and get served before everybody else.
The rungs on the ladder were not totally secure and as such they rotated in your hands as you swung through them.

If you grabbed them the wrong way, the palms of your hands would be pinched against the rungs and cause blisters to form which eventually would break open causing nasty bloody injuries.

Speaking of pushups, one of the other "cadre" was a guy named Jones.
Jones who, for some reason, didn't care at all for Peter's antics.
He would constantly make Peter do pushups which escalated in number as the days went by.
Peter, however, was a fine athlete who had played football at John Adams High School in South Ozone Park, Queens.
As such, pushups didn't phase him at all.
He was a pushup machine.
Finally, in frustration, "Jonesy" announced that he would no longer assess Peter pushups.
Instead of that, he would now make Peter do the low crawl up and down the company street, not a pleasant thought.
The very next day, Jonesy received his orders and was assigned to Alaska.
A week later, Alaska experienced the worst earthquake in its history.
Coincidence?
Who can say for sure?

The Physical Training Test at the end of Basic consisted of five events: the horizontal ladder, the low crawl, the hand grenade-throw for accuracy, the run, dodge and jump, and the mile run.
Early in our training cycle I had noticed a trophy in our mess hall which was to be awarded to the highest scorer on the P.T. Test.
I mentioned to "Sherlock" that I thought I could win that piece of hardware.

He agreed.
It didn't take long to learn who were the good athletes in Bravo Company.
I liked my chances.
The only event I was worried about was the hand grenade throw.
Once I finally learned the proper technique, I knew I could do o.k.
The first four events went off without a hitch and I achieved perfect scores in each
Only the mile run remained.

I had asked one of our Lieutenants to keep track of my lap times with his personal stop watch.

After each lap he would let me know how I was doing.

I knew I was in first place since no one was in front of me, but it became a little confusing later in the run since I was passing runners I had lapped.

At the end of the race, I came to a halt by the Lieutenant.

Suddenly, a Sergeant yelled at me that I should keep going for another lap.

As it turned out, I had had trouble with this same Sergeant a week earlier on bivouac.

I told the Sergeant that I had finished my mile and that the Lieutenant had timed me as proof.

The Sergeant would not change his mind so the trophy was now in jeopardy.

Our Company Commander, Captain Schiano, called me into his office the next day to settle the problem.

James Shavers, who had finished second, was asked what had happened and all he said was, very graciously, "He beat me."

I should have been credited with a perfect 500 score for the five events, but the Sergeant in question would not alter his story so my total was 462.

I would have liked to have had the 500, but it was not to be.

The trophy, however, was mine.

There's a little bit of irony that provides the ending to this tale.

After all the trouble involved, I got the trophy home and placed it on the curb in front of my house while I removed my duffle bag from the trunk of the taxi I had caught at La Guardia Airport.
When I turned back, the trophy had tipped over and broken.
I did, however, eventually get the trophy repaired and it has occupied a place of honor in my basement (Man Cave) for the past 55 years.

Chapter Fifteen

FORT BRAGG

~

After finishing Basic, my next duty assignment was at Fort Bragg, North
Carolina.
It was nothing like Basic.

Based on your Military M.O.S. (Military Occupational Specialty), you
worked a full day from 8am to 4pm, Monday thru Friday.
As a Wrecker Crewman I spent my days at the Motor Pool.
Most of the time there wasn't much to do so the Wrecker Crew
hung out in the farthest corner of the Motor Pool out by the metal
"CONEX" boxes.
(trailer containers).
It wasn't long before I became very bored and after a few days I took
note of the fact that the Base Softball Team would practice across
the road from our Motor Pool.
The Pool itself was enclosed by several strands of "Concertina" barbed
wire to prevent any illegal incursions or unauthorized departures.

One day I happened to come across a small opening in the wire.
By crawling on my belly, I found I could maneuver my way thru the
"fortifications" and go practice with the base team.
After an hour or so the team asked me if I'd like to join up.
I told them that I was only scheduled to remain on active duty for
the normal six-month National Guard tour and much as I'd like to
play, I wasn't about to extend my stay.
The Pistol Team also wanted me to play for them.

I had played against them in a pick-up game and they thought I would be an asset to the team.

I politely declined the invitation and gave them the same explanation I had given the Base Team.

I also told them that in spite of having fired "Expert", I didn't like guns. They then told me, "Don't worry, you won't have to fire any weapons, just play ball."

One very noteworthy milestone in baseball took place during my time at Fort Bragg.

On Father's Day, Sunday June 21, I was watching the nationally televised "Game of the Week" in our Company's "Day Room".

The two broadcasters were the old Brooklyn Dodgers' Captain and shortstop, "Pee Wee" Reese and the great Cardinal's pitcher, "Dizzy" Dean.

The sponsor of the game was Falstaff Beer, a big name at the time.

The teams involved were the Philadelphia Phillies, who were visiting my team, the New York Mets, at Shea Stadium in Flushing, Queens, New York.

It was so hot in the Day Room that all the candy in the room's vending machines melted.

It was just as hot up in New York and the Phillies pitcher, righthander Jim Bunning, was even hotter.

Bunning pitched a "Perfect Game" retiring all 27 batters he faced. Nobody reached first base.

At the time, it was only the 2nd "Perfect Game" ever pitched in National League history.

As I was getting ready to leave the sweltering Day Room after the final out and the victory celebration, the local TV channel put on the 1942 western film, "Ridin' Down the Canyon" starring Roy Rogers, "Gabby" Hayes, Bob Nolan and the Sons of the Pioneers and Trigger, Roy's Gold Palomino.

Needless to say, I sweltered for another hour!

About a month after arriving at Fort Bragg, a rumor started circulating that a new Military Regulation had been issued which would affect our stay on active duty.

The Regulation stipulated that National Guardsmen were to be returned to their home unit upon completion of their M.O.S. training. In some cases, that was significantly shorter than the usual six months.

Two of our barracks buddies, Levine and Sileo, began to pester our First Sergeant to begin processing the guys involved.
After a week or so, the First Sergeant became fed up with their badgering and threw them out of the Orderly Room.
As it turned out, the "I.G." (Inspector General's office) was making a tour of our base and was in our area.

Levine and Sileo wondered what else could be done.
I suggested that it might a good idea to talk to the Battalion Morale Officer.
They asked me if I would mind carrying the ball further.
I said o.k. and made an appointment.
I spoke with the Morale Officer a few days later for about an hour.
I told him about the Regulation and the fact that it directed that all of the National Guardsmen should be sent back to their home unit.
After listening to me plead our case for all that time, he turned to me and said, "Well, Lane, I really can't help you, but if you ever want to "Re-Up", here's some pamphlets that might interest you.
I couldn't believe that this clown wanted to get me Re-Enlist after I had spent the last hour telling him how much we all wanted to go back home!
The next step was to see the "I.G."

I met with a Major from the I.G.'s office a week later and he patiently listened to the oft repeated tale of our plight.
Finally, the Major said to me, "Lane, are you the only one affected by this problem?"
My reply was, "No sir, there are 75 of us National Guardsmen in question."
We started processing out the next day.

Chapter Sixteen

"F" TROOP 1963-1969

I finally bid farewell to Fort Bragg on July 24th after having been on Active Duty for only 4 months and 24 days rather than the usual 6 months.

No sooner had I returned home than I received a phone call from my National Guard Unit, the 102nd Ordnance Company, to report for two weeks Summer Camp to be held up at Camp Drum in Watertown, New York.

Oh, Goody!

We all met at our Armory on a Friday evening and drove up to Camp Smith in Peekskill to spend the night prior to making the all-day trek up to Drum.

Our convoy consisted of about two dozen trucks of various sizes and our two Wreckers.

The Wreckers were supposed to be situated at the rear of the convoy to protect the vehicles and address any problems encountered by them.

Curiously, the Wreckers were not allowed to use the Battery Tunnel into Manhattan since we carried explosive acetylene and oxygen bottles to be used in welding should the need arise.

As a result, we had to use the Williamsburg Bridge to make our East River crossing.

Consequently, we would lose track of the convoy almost immediately and would lag miles behind.

This also occurred as we departed Peekskill the following day.

(By accident, of course) Silly us!

It left us free to make unauthorized stops along the convoy route for our breakfast, lunch and any other breaks we chose to take.
I was assigned to the Wrecker driven by the JAYCOX brothers, TOMMY and DAVEY.

Both the Jaycox's were life-long body builders and I had to ride between them on the whole 400-mile trip.
The cab of the Wrecker wasn't really meant to accommodate three normal sized people let along two body builders and one 159-pound passenger.
One of the charming things about the Wrecker was the fact that the heat from the engine would blow up the back of the cab into the interior.
The problem could be partially alleviated by jamming flattened out cardboard cartons behind the driver and passengers, deflecting some of the heat.

Another unique characteristic of the Wrecker was its floor mounted, five forward gear manual gear shift that was positioned in the middle of its cab.
As the in-between occupant of the passenger compartment, I was forced to straddle that accursed gear shift for the entire 400-mile odyssey.

The Jaycox's were and are two of the nicest guys you'd ever want to meet.
In fact, when my wife, daughter and our newly acquired pussycat, Grubby, moved to Long Island from New Jersey, Tommy and Davey unloaded our rented moving van at our new Commack home.
We were several hours late getting to Commack due to the time it took us to load up the truck in Bogota and the traffic we encountered on the Cross Bronx and Long Island Expressways.
It wasn't until about 10 o'clock in the evening when we finally pulled up in front of our new abode.
Nevertheless, Tommy, Davey and their wives had waited all those hours for us to arrive.

It took the Jaycox's less than half an hour to unload the U-Haul van and put everything in place inside our new hacienda.

Couches, chairs, beds, chests of drawers or dressers, it made no difference to the brothers; they said they enjoyed the workout.

They wouldn't even let Gail and I help them; they knew we were exhausted.

It was like having SUPERMAN and CAPTAIN MARVEL move us in.

Getting back to the Armory and "F" Troop.

Some genius decided to put all the wise guys in our unit into one platoon.

"F" Troop had been born!

Sgt. Frank Patti, a real good guy, was put in charge of us.

Patti was one of the few normal-sized non-coms in the 102nd.

The rest of the Sergeants were either quite obese or very small.

We referred to the latter as "The Seven Dwarfs".

At one of our weekly meetings, a new Lieutenant was assigned to whip us into shape.

We were standing in ranks as the new Lieutenant began to inspect and question us.

The first person he encountered was Dom Consiglio.

"Consiglio, do you know the proper way to raise the flag in the morning?" he asked.

After thinking it over for just a moment, Consiglio replied:

"Pull the cord, Sir!"

It went downhill from there.

Next up was the immortal Peter L. Gardini.

"Gardini, do you know your First General Order?" he barked.

"No Sir" replied Peter.

"Why not, Gardini?"

"Nervous, Sir" responded Peter.

The Lieutenant then made the mistake of trying to soothe Peter by saying, "Don't be nervous, son, we all put our pants on the same way; one leg at a time".

The Officer was unaware that "Nervous, Sir" was Peter's standard excuse for just about any military type question.

After being counseled on the intricacies of sartorial protocol, Peter replied, "Could you repeat that, Sir, I didn't quite understand."

Next up was Ralph "Bouzhie" Mastriano.

Ralph was a good guy, but he occasionally dabbled in some odd "Freelance Pharmaceuticals".

This was one of those times.

No matter what the Officer said, Bouzhie would just stare ahead glassy eyed, smile and weave back and forth.

Now it was my turn.

"Lane, did you shine those boots today?"

"Yes, Sir, I did", I answered.

"What did you use, a brick?"

"No, Sir", I replied, "I usually use a brush and some polish, but if you think I can get better results with a brick, I'm willing to give it a try."

Finally, the Lieutenant faced Hughie Breslin.

"Breslin", he roared, "Do you know who I am?"

Hughie replied, "No, Sir, I wasn't here last week."

We never saw that Lieutenant again.

Summer Camp was a whole different ball game for all concerned.

We would work a full 8-hour day at a Motor Pool, pulling and replacing engines and/or transmissions from any number of vehicles. These vehicles usually came from other units based at Drum for their annual two week "Summer Frolic".

The honest to God mechanics in our unit were pretty good at what they did and for the most part, liked their work.

Our job as the Wrecker Crews was to lift, carry and position the engines and transmissions into the vehicles in need of the replacements.

Occasionally we would even have to leave Drum to retrieve a vehicle that had either broken down or been involved in an accident away from the base.

Now I'm a real believer in the idea that, "When your number is up, it's up!"

In the six years of attending Summer Camp, I saw a base Maintenance Man only once.

A few of us were in our barracks latrine when somebody said, "Look, there's steam coming out of the toilets!"

The Maintenance Man who miraculously was in the building that one and only time, ran around flushing all the toilets and turning all of the faucets wide open.

He then ran outside and around the building to the room that housed the coal fired furnace and hot water heater.

Some bright light had tied down the safety valve on the boiler and it was about to blow.

The Maintenance Man cut the rope holding down the valve just in time.

The safety valve did its job and violently purged itself of the super-heated steam and boiling water.

A few more seconds and we all would have been blown to bits!

Mr. Argo, our Company Warrant Office, decided it would be a good idea for us to march back and forth to our Motor Pool each day although we had any number of trucks at our disposal.

It was a distance of about half a mile.

We were the only Guard unit to do so.

In addition, Argo reasoned that a little military marching music played over our Orderly Room's outdoor speaker would undoubtedly serve to enhance our marching experience.

Enter, Peter L. Gardini.

Peter couldn't stand that s—ty military music and took action to correct the situation.

One day, we were marching back to the Company area to the strains of some of John Phillip Sousa's finest tunes.

Suddenly, there was a loud screeching sound emanating from the P.A. system as if someone had clumsily removed the offending record from the Orderly Room's turntable.

There was a short, pregnant pause.

The next thing we heard was Frank Sinatra's, "Fly Me to the Moon" wafting its way thru the air as we returned.

Peter had somehow gotten to the Orderly Room's phonograph and made his bizarre substitution.

No one, from the Captain, to the Lieutenant, to the First Sergeant, to the Company Clerk had stopped him when he entered the Orderly Room.
Whatever vague and convoluted explanation Peter had given them about his presence there, they basically said, "O.K. Gardini,, do whatever you want, just leave us alone."
Needless to say, Mr. Argo was not happy.
Everybody else thought it was hilarious.
By the way, from that point on we rode the trucks back and forth.

There were so many antics that Peter pulled that I will attempt to chronicle just a few.

One day it was drizzling outside with a chance of heavy rain in the forecast.
and we were all instructed to don our ponchos.
Peter, of course, had a problem with this.

"I hate my poncho", he complained, "I don't want to wear it."
"Listen, Gardini", said Sgt. Fratello, "If they told you to jump out that 2nd story window, you'd have to do it!"
"If I jump out the window, do I have to wear my poncho?" queried Peter.
"Do whatever you think is best", said Fratello.
With that, Peter leaped out the window, his poncho flapping in the breeze as he descended.

Sgt. Fratello then came downstairs to the first floor where my bunk was.
"Your friend Gardini just jumped out the window upstairs" said Fratello with a glazed look on his face.
"He's probably headed for the PX, we're supposed to meet there" I answered.
"Thanks for telling me, Sarge."

One night, our platoon was going to watch "skin flicks" on our barracks wall.
Because my bunk was closest to the wall, I just slipped off my bed and sat on the floor so I wouldn't block anybody's view.
When the lights went off at the start of the show, I was the only one there.
When the film was over and the lights came back on, Peter was sitting next to me wearing only shower clogs and shorts.
This was somewhat disconcerting since he was supposed to be on Guard Duty at the time.
When asked why he was there, Peter recounted some fable about how his relief had showed up early and he had given him his uniform, helmet and weapon.
As usual, he got away with it.

Peter also didn't put much effort into making his bunk in the morning.
As fate would have it, Jimmy Petricone was our Captain's brother.
To make his brother look good, Jimmy would make Peter's bed up for him.
This happened every day until...

Jimmy had KP and couldn't perform his daily bunk making chores.

When the barracks were inspected that morning by the Officer of the Day and the First Sergeant, they found Peter's bed to be somewhat unkempt.

It was so bad that they overturned the bunk and threw all the blankets, sheets and pillows into a pile in the corner.

When Peter returned from breakfast, he saw the abomination, paused for a moment then blithely quoted Goldilock's three bears, inquiring, "Who's been sleeping in my bed?"
The inspectors were not at all amused.
"Gardini, "#@$%^$#&*!@+^#&*%#&*@^#!", they roared, pointing to the mess in the corner.
When they finally finished, Peter replied, "I don't know what happened; I certainly didn't leave it that way when I went to breakfast!!"

BOBBY DONNELLY and I used to bring our hockey sticks up to Drum and would practice taking slap shots at each other from both ends of the barracks at night.
Guys emerging from the showers learned quickly to look carefully before attempting to return to their bunks on either side of the barrack's middle aisle/firing range.

The last day of my last (6th) Summer Camp, the whole Company (200 guys) was getting ready to head back home to Brooklyn.
It was then discovered that the Orderly Room staff had neglected to take down the P.A. system's speaker from the Orderly Room's roof.
Of all the people they could have picked to climb up and bring down the speaker, they chose the one and only Peter L. Gardini.
Peter quickly clambered up the side of the building, removed the speaker and froze.

"What's the matter, Gardini?", inquired the Captain.
"I'm afraid of heights", replied Peter. (Which, of course, he wasn't)
It took twenty minutes to locate a ladder to pluck young Mr. Gardini from his perch.
All the while, most of the 200 were waiting, watching and cursing at him.
Those of us who knew him best thought it was to be expected.
Peter had struck again.
In spite of all these and other shenanigans, Peter was the only one of us to ever get promoted and he never let us forget it.
The Officer responsible reasoned it would give Peter incentive.

Yeah, right!

On the trip home from that last Summer Camp, there was an almost a fatal accident up in Cherry Valley involving one of our trucks.

The truck in question was the "Arms Van" which carried all our weapons and ammunition.

The "Van" lost its steering capability, swerved off the road, clipped the side of a farm house, sheared off an old water pump and came to rest in a muddy field.

When our Wrecker got there, the three guys in the truck were still visibly shaken and perhaps on the verge of passing out.

Other than that, they were unharmed.

Our job was to remove the vehicle in question from that muddy field.

I went into the field to attach the Wrecker's hook to the back of the van.

We've all heard stories about World War I soldiers being stuck in mud and not be able to get out.

(Some were even sucked down and never seen again)

As I approached the rear of the vehicle, I suddenly found I couldn't move either of my feet in the mud because of the suction.

The rest of the crew seeing my plight (and laughing) finally extended the Wrecker's boom and pulled me up and out of the quagmire.

When we eventually extracted the disabled truck, it was time to move out.

A Warrant Officer (not Mr. Argo), who happened upon the scene, was driving an "Econoline" van and did not want to let the three occupants of the truck ride in his van.

He maintained they would dirty his rugs with their muddy boots.

He decided that they should ride back to Brooklyn in the disabled vehicle which was now on our Wrecker's hook and bolstered by a triangular tow bar.

Even so, the truck would sway a little and wasn't safe for passengers.

I told the Warrant Officer I was not willing to transport the three guys in that fashion.

Nonetheless, this Warrant Officer persisted in his reluctance to let the three ride in his van.

I then said, "Please radio my Company Commander to find out what he thinks should be done, Sir."
The guys rode in his van.

In addition, I requested that a Wrecker or two be sent back to meet us along the way since ours was acting up.
Our wrecker finally broke down at dawn the next day by Monticello Race Track.

Just as the sun was coming up, we saw two Wreckers from our Sister Company, the 145th, flying over the hill towards us.
The Cavalry had come to the rescue!

Once all the disabled vehicles had been hooked up (including ours), it was time for us all to go.
As we were preparing to leave, that same Warrant Officer said, "Stop, we can't go anywhere." Perplexed, I asked why?

He replied, "I can't find my flashlight, I'm responsible for it and we can't leave until I do."
Twenty some odd very tired soldiers couldn't leave until this Pin-Head found his "F—-ING flashlight!
Calmly, but bordering on the verge of mutiny, I inquired just how much his beloved flashlight cost.
"That's not the point", he replied.
"Well", I said, "Here's $20, you can stay here if you want and look for your flashlight, but the rest of us are getting the hell out of here!"

Hi-Yo, Silver, Away!!!

As I said, that was my last Summer Camp and a few months later, I was finally discharged on November 6th, 1969.

I had a good time for the most part during those 6 years, met some good guys and didn't allow too much of that Army stuff get in the way.

P.S. I was voted the "Most Hostile" of our 6-year cycle.

CAMP DRUM 1964 N Y

To Bob—
Good Luck and Kindest regards
Dave Sharpe

Chapter Seventeen

WESTERN FILM CONVENTIONS

E arly in the 1970's I started to renew my interest in the old cowboy movies I had enjoyed when I was a kid.

These films were no longer shown on television because the powers that controlled the industry wanted only new, fresh and color fare.

Most of those old-westerns had been made in glorious black and white and were relics from the 30's, 40's and early 50's.

Madison Avenue had no interest in them and "Nostalgia" was years away.

But there existed an underground core of loyal fans who had never forgotten those "Thrilling Days of Yesteryear".

Good friend, ALAN BARBOUR, was in the vanguard of those who struggled to keep the flame alive.

A few nostalgia oriented stores had popped up around the city in lower and mid-town Manhattan which catered to the collectors of movie posters, lobby cards and 8x10 stills (photos).

There also were scores of private 16mm film collectors scattered around the country who had rescued the old westerns and serials from extinction and destruction.

Then in 1972, a number of these collectors got together and decided to hold the first Western Film Convention in Memphis, Tennessee.

Not only did they screen the old films and assemble vendors to exhibit and sell their wonderful western and serial oriented wares, but they also brought back some of the actual stars of those bygone days.

Saddle Aces Lash LaRue, Don "Red" Barry, Russell Hayden, (Hopalong Cassidy's sidekick, "Lucky" Jenkins) and Max "Lullaby/Alibi" Terhune were all in attendance as honored guests.

I didn't make it to the Inaugural Roundup, but I did get to five subsequent conventions in Memphis, Orlando, St. Louis, Charlotte and Memphis again.

My first Memphis Convention in 1974 was probably the best of all. It was held in the historic old Peabody Hotel in downtown Memphis, There were fourteen, count 'em, 14, guest stars scheduled to appear. They included the all-time cowboy great Bob Steele, the greatest stuntman of them all, Dave Sharpe, and his pal Billy Benedict ("Whitey" from the Bowery Boys films and "The Adventures of Captain Marvel"), the truly evil bad guy, I. Stanford Jolley, Monte Hale, Eddie Dean, Lash LaRue, Russell Hayden, "Rocky" Lane's sidekick ("Nugget" Clark), Eddie Waller, singer Johnny Bond, the last of the three "Red Ryders", Jim Bannon and heavy Myron (Mike) Healy. In addition, three of the loveliest leading ladies of the genre, Peggy Stewart, Penny Edwards and Dorothy Fay Ritter (Tex's wife and the mother of John of "Three's Company" fame) graced the roster of stars. "Sunset" Carson was also slated to appear, but could not due to illness.

There were a couple of moments that stood out for me personally at that Memphis Convention.

First was a soft shoe dance and fight routine that DAVE SHARPE and BILLY BENEDICT put on prior to one of the celebrity panel discussions. As they were dancing, Billy accused Dave of stepping on his foot.

Words were exchanged and Billy demanded an apology from Dave.

When no apology was forthcoming, Billy challenged Dave to a fight.

Dave turned to the audience and said, "He has GOT to be kidding."

At that point, Billy swung at Dave who promptly did a complete mid-air somersault landing flat on his back.

The crowd went wild, Dave did a "kip" to get to his feet and the two good friends shook hands to show there were no hard feelings.

The second was the way arch-villain I. STANFORD JOLLEY often stayed in the lobby of the hotel till almost midnight signing autographs and talking to anybody and everybody.

When Stan was introduced at one of the celebrity panels, he addressed those in attendance as follows:

"I would like to thank the convention's organizers for inviting me today in spite of the fact that I'm one of America's foremost SEMI-RETIRED MURDERERS and assure them that I'm ready to go back to work at any time."

I don't think anyone had a better time at the Convention than Stan. (He, by the way, is the father-in-law of Forrest Tucker of "F" Troop fame and dozens of films in which Tucker played both villain and hero.)

Finally, as I've mentioned before, I had lunch with the legendary BOB STEELE.

When he first arrived at the convention, Bob seemed very nervous, probably since he hadn't made any personal appearances in quite some time and

perhaps didn't know what to expect at his first convention.

I ran into Jim Schoenberger, one of the event's organizers, and told him of my concerns about Bob.

Jim echoed my feelings.

At the first panel of stars Jim had introduced the panel by merely saying, "If anyone in the audience doesn't recognize any of the members of our panel, please tell me."

The panel at the time included Dave, Billy, Peggy Stewart and Lash LaRue, I think.

I told Jim that although everybody knew who was who on that first panel, I thought he should give a much more rousing introduction to Bob.

He agreed.

When the time came for the second panel and Jim had introduced all the other guests, only Bob remained.

Jim then quietly spoke these words into the microphone, "Ladies and Gentlemen...MR. BOB STEELE!"

The audience erupted in a standing ovation that must have lasted almost a full minute.

When the tumult finally died down, Bob voiced a resounding "Hi!" into his microphone, all signs of nervousness long gone.

After the panel, I went into the dealer's room, made a few purchases, talked to some friends and got a couple of autographs and pictures.

I was getting hungry, so I went into the Peabody's restaurant to grab a bite to eat.

As I walked in, who did I see sitting alone in a booth by the window but Bob Steele himself.

I knew that this was a once in a lifetime opportunity.

I walked over and asked Bob if I might join him for lunch.

"Sure" he said, "Sit down."

We spent the next hour talking about any number of things.

He mentioned how he missed his father, Robert North Bradbury, who had guided his early career and directed him in dozens of his films.

He said that Ken Maynard thought they were making "Gone With The Wind" when they were doing the "Trail Blazers" series with his good friend Hoot Gibson over at Monogram.

His thoughts on retirement included moving up to the High Sierras for some peace and quiet.

As far as "F" Troop went, Bob said he never had so much fun in his life.

When Forrest Tucker came to Hollywood, Bob had befriended him and took him under his wing.

They've been friends ever since.

Tucker was responsible for bringing Bob into the "F" Troop cast and told him he could work whenever he felt up to it.

When Larry Storch (Corporal Agarn) asked Tucker (Sgt. O'Roarke) what Bob was there for, Tucker told him that Bob (Trooper Duffy) was going to teach him how to keep his butt in the saddle.

Bob said that "F" Troop would have run much longer but for some front office disagreements that eventually doomed the series.

He touched on his role of the nasty "Curley" in the excellent production of the classic 1939 film "Of Mice and Men".

Critics were very pleased with Bob's portrayal.

He thought it might win the Academy Award for Best Picture that year, but that little epic called "Gone With The Wind" got in the way.

About that time a couple of fans came over to the table to present Bob with an honorary "Kentucky Colonel" award.

I asked Bob if we might get these gentlemen to take our picture together before I got out of the way of the presentation.

We took the picture, but while doing so knocked the scroll under our table.

Bob started to reach under the table, but I asked Bob to let me do it for him.

He agreed and I became a stunt double for the one and only Bob Steele.

I briefly entertained the idea of having a 2nd picture taken for protection, but decided against it. (It proved to be a fateful decision)

As I was leaving, I passed a couple of young Memphis Policemen who had been watching what had transpired.

I briefly explained to them who Bob Steele was, but they had no clue what I was talking about.

I left the hotel early the next day to put my luggage in a locker in the Memphis Bus Terminal since I didn't have a flight out for home until later that evening.

As I walked through the door of the bus terminal my camera hit the door and went off.

The result was a double exposure of me, Bob Steele, the floor of the Memphis Bus Terminal and my left foot.

Bob and I are virtually unrecognizable.

I have tried for decades to get someone to correct the problem to no avail.

Perhaps one day...

The other thing I fondly remember about my first Western Film Convention was the Peabody Ducks.

Every morning the hotel would send an elevator to the roof of the building and bring the flock of ducks who lived up there, down to the lobby.

The ducks would get off the elevator, walk across the lobby on a red carpet which had been rolled out for their personal(?) use and jump into the hotel lobby's fountain.

They would spend the entire day there quacking and splashing.

At five o'clock the ducks would jump out of their fountain, waddle across the red carpet, get on the elevator and be whisked up to their home in the sky.

Dozens of people would come down to the lobby twice a day to catch a glimpse of the resident mallards, laugh and take pictures.

Is it any wonder, it was my favorite Convention?

A couple of years later, in 1976, I flew down to Orlando, Florida for my second Western Film Roundup.

As with the previous one, the convention was loaded with guest stars. Dick Foran, Rod Cameron, Ben Johnson, Art Davis, Ray Whitley, Kirby Grant (TV's "Sky King), Eddie Dean, Monte Hale, Chill Wills, Foy Willing and Dan White.

The distaff side was ably represented by the lovely LOUISE STANLEY and the gracious and charming JENNIFER HOLT.

ALAN BARBOUR was the one who first introduced me to Jennifer.

I was wandering around the hotel looking for my roommate, ED HULSE, when I came across Alan, seated on a bench in an alcove, talking to some young lady whose back was to me.

I apologized for interrupting their conversation and it was then that the lady turned around.

Alan then said, "Jennifer, I'd like you to meet a good friend of mine, Bob Lane from New York".

I think Alan excused himself at that point saying he had some convention business to attend to and left me alone with Jennifer.

Jennifer and I spoke together as if we were old friends for 20 minutes or so.

She was a delight to talk to.

Eventually, Jennifer said she was scheduled to appear on one of the panels and I escorted her to the room where the panel was to take place.

She and I ran into each other any number of times in the next few days and on each occasion we passed the time taking pictures and continuing our conversations.

Naturally, fans would approach her for autographs and pictures and she always graciously accommodated one and all.

On one occasion, Jennifer told me she would like to go back upstairs to her room for a rest.

I told her, "Let me get you out of here", since there were still a number of fans hovering around her.

She said, "Would you please".

I walked Jennifer to the elevator and we both went up to our rooms. She on the second floor and I on the fifth.

Jennifer and I would run into each other at two more conventions and we became frequent pen pals.

When we conversed, Jennifer would often remark how pleased she was to see my handwriting on her incoming mail.
She said it was the nicest she had ever seen.

Other guests of note that attended were singing cowboy star DICK FORAN who sang a duet of "Home on the Range" with his young son and perhaps the finest horseman ever to gallop across the silver screen, BEN JOHNSON.
Ben, of course had been a wrangler on a number of pictures and had doubled such cowboy stars as "Wild Bill" Elliott, "Sunset" Carson, Charles Starrett and Robert Mitchum among others.
He became a member of famed director John Ford's "Stock Company" after he had saved the lives of a couple of actors (including John Wayne?) by riding his horse into the side of a runaway wagon preventing it from overturning and perhaps killing all on board.
Ford called him into his office and signed him to a "Personal Services" contract the next day for a VERY, VERY generous salary.
Before he let Ben sign, Ford told him that perhaps he would like for his

lawyer to look over the contract.
Ben, who was probably making about 20 dollars a week at the time, grabbed the contract and immediately signed saying, "I don't need no lawyer to tell me to sign this!"

In addition to being a fine horseman, Ben was also a World Champion Roper.
The night after he had won the Championship, Ben and his buddies went out for a "not so few" drinks
The following day, Ben, feeling quite hung over, was introduced to the crowd as the "Newly Crowned World Champion Calf Roper".
With the applause still ringing in his ears, the gate opened and Ben took off at full gallop in pursuit of his target calf.
Ben swung his loop, threw his rope and...missed the calf completely!
He then sheepishly headed back to the corral dragging his rope on the ground behind him.
When Ben arrived backstage of the arena, there was a little boy standing there staring up at him on his horse.
"World Champion huh?" said the little urchin.
Ben later confided that he looked around and if no one had been there, "I'd have rode that little sucker down!"

Ben Johnson was a class act both professionally and personally.
A fine actor and an Academy Award winner for his role in the "Last Picture Show" Ben was a true stand-up guy.
During the convention, Chill Wills spent a lot of time drinking.
When it came time for his appearance on one of the panels, Chill went into a vulgar speech in which he called his wife, who was in the crowd, everything but the Son of God.
Ben, once he realized what was going on, said, "Sit down Chill, you're making a fool of yourself".
The audience burst into a well-deserved round of applause for this fine Cowboy Gentleman.

To Bob
Your friend
Victor Jory

One night during the Convention, I had been watching the first "Wild Bill" Elliott "Red Ryder" film, "Tucson Raiders," in which Ben had doubled Bill.

I had a question about one of the stunts in the movie and after it ended, I went looking for Ben to ask him about it.

Somebody told me he was in the hotel bar, so I headed down that way. When I got to the bar, I walked up to the bartender to ask if he had seen Ben.

Without me saying a single word, the barkeep said to me, "You're either from New York or Chicago!".

Mystified, I asked him how he had arrived at that conclusion.

He explained, "When you walked in the door you stopped, looked to the left and then to the right before you came all the way into the bar."

"Only guys from New York and Chicago do that!"

The next stop on the Convention Caravan for me was St. Louis in 1979. The one and only KAY ALDRIDGE headlined the array of stars in attendance.

I will address her exploits in a subsequent Chapter so let me concentrate on the other luminaries.

All-time great Stuntman/Director, Yakima Canutt, Don "Red" Barry, the truly menacing Victor Jory, the lovely Joan Woodbury, Jim Brown ("Rip" Masters from the Rin Tin-Tin TV Series), Director Oliver Drake, the alluring Myrna Dell and Leon McCauliffe from Bob Wills' Texas Playboys all lent their presence to the festivities.

VICTOR JORY told many stories about his days in the Hopalong Cassidy movies, his serial appearances in "The Shadow" and the "Green Archer", his role as "Oberon" in "A Mid-Summer Night's Dream" and even an altercation he had with Errol Flynn.

It seems that Flynn had shown up a party given by Victor in a mild state of advanced intoxication.

Errol then proceeded to make the rounds of the married women among

To my friend Bob — good to
see you again. James (Brown
(Lt Rip Masters)

Victor's guests.

When their husbands eventually complained, Victor took Errol aside and

asked politely that he confine his amorous activities to the single females in the house.

At that point, Flynn became somewhat annoyed and invited Victor to continue the discussion outside.

What Flynn didn't know was that Jory had done some boxing up in his native British Columbia and was quite good at it.

At one time, in fact, he was the Lightweight Champion of the entire Province.

Once outside, Flynn swung, Jory ducked, counter punched and knocked Errol on his rump.

Victor then asked Errol what he would like to do next.

The ever-charming Flynn replied, "I think I'd like you to introduce me to some of those single ladies!"

One of the nicest guys I ever met at any of the Conventions was JIM BROWN, (Lt. Rip Masters), of the Rin Tin-Tin TV series.

Over the course of the three days in St. Louis I found myself bumping into Jim on a number of occasions.

In fact, Jim told me that I reminded him of actor Richard Crenna of the "Real McCoys" TV show and the "Our Miss Brooks" radio/television series.

I told him that although I didn't dislike Richard, I was not a big fan either.

From that point on, whenever I came across Jim, he would insist on calling me "Richard".

Thanks, wise guy!

Famed stuntman and Academy Award winning 2nd unit director, YAKIMA CANUTT was another terrific guest.

In the early 30's, Yak often appeared with John Wayne in a number of "Duke's" "Poverty Row", "Lone Star" productions, directed by Bob Steele's father, Robert North Bradbury.

Yak was often cast as the villain in the films as well as serving as Wayne's stunt double.

As a result, he would often gallop after himself in the chase scenes.

It was Yak who staged the monumentally spectacular chariot race in the 1959 version of "Ben Hur" starring Charlton Heston.

Incidently. it was he who taught Heston how to drive his chariot.

When Heston voiced his doubts about his ability to control the chariot, Yak assured him, "Don't worry, Chuck, you're GONNA win the damn race!"

Yak's son, Tap, doubled Heston in the race including the famous leap over the wrecked chariot blocking the course.

Tap was almost killed when he didn't listen to his father's instructions on how to perform the stunt.

Yak told him to make sure that he held onto BOTH the front and the back of his chariot as he hurdled the wreck or he would be pitched forward into his four white horses.

Tap didn't listen, was thrown into the leaping steeds, bounced off the wall of the arena and narrowly escaped death.

The near fatal mistake was incorporated into the final version of the race and it is Heston who is shown climbing back into his chariot after the plummet into the speeding foursome.

I also asked Yak about a number of his own legendary stunts, including the classic when he falls between the horses of a careening stagecoach, slides along the ground underneath all four or six of the horses and the coach itself, grabs onto the back of the stage as it passes over him and climbs back up to the top of the coach to continue the action.

He said that the secret of the "gag" is to make sure the stunt is performed on COMPLETELY flat terrain and that the horses run at full tilt. That way there was sufficient room between the hoofs to allow Yak to clear them safety.

If the stunt is attempted at less than top speed, the horse's hoofs

wobble from side to side as they run, often with disastrous results. Others have tried to use their own slower variation of Yak's effort and have paid the price.

One of my favorite Western Heroes is DON "RED" BARRY, often referred to as the "Cowboy Cagney".
Don got his nickname when he starred in the 1940 Republic serial "The Adventures of Red Ryder".

Don could be difficult to work with and did not want to do the picture. When threatened with suspension, he reluctantly agreed.
While I was seated next to Don in a screening room of the Convention as they were showing a print of the serial, he told me that he hated to come to work every day.
I told him that, "You would never know it, based on what's up there on the screen".

He was just about perfect.

"It's called being a professional" Don replied.

One more thing about Don.

JOAN WOODBURY arrived at the Convention at the last minute, just before she was scheduled to appear on a panel with Don.

As Alan Barbour was escorting the two of them to the room where the panel was to be held, Joan, who had never been to one of these Conventions, voiced her concerns, not knowing what to expect.

Don told her, "Don't worry, they're all just here to love you".

I have a picture of yours truly from the Convention taken with Don on my right and Yak on my left.

It's one of my favorites.

When Ed Hulse and good friend DICK BANN saw the photo, they asked, "Who looks like the real hero here?"

High praise, indeed!

In 1980, Charlotte was the next stop on my Convention "Odyssey". The guest star lineup featured "Sunset" Carson, old friends Jim Brown and Jennifer Holt, Scarlett O'Hara's husband from GWTW and the last "Lucky" Jenkins in the Hopalong Cassidy films, Rand Brooks, director Oliver Drake, the hero of Columbia's "Ranger" series, Bob Allen, "Sky King" himself, Kirby Grant, Lash La Rue and two lovely "Gals of the Saddle", Lois January and Louise Stanley.

During the first night of the Convention, Jim Brown was interviewed by TV station WRET in Charlotte.

I had been speaking with Jim when the young lady doing the interviews approached him.

Jim made some very nice comments about the Convention and the people in attendance, as well as the value of the films themselves.

When Jim had finished talking, the interviewer turned to me and asked if I'd mind saying a few words for the camera.

Even though I was caught off guard, I managed to string together a number of semi-coherent thoughts about the festivities and didn't hyper-ventilate in the process.

The next day, one of the Convention attendees and his wife approached me and told me I had made the 11 o'clock news.

I hadn't seen the broadcast and had no idea how things had gone.

When I got home a few days later, I called the station back in Charlotte and asked them if I might be able to get a tape of the interview.

They told me it would be no problem and would be happy to send it to me.

I asked them how much I should mail them to cover the costs, but they said not to worry, it was their pleasure and there would be no charge.

Can you imagine that happening in New York?

LOUISE STANLEY had made a number of films with and had been married to Cowboy Star Jack Randall, brother of Bob Livingston (Stony Brooke of the Three Mesquiteers series at Republic). Small world, eh?

At both of the Conventions which I attended with her, Louise had sustained some sort of injury prior to leaving home.
In Orlando in '76, she was wheel chair bound with a broken ankle and now in '80, she had a fractured right wrist.
(Couldn't somebody please get this lady a stunt double?)

BOB ALLEN had made his "Ranger" series back in 1936 for Larry D'Amour and showed up wearing his ORIGINAL western outfit including his dark blue, arrow-emblazoned shirt, white neckerchief and hat.
After 44 years, he looked spectacular.

As it turned out, Bob now lived on Long Island in Oyster Bay, only twenty miles away from my home in Commack.
We both took the same flight home to La Guardia Airport in Queens and Bob offered to drive me home.
I declined saying it would take him 20 miles out of his way and that I would take the Long Island Rail Road instead.
Bob said he didn't mind at all and would enjoy the company.
Typical Cowboy Gentleman!
We took a cab to the garage on Queens Boulevard where he had parked his car and headed out to Long Island.
He and I spoke of many things on the ride east.
Bob voiced his opinion that if he had made another 6 films, he would have firmly established himself as a western star.
(I've seen all but one of his "Ranger" films and, in MY opinion, Bob showed definite promise.)
He certainly was a LOT better than some of the guys who saddled up.
Bob had a screen presence, rode well, handled himself in the fight scenes and could read his lines convincingly.
We also spoke of his stage work (e.g. "Showboat") and his John Deere Tractor TV commercial when the narrator asks Bob,

"By the way, how long does a John Deere last?"
With a puzzled look on his face, Bob momentarily pauses then responds, "How long DOES a John Deere last???"
The inference, of course, is that there's no way of knowing since John Deere's never wear out.

When we arrived in my house, it turned out that my Mother and Father in-law were already there.
I took Bob aside when I got the chance and assured him I had no idea that they would be there.
He said it was o.k. and that he didn't mind it in the least.
Bob stayed and chatted for about half an hour.
I invited him to stay for dinner, but he politely declined saying he was anxious to get home.
I thanked Bob for everything and we said our "Good Byes."
After he had gone, I thought to myself, "That's what "Rangers" are supposed to be like!"

My final journey along the Convention Trail was back in Memphis in August of 1982.
Once again, guest stars abounded.

Charles Starrett, the "Durango Kid" himself, topped the list of notables. George "Spanky" McFarland of the "Little Rascals", "Sunset" Carson, Ben Johnson, Harry Carey Jr., Jock Mahoney, Art Davis, noted "Bad Guy" Steve Brodie and stuntman Neil Summers filled out the roster. The feminine side of the ledger was handled nicely by Peggy Stewart, Penny Edwards and of course, Jennifer.
Jennifer had brought a number of her relatives to the Convention including her nephew, Jack Jr., who in spite of a mustache, was a dead ringer for her brother, Cowboy Great, TIM HOLT.

We three took a really nice picture together which I later sent to Jen, once I had it developed.

Jennifer told me that she was having trouble with her eyes and that the camera flash had momentarily blinded her.

In the photo you can see her beginning to wince.

It's still a nice shot of our threesome.

I got a chance one day to speak with villainous "heavy", STEVE BRODIE.

In most of his films, Steve portrayed the "Bad Guy", but on radio he was cast as the hero in two pretty good series.

The one that I had remembered most was "Captain Starr of Space" in which the good Captain zoomed around the galaxy meting out his brand of interplanetary justice.

Steve then reminded me of his second series "Mike Malloy, Private Eye" which had slipped my mind.

This time Steve merely confined his efforts to planet Earth.

I'm not sure if it was a promotion or a demotion.

In either case, the results were the same, the good guys triumphed!

During the Convention, I had a chance to sit down one evening with BEN JOHNSON and stuntman NEIL SUMMERS over a couple of drinks.

There was a "lady" dressed in red "working" the bar.

As we were talking, Ben began to take note of the lady in question.

Eventually, Ben got up, took the lady's arm and left.

Neil turned to me and said, "Even cowboys need love!".

I guess so.

That 1982 Memphis get together marked the end of the Convention Trail for me.

The five that I attended were filled with great memories, lasting new friendships and a hell of a lot of fun.

The stars themselves are all gone now, but the impressions they made, both in their films and in person, were a wonderful part of my life.

Up there on the big movie screen or on my 12-inch RCA television they taught me a pretty good sense of right and wrong.
That, coupled with my Catholic School education, imbued yours truly with a fairly solid foundation in morality.
Their films were pure fantasy and only meant to entertain, but they still demonstrated ideals worth imitating.
I fear for my children and grand-children who have no heroes to emulate or goals to aspire to.
We of generations past were most fortunate indeed.

Chapter Eighteen

NYOKA HERSELF

B ack in Chapter 17, I mentioned KAY ALDRIDGE who played the title role in the great 1942 Republic movie serial "Perils of Nyoka". Her co-star in the film was none other than Clayton Moore who, of course, became TV's "Lone Ranger" seven years later in 1949.

Kay starred in two other serials, "Daredevils of the West" in 1943 with Allan "Rocky" Lane (No relation) and "Haunted Harbor" in 1944 with Kane Richmond as her leading man.

"Rocky" Lane became one of the biggest cowboy stars of the late '40's and early '50's, making almost three dozen excellent "B" westerns. He eventually, believe it or not, became the voice of TV's "Mr. Ed".

Kane Richmond's career spanned three decades from the '30's to the '50's.

His most famous role was that of "Spy Smasher" in the all-time classic 1942 Republic Serial.

Among his other starring efforts was that of "The Shadow" in three movies based on the immortal radio series of the 1940's.

Let's get back to Kay Aldridge, shall we?

I first met Kay at the 1979 St. Louis film convention and we became friends as well as pen pals.

We shared a lot of pleasant moments in St. Louis.

Kay was a lot of fun and she even asked me if I too was in show business. I laughed at the suggestion.

At the convention, Kay made her initial entrance while they were showing a print of "Perils".

She had had a replica of her original costume made and entered the room exclaiming, "That nasty old gorilla, Satan, is still chasing me around after all these years!"

At that point, a figure dressed in a gorilla suit burst into the room and grabbed "Nyoka" in his arms.

Suddenly, cowboy star Don "Red" Barry (Also a guest at the convention) rushed into the room and fired four or five shots at the "Nasty" ape freeing Kay.

The crowd went wild.

The sound of the shots was deafening and the smell of the gun-powder was overwhelming.

(Don "Red" later told me that someone had mistakenly used "full load blanks" instead of the type normally used indoors) I still have the photos of the whole sequence.

In the late 30's and 40's Kay was one of the most photographed models in America.

She was the cover girl on at least 3 LIFE magazines and countless REDBOOK issues as well.

Kay was one of the most beautiful women in the world and a real character.

Jimmy Stewart was her longtime beau and she accompanied him to the 1939 Academy Awards ceremony.

(She also dated Randolph Scott, Sterling Hayden and even Howard Hughes.) The lovely and sophisticated Miss Aldridge even found time to throw up on Errol Flynn while sailing aboard his boat, the "Sirocco".

Quite a busy social life, don't you think?

Kay and her life-long friend, Georgia Carroll, shared a house at one time with Jimmy and his buddy Henry Fonda. (Separate rooms, of course)

The two girls were both Powers models and had become part of the "Navy Blues" sextet from the 1941 picture of the same name.

Georgia later married band leader Kay Kyser and the two lived for many years on the campus of the University of North Carolina in Chapel Hill.

Unfortunately, none of the girls (except Georgia) could either sing or dance so after one more film, "You're in the Army Now" with Jimmy Durante and Phil Silvers (TV's Sgt. Bilko), the group disappeared from the screen.

They, however, continued touring the country, appearing in numerous War Bond drives and making appearances at dozens of military camps.

(They were strictly "Eye Candy" for the boys in uniforms back in WWII.) Two of the other girls, Marguerite Chapman (the leading lady in perhaps the greatest Republic serial of all, "Spy Smasher") and Lorraine Gettman, who as Leslie Brooks co-starred with Rita

Hayworth in the classic 1945 TECHNICOLOR musical "Cover Girl", went on to have long movie careers.

Marguerite often lamented, although she made several dozen other movies, that just about the only photos she's ever asked to autograph, are those from "Spy Smasher".

Like it or not, that's how she'll always be remembered by movie fans.

One of Kay's more memorable roles was that of Betty Grable's rival for the affections of Don Ameche in the lavish 1940 TECHNICOLOR 20th Century Fox musical "Down Argentine Way"

The movie also stars the fabulous dancing Nicholas Brothers and springs the one and only Carmen Miranda on an unsuspecting movie going public.

In the film, Don Ameche reneges on his promise to sell a thorough-bred horse to Betty when he realizes their parents have been feuding for years.

After saying the horse was no longer for sale, Ameche dances with Kay's character who later tells Grable that she has just bought the steed.

When asked how this could be, Kay replies with the delicious retort, "Perhaps it was my DANCING, darling."

Two years after meeting Kay in St. Louis, our family took a trip up to Pemaquid Harbor, Maine in 1981 to visit Terry Hatch's Mom and Dad. At the convention back in '79, Kay had graciously invited me to come and see her at her home in Camden, about an hour north of Pemaquid.

I called her and she repeated the invitation.

She asked us to join her for lunch on her back porch/veranda which had a glorious view of the entrance to Camden's harbor to the north and a small island about a mile away to the east.

She assured us that from there we could, "See all that makes Maine famous."

We drove up to Camden and found Kay's home on a road just south of town on Bay View Street.

Her property contained two buildings, a main house and a three-car garage with a loft apartment on the second floor.

The garage housed a vintage Rolls Royce, a Bentley and Kay's own personal automobile.

The main house was connected to the town water supply during the warm months May thru October.

When the weather turned cold, the town would turn of their water supply lest the pipes freeze.

Kay would then migrate to the apartment above the garage which had access to its own private well.

It was a small but cozy dwelling that even contained a secret panel behind one of her bookcases.

(I imagine the area was used for storage)

The apartment had doubled as her late husband's (artist Richard Derby Tucker), painting studio, complete with skylight.

He was of the opinion that the morning light was at its best from there.

When we arrived, Kay had one of her friends give us a ride in her Rolls while she prepared a light lunch for us.

Upon our return, we sat down in Kay's living room and I gave her some photos I had gathered over the years, including a delightful lobby card of the whole cast of "You're in the Army Now".

In the shot, Kay and Jimmy Durante seem to be having a lot of fun even though the photographer was trying to get a semi-formal portrait.

There also was a LIFE Magazine spread entitled "Models Go to a Party".

In it, Kay seems to have taken over the festivities and gets the majority of the article's attention.

In the midst of perusing her photos, I showed Kay my album of pictures I had taken at other conventions.

Included in the array were photos with the stars of those get togethers, which, of course, featured other leading ladies such as Peggy Stewart, Joan Woodbury, Penny Edwards, Dorothy Fay-Ritter, (Tex's wife and John's mother) Louise Stanley and good friend, Jennifer Holt.

Without deigning to even look up from the album, Kay murmured in a soft and pseudo-syrupy tone, "It appears that you have been unfaithful to me from time to time, Robert."

I couldn't help but laugh at her sly aside.

There was one other color advertising shot from a LOOK Magazine which I wasn't quite sure was Kay, she looked totally different.

After looking at it, she assured me that it was indeed her.

She told us that one of her strong points as a model was the ability to change her looks to suit the spirit of the session.

That's one of the traits that made her so successful in the fashion world.

She could go from innocent and wholesome to coy to dramatic to sexy and alluring, depending of the requirements of the shoot.

When it came time to eat lunch we adjourned outdoors and spent the time in cordial conversation.

While we were finishing our meal, Kay disappeared for a while and I went back inside to take a few photos of the interior of the house.

Kay, ever conscious of her figure, had a note pinned to her refrigerator which said: "A moment on the lips, forever on the hips"

As it turned out, Kay had gone upstairs to change into her "Nyoka" costume, but unfortunately it had fallen off its hanger in her closet and had gotten too wrinkled to wear.

When Kay reappeared, we took some snapshots together out on the porch with the harbor view in the background.

She even showed us the scar on her leg she had suffered while filming "The Tunnel of Bubbling Death" sequence in the serial.

(It was caused by dry ice not the fiery "Bubbling Death")

Once that was done, I asked Kay if it would be alright to take some movie film with my trusty Super-8 movie camera that my wife, Gail, had given me as an engagement present back in '66.

I had intended to take generally panoramic shots of the house and especially the view from the veranda.

Kay thought instead that I wanted to film her, and in a flash, she started cavorting around the deck and playing to the camera.

I later said to my wife, "Did you see what just happened?"

As soon as I turned the camera on, Kay dropped forty years right in front of our eyes and proceeded to make love to the camera.

It was magical to see.

The camera loved her in return as she exhibited the beauty and talent that had made her so successful as one of America's finest models.

I'm so glad we were able to capture that moment.

Soon it was time to go, and after Kay autographed a bunch of 8x10s, we said our "Good Bye's"

As she had explained earlier, Kay had a plane to catch that evening and her ride to the airport was due in a couple of hours.

The afternoon couldn't have gone better as Kay had extended her southern hospitality to Gail, Chrissy, Bobby and I.

She was as charming and gracious as I could have ever hoped for, a true Southern Lady.

Kay and I continued to write to each other and her letters and cards are among my most cherished possessions. Most of the letters and cards were hand written while others were of the type written variety. After completing them, however, Kay would remember some additional thoughts and scribble them around the margins of her original typed text.

There was one other incident Kay told us about that really epitomizes her playful personality.

It seems that Kay was travelling cross country during WWII when one of the soldiers on her train struck up a conversation with her over lunch.

When the meal was over, Kay autographed a napkin for the GI questioning if it was "her looks or the pork chops" that had prompted his attention.

Many years later, Kay was appearing at a charity auction up in Maine when a woman approached her prior to the event.

The lady revealed that she was the wife of that soldier, who had not only kept the napkin, but also, on numerous occasions, related the tale of that long ago train trip.

She said her husband was in the audience and had insisted they attend. Kay, typically, said she would address the situation.

Before the actual auction began, Kay stepped up to the microphone to say a few words about the fine work the charity in question was doing and urging everyone to be as generous as possible in support of their efforts.

As she was finishing her speech, Kay mentioned that there was an old and dear friend of hers in the crowd, and after telling the story of their long ago luncheon, loudly proclaimed, "Now, George, you come right up here and let me give you a great big kiss!"

He did and she did.

As I said, she was a character!

I consider myself extremely fortunate to have known this charming lady and to have corresponded with her for all those years.

"Nyoka" was quite a gal!

Chapter Nineteen

RADIO CONVENTIONS

A s previously mentioned, RADIO was "THE" home entertainment medium
from the 1930's thru the early 1950's prior to the arrival of TELEVISION.
It was an extremely personal, warm and intimate method of
communication.
Radio became part of the everyday fabric of life.
Families would gather round their sets on any given evening to listen
to stories and personalities that they welcomed into their homes as
honored guests.
You could even say that people actually "watched" the radio since
it was not unusual for entire households to stare at the lighted dial
while visualizing the programs in progress.
There are those who still maintain that the "images" on radio were
much clearer and more vivid than those on early TV.

Many a housewife would go about her day time activities listening
to such shows as "Arthur Godfrey", "Don McNeill's Breakfast Club",
"Dorothy and Dick", "Ma Perkins", "Helen Trent", "Young Dr. Malone",
"Wendy Warren",
"The Second Mrs. Burton" (Not Elizabeth Taylor), "Lorenzo Jones",
"Our Gal Sunday" and dozens of others.
Radio allowed a person to be entertained while not requiring full
and undivided attention, unlike the hypnotically visual "Boob Tube".

Unfortunately, as television became more dominant and widespread,
radio's popularity fell into decline.

Many of the stars and series that had thrived on radio migrated to the newer venue however.

For a while there were versions of many shows on both media.
Slowly and inexorably, however, Radio morphed into nothing more than news programs, recorded music, sporting events and incessant talk.
Radio's golden age ended with a final broadcast of "Yours truly, Johnny Dollar" on September 30th, 1962.

It was a sad ending for a form of entertainment that had helped to sustain the country through the Great Depression, World War II, the Korean War and he beginning of Vietnam.
Luckily, many people had never forgotten how wonderful Radio really was.

In 1975, an organization called "Friends of Old Time Radio" put on its first convention and brought back some of the stars of the "Audio Airwaves".
There were Autograph Sessions, Photo Ops, Panel Discussions with the audience in attendance and best of all, recreations of some of the old shows with many of the original cast members.
I didn't become aware of these conventions until 1993.
I had purchased "Reel to Reel" recordings of a number of the old shows from private vendors starting about 1968, but didn't know about the conventions.

In '93, FOTR was about to hold its 18th annual get together at the Holiday Inn just North of Newark Airport.
I have no idea how I heard about it, but I learned that the original cast of "Tom Corbett Space Cadet" were to be the featured guests.
That show had originated on Television and was so popular that a Radio version was created soon after.
I'm not sure, but it may have been the first program to make this reverse migration.
Both shows starred FRANKIE THOMAS (Tom Corbett), JAN MERLIN (Roger Manning), AL MARKIM (Astro) and ED BRYCE (Captain Strong) as the principals.

The highlight of the Convention was the cast's re-creation of the radio episode "Asteroid of Danger".

Even JACKSON BECK, the original announcer of the series, was on hand to join in the fun.

When a "do over" of the show's rousing opening was necessary, the director chided Beck saying that Jackson probably did not have another "take" in him, Beck responded with an even more vigorous rendition in his classic stentorian style.

The rest of the episode, including sound effects, music and commercials, went off without a hitch and was rewarded with thunderous applause.

I had a chance to speak to FRANKIE THOMAS after the show and he said he was thrilled that the concept still "played" after all those years.

"Cream always rises to the top" was my reply.

Frankie was now a noted Contract Bridge authority and was also writing new Sherlock Holmes books which were well received.

A few years earlier I had sent some 8x10 photos out to Frankie from his days in the 1939 "Nancy Drew" series starring Bonita Granville.

Frankie played Nancy's beleaguered boyfriend Ted Nickerson.

At the time, my daughter, Christine, was heavily into the Nancy Drew books and I thought she would get a kick out of the signed photos.

One night I was down our basement when my wife, Gail, called down to me and said, "Frank Thomas is on the phone."

It was the middle of the baseball season and there were two ballplayers with that name who entered my mind.

Somewhat bewildered, I went upstairs to take the call.

When I realized it was "Frankie" not "Frank" who was calling, it began to make sense.

It seems that I had included my name and phone number in the package I had mailed out to California.

Frankie had misplaced our address, but still had our phone number. He graciously had called to get our address so Christine would not be disappointed.

We spoke for about half an hour about everything from "Nancy" herself, "Bonnie" Granville to the "Holmes" books to some new videos of the "Space Cadet" series to his Contract Bridge Column.

Although we had never met at that point, it was like we were old friends.

I would have put Christine on the phone, but it was past her bed time and she was sound asleep.

In addition to the Nancy Drew pictures, I also had sent along a portrait of Frankie's dad, the fine character actor FRANK M. THOMAS, which I thought he might like.

Frankie told me that his dad was still alive and as soon as he had some copies made he would send the original back autographed by his father.

What a nice gesture!

No wonder he had graduated at the top of his class at "Space Academy".

JAN MERLIN was another of the "Cadets" who guested at the Convention.

Jan's character, "Roger Manning" was the bad boy of Tom's Polaris crew.

Whenever there was a problem, Roger would somehow make it worse. He was a cocky, brash, irascible rogue who nonetheless managed to pull together with his crew mates when the chips were down.

Jan, in person, was much the same as his TV persona.

I ran into Jan in the hallway of the hotel and asked him if he would sign a classic photo of the three Cadets against the backdrop of Space Academy.

Jan initially asked if I could wait a few minutes because he was "on his way to the can".

Reconsidering in spite of the pressures of the moment, Jan inscribed the 8x10 with his trademark tag line, "Aw, go blow your jets!! from Roger Manning – Jan Merlin."

The next day, I stopped by Jan's autograph table and with him no longer under pressure, had a picture taken with him.

Jan's wife, Barbara, had accompanied him to the "Con" and during a lull in the autographing, I managed to talk to her for a few moments.

"Is Jan pretty much the same as "Roger" at home?" I asked.

She nodded her head and confessed that he was.

In spite of everything, you couldn't help but like Jan/Roger.

He was exactly what you expected him to be.

That 1993 Convention was the first of many for me.

Over the course of the next 18 Years, I managed to attend about 10 more.

One of the reasons I'd make the trip over to Jersey, in addition to the Conventions themselves, was to re-unite with some of my old friends. I would usually roam around the dealer's rooms, make a few purchases, take some pictures with the guests while having them autograph a picture or two and then have lunch with my buddies.

It was about the only time we had a chance to get together since most of them lived in Jersey or Manhattan, while I called Long Island home.

Usually Ed Hulse, Sam Sherman, John Cocchi, Paul Becton, Mark Heller and I would chow down in the hotel's restaurant while regaling each other with narratives of our lives since we had last gotten together.

The main attraction, of course, was the chance to meet and talk with the stars of Radio's bygone days.

LON CLARK, who was Radio's "Nick Carter Master Detective" and "The Comic Weekly Man" among hundreds of other character roles was one of the first I encountered.

While speaking with Lon, I mentioned that I had seen him in a production of "Abraham Lincoln" starring John Ireland back in the summer of 1958 at the John Drew Theater out in East Hampton on Long Island.

That year I was a camp counsellor (Chief Bob) at Camp Grant in Calverton.

We had taken a number of the campers out to see the play and were seated in the balcony of the theater.

I really wasn't paying too much attention to the play itself since there was a cute little usherette tending to us and I was much more interested in her.

Suddenly, I heard a familiar voice emanating from the stage behind me.

NICK CARTER!!!, I exclaimed to myself.

I looked around for a program to check out the cast list, and sure enough it was Nick himself, LON CLARK.

I was really excited to hear the voice I had heard for years on Radio. I turned to tell the young lady about my good fortune, but she was gone.

Never saw the young lady again.

Lon said he had forgotten all about that summer show and he thanked me for bringing back a pleasant memory.

BOB HASTINGS, who was "Archie Andrews" on the Radio and a member of McHale's Navy on television was another real good guy. His brother, Don, was the Video Ranger on "Captain Video" back in the earliest days of Television.

While Ed, Sam, John and I were having lunch one day, we noticed Bob sitting by himself at a table across the room.

We asked Bob to join us and spent the next half hour or so listening to him tell us about his career.

One of the more amazing stories Bob related was how he and Dick Van Patten as children would routinely be put on a train in New York and travel to Chicago and other cities by themselves to appear in a play or Radio show.

Often, they would be the only ones in their families gainfully employed. Someone at the other end would pick them up and care for them during their stay.

Their families could not afford the added expense of accompanying them.

This was still the Depression and money was hard to come by.

One of the questions I asked Bob about was a day time TV science fiction series he had appeared in back in the mid 1950's.

I didn't see too many episodes back then since I was in high school by that time and had track practice just about every day.

For the life of me I could never remember the name of that series.

"Atom Squad" replied Bob, clearing up the mystery.

We thanked Bob for spending some time with us and for all the hours of enjoyment he had provided us with over the years.

We insisted on paying for Bob's lunch over his protestations and let him return to the Convention room where he was due to appear on a panel.

GALE STORM of "My Little Margie" TV fame, made her first appearance at the 1995 FOTR Convention.
"Margie" was originally intended to just be a summer replacement for the all time TV classic "I Love Lucy" in 1952.
The show became so popular that it not only earned a regular spot on the 1952 fall schedule, but also spawned a simultaneous radio series as well.
Gale herself proved to be as much fun in real life as she was on TV.
She had recently recovered from some extensive surgery and, for the first time in years, was pain free.
Gale, whose real name was Josephine Owaissa Cottle, came by her stage name in a most unusual way.
It seems she had entered a "Gateway to Hollywood" contest in 1940 and the winner, whoever it might turn out to be, would be given the "Gale Storm" "Nom de Cinema" and a one-year movie contract.
Her future husband, Lee Bonnell, won his part of the contest and became "Terry Belmont".

CYNTHIA PEPPER had appeared with Elvis Presley in the epic 1956 musical flick "Kissin' Cousins" and they became good friends.
Cynthia later had her own TV series "Margie" which was based on the 1946 Jeanne Crain Technicolor picture of the same name.
Cynthia eventually wound up on "My Three Sons" show as Tim Considine's girlfriend, Jean Pearson.
The first time I met Cynthia in 2002, she was volunteering at the Elvis Presley Museum out in Las Vegas.
During the Convention, I was wandering around the various dealer's rooms when I happened to duck into one where there was only one lady sitting by herself.

I immediately recognized Cynthia and, just to be sure, checked the name on the door as I entered.
I introduced myself and we struck up a conversation.
Fortunately, only a few people came in to interrupt us and we talked for quite a while.

Cynthia blushed a little when I told I had had a teen age crush on her in my youth.

She did nothing to change my opinion or alleviate my "crush".

I ran into Cynthia briefly a couple of years later at a subsequent FOTR Convention, but we could only speak for a few moments since she was seated in the audience preparing to appear on a panel.

When I re-introduced myself, Cynthia said that she indeed remembered me and was glad to see me again.

She told me that after the FOTR Convention, she was heading across the river to Manhattan for the "Comicon" Convention the following week.

I remarked to her that, "If you think you've seen some strange people here, wait until you get over there!"

She laughed and I continued, "Please be careful."

Cynthia nodded and thanked me for the insight.

ELENA VERDUGO was quite a character!

Back in the 1500's, her family had been given a land grant from the King of Spain which encompassed a great deal of Southern California.

Naturally, that land grant had ceased to exist several centuries ago.

Elena herself proved to be a lovely and vivacious lady with a terrific sense of humor.

When I finally got a chance to talk to her at the 2000 FOTR Convention, we immediately found we were kindred spirits.

No matter the subject, Elena and I seemed to agree on just about everything.

Our conversation lasted for quite a while and was seldom interrupted

COLUMBIA PICTURES presents JOHNNY WEISSMULLER as Jungle Jim in THE LOST TRIBE with Myrna Dell, Elena Verdugo, Joseph Vitale   49/268

by the attendees of the Convention.

We discussed many things from her early career as a dancer to her film appearances to her Radio show "Meet Millie" which became a hit TV series.

On Radio, "Millie" was originally portrayed by Audrey Totter, but when the Television version became more popular, it was decided not to have two different actresses share the role.

Incidently, Millie's mother was portrayed by Florence Halop, the sister of Billy Halop of "Dead End Kids" fame.

Millie's friend, "Alfred Prinzmettle" was portrayed by Marvin Kaplan and he and Elena have remained buddies for over 40 years.

Elena appeared in a number of Universal Studios horror films in the late 1940's and starred with Gene Autry in one of his first color films for Columbia Pictures, "The Big Sombrero" in 1949.

In retrospect, Elena said that she probably could have done more with her career, but had no regrets.

Her most famous TV role was that of "Consuelo Lopez", the office assistant to doctor "Marcus Welby" as portrayed by Robert Young.

Elena received a well-deserved "Prime Time Emmy Award" nomination for best supporting actress for her role as "Consuelo".

When it came time to go, I asked Elena to autograph a couple of pictures for me and one for my wife, Gail.

She signed my two with nice personal sentiments even adding an "OLE" to one with her dressed in a mildly provocative exotic costume.

Since we had such a great time together and laughed so much, it was hard to say "Good Bye".

When I took the picture that Elena had autographed for Gail, I did so without glancing at the photo.

Elena stopped me and said, "Take a look at what I wrote".

There on the 8x10 over her signature was the inscription: "Dear Gail, Good Luck with Bob!"

VERY FUNNY, ELENA!

To Gail -
Good luck with Bob -
Elena Verdugo

STAR OF THE 1950's "MEET MILLIE"
SERIES ON BOTH RADIO AND TELEVISION

Chapter Twenty

LONE PINE

~

The year is 2005 and I finally acceded to the wishes of my buddy ED HULSE and flew out to California for the 16th Annual Lone Pine Film Festival.

Ed had been trying to get me to attend the Festival for over a decade, but I had been unable to go for a number of reasons.

I flew out of JFK on the Wednesday prior to the Columbus Day weekend.

As it turned out, it was the Jewish Holiday of Rosh Hashanah and as a result the American Airlines Terminal was virtually deserted. Weird! After a five-hour flight to LAX, Ed and another old friend, MARK HELLER, picked me up and we went out to grab a bite to eat in Hollywood.

Later that evening, Ed took me to the home of WOODY WISE in Burbank where we spent the night.

Next morning, Ed and I began the drive up to Lone Pine about 200 miles northeast of Los Angeles in the Owens Valley.

Along route we made stops at two other famous movie locations.

The first was "Vasquez Rocks" and the latter was "Red Rock Canyon" right next to Highway Route 345.

Half way to Lone Pine we stopped for lunch at the Diner in Mojave. As we were getting out of our car, who did we bump into but another old friend, DICK BANN.

I hadn't seen Dick in about 15 years and he too was on the way to the Festival.

Dick is now the Film Co-Ordinator for Hugh Hefner at the Playboy Mansion and spends a great deal of time there.

Red Rock Canyon has been and is still is used extensively from the 1940's "Flash Gordon Conquers the Universe" serial starring "Buster" Crabbe and the "Mummy" series with Lon Chaney Jr. to the present time.

We pulled into Lone Pine after our 4-hour drive and checked into our motel, the Best Western Frontier, about a mile south of town.
Some of the celebrity guest stars of the Festival were also staying at the same motel.
Every morning I would walk out the door of my hotel room and be greeted by a truly magnificent sight.
Across Route 345 from the motel was a panoramic view of the Sierra Nevada Mountains (about 10 miles away) which was used as the title background for the very first "Hop-A-Long Cassidy" movie in 1935.
The only difference between the 1935 shot and the one I took was due to the fact that mine was in full color.
Even in October, the distant mountain peaks, including Mount Whitney itself were capped by early morning snows.
What a sight to behold!

Upon arriving at the Festival Headquarters that first day, it was necessary to register for the Convention and receive an official I.D. badge.
In addition, it was also time to sign up for the various guided tours into the "Alabama Hills" about two miles west of the center of town.

The "Alabamas" have been used for hundreds of movies, TV shows and commercials for over 80 years.
Just about every major film star has worked in the Hills including Tom Mix, Hopalong Cassidy, Gene Autry, Roy Rogers, Errol Flynn, Randolph Scott, Cary Grant, Humphrey Bogart, Gregory Peck and scores of other movie greats.
The Hills themselves have been used to portray India, Alaska, the planets Saturn and Krypton, Tibet and every Western locale imaginable.
In fact, about half of the 66 Hopalong Cassidy oaters were made there. Additionally, Bill Boyd ("Hoppy" himself) and his 3rd wife, Grace Bradley, honeymooned in a log cabin in the hills which has become known as the "Hoppy Cabin" and has appeared in any number of westerns.

The "Hallmark" film that was shot in the "Alabamas" was the all-time classic "Gunga Din" starring Cary Grant, Douglas Fairbanks Jr. and Victor McLaglen. Other greats include "Lives of a Bengal

Lancer", "Bad Day at Black Rock", and "High Sierra" and "Charge of the Light Brigade".

After registering at Festival Headquarters, it was time to seek out some of the guest stars at Statham Hall and collect a few autographs After talking to the stars about their careers and present-day activities, it was time to purchase some CD's, DVD's, VHS tapes and paper goods.
(Movie posters, lobby cards and 8x10 photos etc.)

The focal point of the Festival in the town itself is the Dow Villa Motel. All the Big Stars have stayed there through the years while making movies.
"PACKY" SMITH, one of the prime movers of the Festival, has occupied the same room of the motel during the Convention for the past sixteen years.

On the first night of the convention, Ed was invited to see the site of the new Jim and Beverly Rogers Lone Pine Museum of Western Film History which was still in the earliest stages of construction.
There were only bare floors and the skeletons of future walls to be seen at this juncture.
Ed managed to wrangle an additional invitation for me so I was also able to attend the coming out party and buffet.
The directors spoke and gave a brief insight as to what the Museum hoped to be upon completion in 2006.
(It turned out to be everything they could have wished for)
The second night, just about everyone dressed up in their best cowboy garb on the street in front of the "Dow".
Some of the Festival attendees had duplicated the classic western outfits of their favorite "Saddle Aces" down to the last button.

You could run into imitators of "Wild Bill" Elliott, Roy Rogers and Dale Evans, Hopalong Cassidy, the Cisco Kid, the Lone Ranger and Tonto, Zorro, Paladin, Charles Starrett (The Durango Kid) and even "Rooster" Cogburn.

Believe it or not, I had happened to come across a really great cowboy shirt of my own on Sunrise Highway on Long Island, just about as far EAST as you could get from Lone Pine, California.

Some of the imitators were so impressed that they inquired if I was supposed to be anyone of note and asked me where I had gotten my cool duds.

When I told them from whence came the shirt, they couldn't believe me.

When they asked who I was supposed to be, I informed them that I was the mysterious drifter who you were never sure was a good guy or a bad guy.

I revealed to them that I was the truly notorious "Schizophrenic Kid".

They tended to regard me with strange looks on their faces after that.

The tours of the "Alabamas" were absolutely fabulous.

What the Festival Committee would do was to first go out into the Hills and scare away the mountain lions for the safety of the attendees.

Next, the Committee would set up podiums containing 8x10 stills from a given picture at the actual camera location where the shot was taken.

Perhaps the most famous and recognizable photo of all was that of Gene Autry and Smiley Burnette on horseback from the 1937 film "Boots and Saddles" which was taken next to the oddly shaped "Gene Autry Rock".

(More about that "Rock" later)

Some of the guest stars who graced the Festival were NOEL NEILL (Lois Lane of SUPERMAN fame), MORGAN WOODWARD, the infamous "Man with no eyes" in "Cool Hand Luke", PAUL PICERNI, one of TV's Eliot Ness' "Untouchables", ace stunt man NEIL SUMMERS and RICHARD ANDERSON, he of the "Six Million Dollar Man" and "The Bionic Woman".

I tried to convince Noel Neill that since she had portrayed "Lois Lane" in both the two "Superman" movie serials and the TV show and my last name was "LANE" that we were somehow related.

She didn't think so.

One of the real highlights of the Festival was the "Panel of Stars" discussion conducted by Ed Hulse.

In addition to asking members of the Panel about their career memories, Ed also introduced Hoppy's widow, GRACE BRADLEY BOYD, from the audience much to the delight of all in attendance.

The legendary B-western leading lady, PEGGY STEWART, who is one of the Festival's Co-Ordinators, was a real delight.

Peggy regaled the attendees with stories about her co-stars "Sunset" Carson, Gene Autry, Lash La Rue, "Wild Bill" Elliott and ex-hubby Don "Red" Barry.

Peggy, along with Dale Evans and old friend Jennifer Holt made dozens upon dozens of "Shoot 'em ups".

Where would the B-westerns of the 1940's been without them?

Every evening there would be screenings of some of the great films of Tom Mix, Tim Holt, Hopalong Cassidy, Roy Rogers, Gene Autry and even Tom Tyler (of Captain Marvel fame), all shot in the "Alabamas".

ANN RUTHERFORD who was one of Gene Autry's first leading ladies and who later became Mickey Rooney's "Andy Hardy" on again off again girlfriend "Polly Benedict", was a great guest.

Ann's most famous role, of course, was that of Scarlet O'Hara's sister, "Careen", in the immortal epic "Gone With the Wind".

On the panel, Ed had to be aware of the fact that Ann, once asked a question, would ramble on for quite some time.

It was best to have packed a lunch whenever Ann began to speak.

On the last day of the Festival there was a great parade up Main Street. It started at the High School and ended at the only traffic light in town. If you make a left at the light it puts you on Whitney Portal Road and takes you thru the "Alabamas" to the distant Sierra Nevada Mountains which contain Mount Whitney itself, the highest peak in the lower 48.

Only Mount McKinley in Alaska is higher in all of the USA.

Vintage cars containing all of the Celebrity Guests and a grouping of all the Cowboy Star imitators were the highlights of the event.
Lone Pine itself was well represented by a classic, horse drawn Steam Fire Engine, featuring a "Troika" of three white equines.

Some of the imitators had asked me if I wanted to join them in the Line of March, but I declined.
I preferred instead to stand in the crowd lining the street in front of the "Dow" with BONNIE BOYD and take pictures of the whole spectacle.
It was the right choice.
After the parade, it was decided to drive out to the Alabamas to take some group photographs.
Ed, Dick, Packy, Bonnie, Woody, Mark and I were going to pile into Packy's van for the excursion.
Unfortunately, I wasn't wearing my super-groovy shirt, hat, neckerchief and gun belt so I had to borrow Ed's Rent-A-Car and go back to the motel to pick them up.
There was no time to get dressed in the whole rig, so I just threw them in the car and rejoined the group.

We visited "Lone Ranger Ambush Canyon", the remnants of the "Gunga Din" Elephant Bridge and the site where the Thugee Temple in that film was once located. (Temple Pocket)
It's too bad since it was a magnificent edifice.

Naturally the structure itself is long gone since the rules that govern the Alabamas dictate that any buildings constructed for a film must be removed upon completion of the production.
This directive helps maintain the natural and pristinely primitive beauty of the ancient hills.

My favorite picture taken on that trip into the hills was one that Ed took of me crouching behind a rock wielding my trusty "Texan Jr." cap gun and aiming up in the direction of "Gene Autry Rock".
Unfortunately, if you look REAL close, you can still see my ever present blue, red and white striped Smithtown High School La Crosse shorts.

This "Wardrobe Malfunction" is due to the fact that all I had time to put on was my shirt, neckerchief and Stetson hat.

In spite of this glitch, the shot provides a panoramic view of the western Alabamas with the majestic Sierra Nevadas in the background.

We took a couple of dozen photos of our group in the hills which truly capture the spirit of our brief foray into that marvelous landscape that is the Alabama Hills.

After a "Farewell Dinner" later that evening, it was time to say "Adios" to Lone Pine, my new "Compadres" and my old friends.

The next morning, we said our "Good Byes" and headed home.

Bonnie and the others tried to convince me to return in 2006, but I declined.

There was no way I could hope to duplicate the wonders of the 2005 Festival!

I'm so glad Ed convinced me to come out to California and attend the Festival.

It was everything he said it would be and more Every time I happen to see a film on television or in the movies that were shot in the Alabamas, I find myself virtually ignoring the actors and the plot.

I concentrate instead on the scope and grandeur of the fabulous Alabama Hills.

If you ever get a chance to venture out into the Alabamas, don't pass it up!

It truly is a "Never-Never Land".

Chapter Twenty-One

REUNION 2010

F ast forward 56 years to September 25th, 2010 and an Our Lady
of Angels Reunion for all of the grammar school's graduates,
including the class of 1954.

Kevin Farrell came, as well as Margaret McCormack (and her younger
sister, Ann), J.P. (Jack) McGuirk, Joan Moloney, who came up from
Florida, plus Mary Dell'Accio, who drove in from Pennsylvania and
attended with her brother and son.

Ray Flood couldn't make it since he was headed down to Florida to
see his son and Tommy Nacinovich's Mom, Val, had passed away on
the previous Friday and he wasn't up to it.

My wife and I had driven into Bay Ridge to attend the one-night
wake that Sunday evening to pay our respects to that very nice lady.
The Reunion itself kicked off with a celebratory Mass in the
church on 73rd

and 4th and one of our old parish priests, FATHER LABITA, was one
of the celebrants of the service.

After the Mass, the 200 or so old graduates went around the corner
to the school itself to kick off the get together.

The festivities were held in the new gym, which wasn't built until
several years after we graduated.

I was worried that they were going to use the OLD gym on the fifth
floor for the occasion.

That venue was a bizarre structure in which nobody ever wanted to
play basketball or do anything else. (even "Shebelgar")

The ceiling was too low for basketball and sloped down at the edges by the walls so that any shot taken from there with any arc in its trajectory was doomed to failure.

But, let's go back to the reunion itself.

The six of we '54's reminisced about our time at OLA, told stories about our teachers, especially Sister Mary Arthur, and brought each other up to date on our lives since graduation.

KEVIN FARRELL and I had gone to high school together at La Salle Academy in NYC on the lower East Side.

He still lived in Bay Ridge and had become Chief of Detectives for the borough of Manhattan under Mayor Rudy Giuliani.

Not only that, but one day Giuliani had called him into his office and told him that he was now the head of the Department of Sanitation.

"But I'm a Cop", protested Kevin.

"YOU'RE NOW THE HEAD OF THE DEPARTMENT OF SANITATION!", re-iterated Rudy. End of that conversation!

MARGARET McCORMACK (Pacelli) still resides in Bay Ridge, four blocks from where she lived while attending OLA.

Margaret was a very quiet, docile young lady when I knew her and remained so until one day in high school, her teacher said something with which Margaret strongly disagreed.

A discussion ensued, and Margaret, uncharacteristically, refused to back down.

From that point on, Margaret emerged from her shell and her whole personality changed to a confident, pleasantly gregarious young woman.

MARY DELL' ACCIO (Holohan) had been the first of the girls to "blossom".

As such, many of the boys flirted with and were sometimes even a little cruel to her.

In speaking to her during the Reunion and after by phone she said she was very lonely at OLA.

She lived on a block with no children to play with in the very farthest southeast corner of the parish.

Most of the girls lived below 4th Avenue, north and west of the school. As with all schools, there were cliques.

The fact that Mary lived where she did and was one of the few non-Irish girls in our class, didn't help.

Happy to say that Mary and her husband have been together for 49 years and she was thrilled to come back to the Reunion.
JOAN MOLONEY (Donohue), lives in Florida and mentioned that my name had come up in a recent conversation she had had with REGINA FOLEY, one of the girls who couldn't make it.

I found this very strange because I'm virtually certain I NEVER spoke a word to either of them in all of my eight years in OLA.

They were GIRLS, and I had no use for them.

As far as I was concerned, GIRLS were weak guys with long hair who dressed kinda funny and talked a lot. (Still not sure)

Joan said she has our "Graduation Program" from 1954, and promised to send me a copy. (I didn't even know we had one.)

Getting back SISTER MARY ARTHUR

I had called a number of classmates, including Tommy and Ray, to see if they were coming to the Reunion.

I was home sick from work, courtesy of the little urchins at BOCES and their whole new set of germs they had brought back with them from summer vacation, so I had the opportunity to make the calls.

Ray's family has owned Flood Realty in Bay Ridge just about forever. I called the office to speak to Ray, but he wasn't there.

I wound up talking to his partner, Jim Clark, who graduated in '52, two years before Ray and I.

Jim and I spoke for some time about our experiences at OLA and I eventually asked him who he had had for his 8th grade teacher.

After a short pause, he answered, "SISTER MARY ARTHUR".

We then proceeded to swap Sister Mary Arthur stories for the next 20 minutes.

Jim then said, "Would you like her phone number up in Wellesley Mass.?".

Stunned, I told him, "I'd love to have her number and talk to her".

(God knows, she had had MY NUMBER!)

After I hung up with Jim, I called Sister and left a message on her answering machine.

An hour or so later the phone rang and it was the great lady herself.

I introduced myself and told her Jim Clark had given me her number.

We spoke for about half an hour and talked of many things including the infamous "crayon" incident.

I didn't recognize her voice as such, but there was no mistaking that "Boston" accent.

I told her I would send her some pictures I had of our "official" graduation photos as well as current pictures of my wife and I, our kids, grand-kids and even some photos of our most recent vacations.

I included a three-page letter discussing some of the things we had spoken about.

It seems that Sister couldn't make the Reunion, due to a prior com-mitment, but she does get down to NYC occasionally as part of her official duties and I asked if we might get together for lunch/dinner. She said she'd love to.

Now I always thought that Sister was about 10 to 15 years older than we.

That would make her about 85.

Well, I spoke a couple of the "younger" nuns (Only in their 70's) at the Reunion and they assured me, in no uncertain terms, that Sister Mary Arthur was, in fact, NINETY-five.

She still works in the hierarchy of the Sisters of Charity, is a driving force on a number of National Committees and God knows what else she does in her spare time.

The hell with the "Energizer" bunny, give me Sister Mary Arthur!!!

There is one other Sister Mary Arthur story I'd like to relate As I was leaving the Reunion, I saw Jim Clark talking to some other grads.

I walked over and introduced myself since we had never actually met, but had only spoken that one time on the phone.

In the course of our conversation, Jim told me about Sister Mary Arthur's Golden Jubilee (50 years as Sister of Charity) celebration up in Wellesley.

It seems that, 20 years ago, both Ray and Jim made the trip up for Sister's big event.

Jim had dressed up as "Clark Kent" and when Sister saw him, she was not happy.

She asked him how he could this to her on this, her special day.

Jim said to her "If you think this is something, wait until you see Ray!".

Sure enough, Ray had come as "Superman".

I'm sure that didn't improve Sister's frame of mind one bit.

As if that wasn't bad enough, the local newspaper ran the picture of them on the front page of the following days edition, under the headline...

"SUPERMAN MEETS SUPER-NUN".

After talking with Jim for a while, I fully intended to make my exit and head for home.

As I approached the door, I noticed a number of people coming down the stairs that led to the upper floors of the school itself.

I thought to myself that this would undoubtedly my last chance to visit the actual "Inner Sanctum" of my "Alma Mater".

I took off up the stairs and was transported back to those "thrilling days of yesteryear".

Things had changed, of course, but not as much as I had feared.

The hallways and classrooms were still very recognizable and familiar, in spite of the passage of all those years.

Things looked so much smaller than I remembered, but that's only natural considering how much bigger WE ALL had become.

I even went down to the auditorium where we occasionally saw a movie such as "Sitting Pretty" with Clifton Webb as "Mr. Belvedere", or "Prisoner of Shark Island" about Dr. Samuel Mudd, who inadvertently had helped John Wilkes Booth after he had shot Abraham Lincoln.

The auditorium was also used for some Sunday Masses, some plays such as "A Christmas Carol" and our spectacular "Flash Gordon" epic.

We also celebrated days like St. Patrick's Day with some live shows of song and dance.

As a matter of fact, while I was standing around talking with my classmates, a girl (woman) named GLORIA PASTORI came over to say hello.

Gloria was a year older than we, but she had sung in a number of those shows.

She had a great voice.

One year, one of the Irish priests, (I believe it was Father McKenna) to justify her participation in the St. Patrick's Day festivities, decided to "Re-Christen" the very Italian Gloria as "Gloria O'Pastori".
The other thing we used the auditorium for was daily "Choir Practice". Mr. Frederick T. Short was our choir director and played the church organ for the 10 o'clock High Mass on Sunday, at which the choir sang. Sometimes, during practice, I would change my voice to imitate cowboy
movie star, Tex Ritter. (father of John Ritter of "Three's Company" fame) My Mother HATED the way Tex sang.
She always referred to him as, "That cryin' guy".
Needless to say, Tex's voice did not lend itself to liturgical harmony. Whenever Mr. Short or Sister Mary Eunice, our moderator, would get close to me while searching for the irritating, discordant sound, I would revert to my normal voice to remain undetected.
I shudder to think what would have happened had I been caught.
I believe Mr. Short also played the organ and was involved with the choir at St. Patrick's Cathedral, at least that was the legend.
(I wonder how we stacked up against that group?)

Every year at Christmas time, we would get dressed up in red and white cassocks and surplices and go over to the Fort Hamilton Veteran's Hospital to sing a few carols for the "Vets".
It was very pleasant and, as I remember, very well received.
The place was warm and bright and tastefully decorated for the holidays.
(I understand it fell into disrepair in later years and eventually closed.)

It's really a shame, since we owe those guys of that generation so much.

I should also mention that after the "Reunion" Mass I had gone up
the old winding stairs into the church's choir loft.
I introduced myself to the fellow who had played the organ during
the service.

He had his young son with him and the boy had quietly played with his toys on the floor by the organ through the entire Mass.

The organist said that some former choir boys have occasionally come up to the loft to see if they could find their initials that they had carved into the benches where we sat during Mass. They invariably did.

Not much had changed up there in the intervening years.

It was somewhat scruffier, but the only noteworthy change was that they had moved the organ from the back wall of the loft to the front, closer to the main part of the church.

I exited the church, walked over to the school, met with my classmates, took the tour of the floors of the building, ending up in the auditorium.

After visiting the auditorium, I finally left OLA, but I knew that I had, after so many years, at long last, come home.

We, the class of '54, were extremely fortunate to have attended OLA when we did and to have had the teachers and memories from that era.

Of course, that time will never come again, but sharing some of those bygone experiences, both good and bad, brought us together once again, if only for a few hours.

We're planning to have a reunion of only our '54 class in the not too distant future.

If each of the attendees and those others who couldn't make it this time can drum up one or two others, we should be able to put together a pretty good-sized group.

Who knows, maybe we can co-ordinate it to coincide with one of Sister Mary Arthur's trip down to NYC?

Wouldn't that be something!

If not, we would probably have to use a Boston based limousine service to transport Sister down and back.

We also might put her up in a local hotel for the night, since a round trip in one day would be awful lot to subject her to.

I figured if a number of us each put up a hundred dollars or so, we can get it done.

Jim Clark suggested that she bring another nun along with her to keep her company on the trip.

Five hours alone each way can be pretty tedious for anyone, let alone a ninety-five-year-old nun with a pacemaker.

I've even fantasized about chartering a helicopter to ferry her back and forth, but decided against it.

But the best method, I think, is for Sister to take the shuttle flight from Logan Airport outside Boston to La Guardia here in NYC.

It would seem to be the fastest, cheapest, and most convenient way to have Sister travel.

The other possible option is a flight into JFK, if one is available.

In any event, I could pick her up at the airport and drive her to the Reunion and back.

Think of it, Sister Mary Arthur, FLYING NUN!

Sister Bertrille, eat your heart out!

Chapter Twenty-Two

REUNION 2012

In the two years that followed, I contented myself with such mundane and pedestrian activities as Quadruple Bypass Surgery and the installation of a nifty "Pacemaker" to regulate my heart beat.

Once I had put those fun experiences in my rear-view mirror, it was time to get going on the Our Lady of Angels class of June '54 Reunion. I tried a number of times to contact JOAN MOLONEY using the E-mail address she had given me back in 2010, but had no luck.
Finally, one day, for no reason at all, the very same address worked. That started the ball rolling.
Joan had kept in contact with a couple of our classmates, while I busied myself tracking down as many of the others as I could.
Between the two of us we managed to locate over 25 ex OLA'ers.
Joan knew the whereabouts of MAUREEN TREANOR and REGINA FOLEY while I had maintained contact with KEVIN FARRELL and TOMMY NACINOVICH.
Both MARGARET McCORMACK and MARY DELL'ACCIO as well as J.P. McGUIRK had come to the '10 reunion, so we knew where they were. Some of the others were a little or a lot more difficult to locate.

Joan also knew where JIM LUNDRIGAN lived since her husband Jack had often communicated with him over the years.

Margaret McCormack's sister, ANN, married BOBBY LENTO (an old ball playing buddy of mine from the P.S. 102 under 5-foot team days) and his cousin, MARY ANN LENTO, was actually one of us.

Mary Ann still lived in the neighborhood although not in the OLA parish.

Mary Ann was incredibly helpful in locating our classmates who had gone on to St. Joseph's Commercial High School, as she did.
These included IRENE PURCELL, BONNIE McTIERNAN, GAIL GALLAGHER, and EILEEN O'REILLY.

Back in 1962, I had escorted a lovely young lady named DOROTHY MONTUORI to her prom at St. Joseph's College.
As it turned out, three of my OLA classmates, namely KATHLEEN MURPHY, ELAINE ZISK and REGINA FOLEY were also at that prom.

I'm not sure if I spoke to any of them that evening, but by finding their yearbook and their ALUMNI NEWSLETTER online, I was able to learn each of their married names and track them down.
MAUREEN TREANOR also went to St. Joe's, but because of financial constraints, she didn't enter until a year after the other three.

When the 1962 St. Joe's graduating class held their 50th Reunion in April 2012, Maureen went too.
It seems she had maintained a close relationship with her OLA class-mates thru her college years, in spite of graduating a year later.

ELAINE ZISK was an interesting challenge.
Elaine was universally accepted as the smartest girl in our class.
I had often wondered why she hadn't won a scholarship to our local Diocesan High School, St. Brendan's.
I always had thought that she had had a bad day and failed the test.
GERRY FITZGIBBON, who did go to St. Brendan's, told me the real story.
It seems that Elaine had decided that she was going to Fontbonne Hall, a very prestigious venue, right in Bay Ridge on Shore Road and 95th St.
As a result, Elaine took no other entrance exams.
She was very determined.

Strangely enough, the way Fontbonne selected their students was somewhat odd and unique.

Once a pre-determined number of worthy applicants was reached, no more would be considered for entry.

It was first come, first served.

Although the "Official" reporting time was 7:30am, applicants started showing up at 2:30am to assure themselves of a spot in the incoming freshman class.

Elaine, somehow, was not aware of this.

When she arrived at the announced starting time, all the slots had long been filled.

No amount of pleading, cajoling and/or arm twisting by her teachers, parish priests or anybody else could alter the school's decision.

As a result, Elaine wound up attending Bay Ridge High School on 4th Avenue and Senator Street, walking distance from her house on Ovington Avenue.

The happy ending to this story is that Elaine eventually re-surfaced at the University of Texas in Austin and they are now naming scholarships after her.

Way to go, Elaine!

In a curious co-incidence, it turns out that TOMMY NACINOVICH'S roommate at M.I.T. married DOROTHY DE NAVE, also one of our grads. Tommy and Dorothy met at a M.I.T. alumni function and in the course of their conversation learned of each other's OLA roots.

Dorothy couldn't attend our re-union since she and her husband were on a cruise and wouldn't return until October 6th.

She, like a number of others who couldn't make it, can't wait until our 60th in 2014.

Speaking of cruises, KATHLEEN MURPHY returned from hers at 6:00am up in Boston on the morning of the reunion.

She went home, changed and drove down to Bay Ridge, arriving at 2pm. That's dedication!

BONNIE McTIERNAN came in all the way from Tulsa, Oklahoma. Her husband worked for American Airlines and was transferred there a number of years ago.

BILLY ROYALL was a bit of a challenge to locate.
I figured I might be able to track him down through his brother, PEYTON, not exactly a common name.
But, Tommy Nacinovich, told me that Peyton wasn't his real name.
Evidently it was GEORGE, the same as his father.
To avoid confusion, everyone called him by his middle name instead.
Having no luck there, I decided to look up BILLY (WILLIAM) directly.
There were over 250 WILLIAM ROYALL's in the country, but only 27 in our age-group.
The search engine I used not only gave ages, addresses and some-times phone numbers, but names of relatives as well.
When I got to the 7th WILLIAM ROYALL, it listed his son's name as Michael PEYTON Royall. Gotcha!!!

I called Billy and told him about the reunion and sure enough, he came.
It turned out that the day of the reunion (September 22nd) was also Billy's birthday, so naturally we all serenaded him by singing "Happy Birthday".
It was a nice touch.

IRENE PURCELL had taken a "Medication Induced" fall a couple of weeks prior to the event and had sustained some pretty severe facial injuries, but she came with her 80-year-old brother, Rod.

By the day of the reunion, most of the bruises had healed except for her chin, which was still heavily bandaged.

JOAN MOLONEY came up with the idea of making picture ID badges for all who were coming to the get together.
She used the individual pictures from our group graduation photo so we could recognize one another after so many years.

For some reason, a couple of my co-workers at Western Suffolk BOCES suggested that we take the group graduation picture as a whole and make some laminated place mats for one and all.
It seemed like a great idea.
Once again, it was Joan to the rescue.
She got them made up, arrived at the restaurant an hour early and got everything ready by the time our classmates started to arrive.

What a gal!!

There was one final touch I thought would be nice.
I went to Cedarhurst Paper Party City and had a laminated banner/
poster made up for the occasion.
It was 12 feet x 15 inches in length and read:
"OUR LADY OF ANGELS – CLASS OF JUNE 1954"
I thought it might be too big, but as it turned out, it was just perfect.
(After the party was over, Joan had the presence of mind to take
down the banner and save it for the upcoming 2014 Reunion)
Again, what a gal!!

In choosing the Reunion's restaurant, I had sought the advice of
KEVIN, MARGARET and MARY ANN, since they all still lived in the
neighborhood.
I thought it was advisable to choose one close to the school, if possible, that way I wouldn't have to give anybody directions.

Margaret couldn't make it, but Mary Ann and Kevin suggested we
meet at a place called "The Greenhouse Café", only a few blocks
from OLA on 3rd Avenue and 77th street.
I had gone to high school with Kevin at La Salle Academy in NYC and
had kept in touch with him over the years.
I had not seen Mary Ann since our grammar school days and had no
idea what she looked like.

As it turned out, I was about a half hour late arriving for our 12-noon
appointment because of the traffic coming in from Long Island.
(God bless the Long Island Expressway and the Belt Parkway.)
Finding a parking space close to the restaurant was a bit of a chore,
but I found one on 4th Avenue about a block from the Greenhouse.
When I walked in the door, Kevin was on his cell phone speaking to
my wife, Gail, concerned about my tardiness.
Kevin and Mary Ann had introduced themselves to each other
and were catching up on old times over drinks at the bar when I
finally arrived.
I spoke to my wife to assure her I had arrived safe and sound.

The restaurant itself was absolutely terrific.

It seemed both of them had dined at the Greenhouse on previous occasions and they were very pleased with it.

Kevin also knew one of the Maitre d's (Pablo) and appreciated his services.

After reminiscing for a while about our days at OLA, we all agreed that this place would suit our needs just fine.

Kevin introduced me to one of the owners, Bobby Daquara, and I signed a contract for September 22nd for approximately 20 grads and guests.

The final number of attendees would be decided upon a week before the event.

This would allow the restaurant to anticipate the proper amount of food and to have sufficient staff available.

As luck would have it, my wife's old friends, Mary Ann and Pat Harmon had flown in from Ohio a few days earlier and were staying in Jersey.

We decided to meet the following week half way between our locations and I thought the Greenhouse in Bay Ridge would be the perfect spot.

It would also give me a chance to check out the place.

It couldn't have been better.

All that remained was to collect the money from everybody and get a cashier's check for the bill.

It worked out to about $50 dollars per person, very reasonable.

Everybody came through with flying colors and the final count was 21 grads and 8 guests, (Total – 29 attendees.) Yay Us!

One other thing that I did was to get in touch with OLA to get permission to use the school's parking lot, since finding a parking spot in Bay Ridge can be very, very difficult.

I eventually spoke to Msgr. Noone, an OLA grad and Sister Mary Arthur alumni, and he said there would be no problem using the lot since it would be open for 5 o'clock mass that day.

The day of the Reunion finally arrived and I held my breath, waiting for something to go wrong.

I got to the restaurant at noon, about an hour early.

Joan was already there and had set out the place mats and all the photo ID's.

She, my wife and I hung the banner and waited for our classmates.

It seemed as if everybody arrived almost simultaneously and the party began.

MARY ANN had picked up EILEEN O'REILLY to make sure she got there.

The name tags were a Godsend and allowed everyone to get reacquaintted immediately.

Cameras flashed again and again as 58 years melted away.

Hugs and kisses ran rampant.

The food was great, the service was excellent and the restaurant even threw in some hot hors d'oeuvres for free.

As part of the package we were entitled to an "Occasion" cake.

I wanted to write on the cake:

"WELCOME BACK OUR LADY OF ANGELS CLASS OF JUNE 1954 – YAY US!"

Our Maitre d', Pablo, advised me that all that writing would not fit on the cake that came with the package.

I told him to please get a larger cake and I didn't care if it cost more, I would take care of it.

He did and I did.

The hours flew by and we lost all track of time.

Eventually, I asked everyone to go outside for a group picture since there were too many of us to get a decent shot inside.

KEVIN helped me move the bench that was outside the restaurant for use in the photo.

MARGARET, MARY ANN and I sat on the bench in the foreground while everybody else stood behind us.

What a group!

After the picture was taken, we all went back inside since it was time to cut the cake.

Everyone insisted that I should be the one to do the honors.
As I was cutting the cake, my classmates decided to serenade me with "The bride cuts the cake… the bride cuts the cake…"
I responded with a totally inappropriate digital gesture.

There were a few disappointments, however, since TOMMY NACINOVICH, RAY FLOOD and JIM CLINE didn't make it to the re-union. Jim had misunderstood the time and called us at the restaurant to say he wouldn't be able to make it up from Philadelphia before we left. He said he will definitely make the next one; we'll see.

There were also some bright spots too, since MADONNA O'BRIEN, MAUREEN TREANOR, HELEN McGREGOR, DOROTHY DE NAVE, BARBARA DE MARCO and EILEEN TUBMAN are all looking forward to the 2014 re-union.

I eventually called RICHIE GIUSTRA to try and coax him into coming in 2014, but the best I could get from him was a, "We'll see".

Incidently, of all the grads who did attend, it seemed to me that KEVIN FARRELL and AUDREY MOFFITT had changed the least and were the most recognizable. (Just my opinion, folks)

It was ultimately decided to wait until 2014 rather than 2013 for our next get together since it will be our 60th anniversary and will be a nice round number.

The instructions I gave to everyone who plan on attending were plain and straight forward: "DON'T DIE!"
Anyone failing to heed my edict will have to bring a doctor's note to gain admission.
"YAY US!!!"

Chapter Twenty-Three

A VISIT WITH SISTER MARY ARTHUR

I n May of 2013, one of our grand-daughters, Olivia, made her First Holy Communion.

At the party after the ceremony, her parents (Bobby and Dawn) mentioned that Olivia was entered in a Gymnastics competition the weekend of June 7-9.

Unfortunately, this conflicted with a hockey tournament of little Bobby IV.

The tournament was going to be held that same weekend up in Marlboro Mass.

Our son, Bobby III, said he was going to drive up to Marlboro early Friday morning and then drive back to Long Island to attend Olivia's competition.

Bobby IV would stay with the parents of one of his teammates at the hotel.

After Olivia's competition was over on Saturday, Bobby, Dawn and Olivia would then pile in their car and motor back up to Massachusetts to try and catch the remaining games in Marlboro.

I told them I thought that this was foolish and that I would take Bobby up to his tournament.

One of the reasons I volunteered to do this was the fact that Marlboro was only about 20 miles west of Wellesley Hills where Sister Mary Arthur lived

in the Elizabeth Seaton Residence of the Sisters of Charity.

I called Sister to see if she would be available and she said she would be.

I told her I wasn't sure if I would be coming on Saturday, the 8th, or on Sunday the 9th.

It all depended on how the games were to be scheduled and I told Sister I would let her know when I found out for sure.

I also called KATHLEEN MURPHY (Bernegger) to see if she wanted to tag along. Kathleen lives about 20 miles west of Marlboro and I knew she would come if she could.

As it turned out, Kathleen was only available on Saturday and the schedule only allowed me to go on Sunday. Bummer!

Little Bobby's team had advanced to the tournament playoffs and would indeed have a game or two on Sunday depending on the outcome of the morning's game.

Fortunately, Bobby and Dawn had arrived late Saturday afternoon after the completion of Olivia's tournament.

That allowed me to call Mary Arthur and make arrangements for Sunday.

Olivia had done fairly well, but not as well as she would have liked.

As a result, Olivia didn't make the trip up to Marlboro.

Although she is a fine gymnast, Olivia, I'm afraid, is also a bit of a "Drama Queen", or would "Drama Princess" be more appropriate?

I called Sister and asked her if it would be alright to come over to see her about one o'clock or so.

She said that would be fine inasmuch as morning Mass would be over and it would not interfere with lunch either.

I drove to Wellesley Hills and along the way picked up some flowers.

Once I arrived on the grounds, I parked in front of the main building and went to the front desk.

The Nun who was acting as receptionist told me that Mary Arthur was next door on the second floor of the "Elizabeth Seton Residence".

I walked over and took the elevator up to floor number two.

When I exited the elevator, I asked one of the attendants where I might find Sister.

She took me to Mary Arthur's room, but she wasn't there.

The attendant said, "Sister is probably still in the lunchroom down the hall".

We went down to the lunchroom and there was Mary Arthur sitting with a few other Nuns.

I introduced myself and Sister told her friends that I was one of her students from Our Lady of Angels in Brooklyn.
"From 1954", I added.

The Nuns where duly impressed. (Take that, Penguins!)
After a few more moments, Sister and I made our way back to her room and sat down to talk.
(Sister used a walker to get around, but I got the impression she could navigate just about as well without it if she wanted to.)
We spoke of many things and I gave her the flowers I had purchased, as well as a birthday card on which I had signed all the names of the '54 graduates with whom we had been in touch.
I included all who had attended the past September's reunion and even those who couldn't make it.
Sister's 98th birthday was going to be on June 17th, so I was a little bit premature.
The card itself was designed for an eight-year old girl, but I wrote a "9" with a red magic marker in front of the "8" in honor of Sister Mary Arthur's upcoming ninety-eighth.

Sister told me many things about her life, her family, how she became a nun and her time at Our Lady of Angels, both as teacher and as principal.
She also told me her real name is Dorothy (McCarthy).
It seems that Sister did not attend Catholic school as a child, but started running errands for the nuns at St. Joseph's School.
Through that association, she became friends with some of the Jesuit priests in the parish.
As she grew, she became interested in their religious calling.
When she told them of her interest, one of the priests gave her some literature to read and the rest is history.

Sister had also taught dancing as a young lady prior to entering the convent.
In retrospect, that did not surprise me.
Even as a kid, I remember her moving gracefully about our classroom in spite of the constraints of her nun's habit.
Speaking of the habits the nuns wore, Sister told me that, no matter the weather, she was never uncomfortable.

I must admit that I found that awfully hard to believe.
All those layers and that starched collar and bib would certainly seem to be VERY uncomfortable indeed.

In regard to her early days as a dance instructor, Mary Arthur related the fact that several of her pupils had even won National Championships back then.
That didn't surprise me either.
Sister was always a supremely dedicated and relentlessly driven woman.
No one who had ever had her for a mentor would argue with that.
On occasion, someone would try to dissuade her from her chosen course of action. Needless to say, they met with absolutely no success.
As she said,
"Can you imagine ANYONE trying to talk me out of ANYTHING?"
Not me!

Sister came from a family of three other sisters and one brother.
Her youngest sister also joined the Sisters of Charity and took the name, Sister Peter Claver.
In fact, whenever Mary Arthur referred to her sibling, she always called her "Peter Claver".
I don't think that Sister ever mentioned Peter Claver's real name.
Sister allowed me to take a picture of a snapshot with the two of them in full "Battle Gear" from many years ago.
Back then, we were not allowed to take pictures of any of the nuns.
Just prior to my making the trip up to Massachusetts, Ray Flood had E-mailed a picture of Mary Arthur from those days that someone did actually manage to take.

He sent the photo to all the '54 graduates with whom we had been in contact.
In the picture, Sister is smiling.
I almost didn't recognize her.
To the best of my recollection, I don't EVER remember Mary Arthur smiling when we had her in eighth grade.
She was ALWAYS very intense.

When Sister and I were sitting in her room, I noticed that very same picture on her dresser.
I told her about my inability to recognize her in the photo and why that was the case.
When I told her of her perceived intensity, she laughed.
Thank goodness!

Incidently, her brother became a priest as well and I'm afraid, I must admit, his name has slipped my mind.
(I think I'll call Jim Clark and ask him if he can shed any light on the situation.)

After spending over an hour with Sister, I felt it was time to go.
I thought Mary Arthur might be getting tired and I had a long drive ahead of me back to Long Island.

I asked Sister if we might take a few pictures together and she agreed.
Just about that time, one of the nurses passed by and I asked her to do the honors.
The lady said she would so Mary Arthur and I went out to the main area of the floor where the light was better.
As we were preparing for the photos, I remarked to the lady who was to take the shots:
"Sister was the best teacher we ever had and back then she could really hit".

At that point, Mary Arthur raised her right hand and said, "AND I STILL CAN!"

Once the pictures were taken, Sister and I walked to the elevator and I thanked her for all she had done for me and for all her students through the years.
I gave her a hug and said, "You're the best, Sister."
I think she then gave me a kiss on the cheek, but I'm not sure.
The elevator came and I got on and headed for home.
What a wonderful visit.

This truly was and is one great lady!

All the children who were fortunate enough to have Sister Mary Arthur McCarthy pass through their lives were blessed beyond their comprehension.

Thank you, Sister.

Chapter Twenty-Four

REUNION 2014

~

Two years had now passed since our first Reunion in 2012 In the interim we had lost two of our June '54 classmates.

MARY ANN NASTRO and REGINA FOLEY had gone on ahead to set up for our "Big Reunion" in the "Hereafter".

No sooner had I sent out the notices of the September 20th date than Rosemary Fox and Kathleen Murphy sent in their checks.

As in 2012, the confab was to be held at the Green House Café in Bay Ridge, four blocks from our Alma Mater.

Unfortunately, a number of our Grads were reluctantly unable to attend. Mary Dell'Accio, Audrey Moffit, Irene Purcell, Billy Royall, J.P. McGuirk, Dorothy De Nave, Helen McGregor, Madonna O'Brien, and Maureen Treanor and Barbara Barrett couldn't make it for a variety of reasons, both medical and logistical.

Speaking of Barbara, the way I found out about her was a little unusual and enlightening I was searching for St. Saviour's 1958 yearbook since I thought some of our girls may have gone there.

There were just a certain number of Catholic High Schools in Brooklyn back then, so I was checking as many as possible looking for leads.

I never did find St. Saviour's book, but I did come across their Alumni Newsletter which mentioned Barbara and the fact her husband was a "John McCormack".

I called Margaret and asked her if the "John" mentioned is her brother, John. When she said "Yes", I asked her, "When were you going to tell me?" Small world, huh?

Fortunately, Joan Moloney and husband, Jack, made the trip up from Florida

once again and brought the large "Our Lady of Angels" banner from our 2012 get-together.
Jack also made another set of ID-tags for the occasion. Thanks Jack.

Mary Ann Lento, Rosemary Fox, Kathleen Murphy, (who drove down once more from Massachusetts), Kevin Farrell, Tom Convey, Geraldine Fitzgibbon, Margaret McCormack and Gail Gallagher also returned.

My wife, Gail, sat with Margaret and Kevin and had a great time reveling in the fact that she was the youngest attendee by about five years.

As was the case in 2012, we had wonderful weather for the Reunion and everyone enjoyed themselves immensely.
The food and service were up to the usual Green House standards and there were no complaints on either score.

Bonnie McTiernan made a return trip from Oklahoma and Jim Cline finally got the time right.
Ray Flood, however, did not.
Luckily, he and his wife, Joyce, showed up at about 4 o'clock, just in time to get fed and "schmooze".
Ray thought the festivities were scheduled for that evening in spite of the multitude of E-mails I had sent to one and all over the prior six months.
In those E-mails I made sure to mention the time and place of the party.
Read the memos, Ray!!

Carolyn Gregorio had neglected to mail her check, but we knew, thanks to Rosemary, she was coming and would pay upon her arrival.

The final totals were 15 grads and 5 guests.
Oops, make that 14 Grads.
Jim Lundrigan never did show in spite of the fact he had paid in advance.
We waited and waited, but Jimmy never put in an appearance.

When I got home, I decided, on a whim, to try and find Jim's 1958 yearbook on "Classmates".

Jimmy had won a baseball scholarship to Holy Trinity High School when he graduated from OLA.

I found the yearbook and his senior year graduation portrait, but no trace of him on the baseball team.

There were a goodly number of nifty shots of the baseball team in the book, but none of Jim.

While I was looking at the baseball photos, I noticed some pictures of the track team on the opposite page.

One of the photos showed a "Trinity" runner in the middle of a pack at the beginning of a 500-yard race.

Leading that pack was a runner from my school (La Salle) who looked familiar.

It took me a second or two to realize that the leader in question was none other than little Bobby Lane himself 56 years and 100 pounds ago.

I can assure you that this was a very unusual image since I seldom was in the lead in any race I ever ran.

I had never even practiced at that distance and had no idea what the proper

pace should be.

As a result, I took off way too fast and wound up in the front of the field when the photographer took his shot.

After setting the pace for a few laps, I faded badly and finished dead last, but that photo makes me look like a world beater.

Getting back to the Reunion itself, the day was a total success and everyone seemed to think we should do it all over again in two years.

There was even talk of taking a cruise together next time; We'll see.

Getting together with my classmates was a real treat for me and made all the work making our 60th Reunion a worthwhile venture and truly rewarding.

See you all (plus a few more) in 2016?

Chapter Twenty-Five

FUN AND GAMES

A great deal of time during my younger years was spent playing sports of one sort or another.

It kept me out of trouble and afforded me a lot of pleasure to boot.

Most of the time it was SOFTBALL, but PUNCHBALL, STICKBALL and BOXBALL all figured into the equation.

HOCKEY, FOOTBALL and BASKETBALL eventually entered the picture too.

My first experience with playing ball came when I spent a summer at Camp St. Joseph's Villa in Hackettstown, New Jersey in 1949.

During my stay there, I was introduced to sports in general.

My initial exposure to softball was when I made my first of a lifetime of mistakes in the world of athletics.

I was on first base having walked when the next batter got a base hit.

There was a runner in front of me on second base and since I was a lot faster than he was, I ran past him on my way around the bases.

Upon arriving at home plate, I was informed that passing a runner on the basepaths was against the rules and I was "out" as a result. (Mistake number one!)

In the ensuing years, I made more than just a few more.

But, that's one of the ways you learn, both in sports and in life.

I really didn't pay too much attention to sports for the next two years.

My Father, Robert Lane Sr., had died back in 1943 as a result of injuries that he incurred while a member of the NYFD.

He was a fine ballplayer, but he wasn't there to mentor me while I was growing up.

Who knows how different my life would have been had he survived?

Finally, in 1952 I began to collect baseball cards and watch games on our 12-inch RCA television.

I also began to attend the summer playground sessions of P.S. 102, a couple of blocks away from our apartment house on Ovington Avenue. The school had two teams, the UNDER FIVE FOOT team and the OVER FIVE FOOT one.
Needless to say, I wound up on the former.
I started out as a third baseman, but eventually wound up on first.
My teammates included Bobby Lento (p), Stevie Marks (1b), Robbie Weissfield (2b), and Bobby Campbell (of).
In addition to playing softball, John Cuff and I played a lot of stickball.
It was John who really taught me to basics of the National Pastime.
We played quite a bit and I seldom won, but that wasn't the point.
We had fun and I learned a lot.
Another good friend, Richie Giustra, actually played for the Our Lady of Angels TYRO baseball team.
Richie was the second baseman while Jack Fitzgibbons (c), Jim Lundrigan (1b), Ed Phelan (of) and Danny O'Connell (ss) rounded out the squad.
I never tried out since, at that time, I had little interest in the game.

My first exposure to HOCKEY came one winter evening in 1952.
I was watching television and came across a very odd activity on WPIX, Channel 11 in New York City, the DAILY NEWS STATION.
Note: There were only 7 stations on the air at that time.
They were: WCBS (Channel 2), WNBT (Channel 4), WABD (Channel 5), WJZ (Channel 7), WOR (Channel 9), WPIX (Channel 11) and WATV (Channel 13) from Newark, New Jersey. (Wherever that was?)
This strange game was played on some sort of white surface by players who seemed to slide along while chasing a little black disk as they smacked it around with long wooden sticks.
At each end of the arena, there was an oddly dressed individual standing in front of a small cage.
Suddenly, one of the teams shot the little black disk past this bizarre creature and into the small cage.
At that point, the team that had just scored all raised their sticks and began to dance around and hug each other.
I had never seen anything like it.

It was HOCKEY and it was love at first sight!

The next day I went up to my local hardware store and asked them if they sold those peculiar little sticks.

When they said "yes", I immediately bought one for the price of ONE DOLLAR.

Very quickly, the guys on our block followed suit and we began to play in the street on our roller stakes in front of my apartment house.

Initially, we used the fabulous "SPALDEEN", but quickly adopted a roll of black friction tape for our "puck" since a real regulation one did not slide well on the black street pavement.

There weren't too many cars parked on our block so we had plenty of room to play.

If there was a car that happened to be in the way, we would ring the owner's door bell and ask him to please move it.

In the winter, we would play until dark (and sometimes a little longer) if we happened to be under a particularly bright street light.

We would also often shovel snow off the street so we could play.

When my Mother re-married after I graduated from OLA in June '54, I didn't play Hockey anymore.

We moved to the Kings Highway area of Flatbush and Roller Hockey was nowhere to be found.

I did, however, continue to play Softball in PS 197's Summer School. At that point in time I was strictly a "Punch and Judy" hitter who would hit the ball on the ground and run like hell.

I had, by that juncture, developed into a pretty damn good center fielder and was voted to the "All School Yard" team chosen by a fellow named Barry Barenhoff, who I think was a high school teacher.

It was a strictly "unofficial" designation, but I was honored to have been selected.

During my high school years, 1954-58 most of my time was spent running Cross Country up in Van Cortlandt Park in the Bronx and both Indoor and Outdoor Track.

Since I weighed less than 100 pounds as a Freshman, I was eligible to compete in the "Sub-Midget" Class in "CHSAA" events, mostly relays.

Our relay team was pretty good, but the teams from Rice, St. Francis, Loughlin, and Mount St. Michael were every bit as good if not better. Occasionally we would take home a medal for our efforts.

My Sub-Midget teammates were usually Gene Corcoran and Henry Cahill.

(Henry and I still keep in touch.)

Others who ran with us at one time or another were Phil Kelly and Michael Curry.

Every once in a while, I would run as an individual with varying degrees of success.

Since daily track practices would usually run until very late in the afternoon I didn't get home until after dark.

Interestingly, my trip back to home on the "Brighton" line would take me right past the Prospect Park station on my way to my Kings Highway stop.

The Prospect Park station was the closest to Ebbets Field, home of the BROOKLYN DODGERS.

I never thought to get off the train even on the days when there was no track practice and catch a game.

I guess I thought there would be plenty of time to catch games after my graduating from La Salle.

We all thought the Dodgers would always be a part of Brooklyn. WRONG!!!

Of course, the Dodgers up and left Brooklyn for Los Angeles after the 1957 season and destroyed the borough's unique identity.

This betrayal happened only two years after the Dodgers won their only long awaited World Series Championship in 1955.

Note: When I lived in Bay Ridge back in my OLA days, EIGHT of the Dodgers lived in the neighborhood within walking distance of my apartment.

PEE WEE REESE, the Dodger Captain, DUKE SNIDER, CARL ERSKINE, PREACHER ROE, RUSS MEYER, RUBE WALKER, BOBBY MORGAN and BILL ANTONELLO all called Bay Ridge home during the baseball season.

Antonello, in fact, was a native-born Bay Ridger whose dad was the Superintendent of an apartment building a few blocks away from my abode on Ovington Avenue.

There may have even been a few more Dodgers who lived in the general area such as CLEM LABINE and BEN WADE, but I never found out.

One of my friends, Drew Adams, was actually the nephew of Dodger pitcher RALPH BRANCA.

I started to play BASKETBALL, at which I was not good (could not shoot!) and TOUCH FOOTBALL after we moved.

I turned out to be a pretty good pass receiver and enjoyed scoring touchdowns.

The guys I most frequently played with were AL PACHECO, Eddie Illions and Tony Marino. (In my lifetime I think I've known half a dozen Tony Marinos)

When Al and I first met on the basketball court, it was chaos.

We were both hard-nosed players and would beat the hell out of each other.

(He couldn't shoot either)

Eventually we started to play both basketball and football together and became good friends.

One Tuesday afternoon I became fed up with being the aforementioned "Punch and Judy" hitter and decided a big change was in order.

I decided to become Mickey Mantle.

I adopted Mickey's stance and the very next day (Wednesday) I emerged as a power hitter.

What happened was that by patterning myself after Mantle at the plate, I accidently started doing things MECHANICALLY correctly in the batter's box.

Instead of wrapping my bat around my ear, I now held it straight up and down at my shoulder (like Mickey) and the ball started jumping off my bat.

I had become a slugger and long ball hitter overnight.

It wasn't until a couple of years later when I read TED WILLIAMS' book, "The Science of Hitting" that I learned what I was really doing right.

(and wrong too)

One of the most curious incidents in my career occurred shortly after I began to display my new found power hitting prowess.

I was approached by one of my neighbors, pitcher Paulie Abrams, to play on a tournament team he and his catcher Gene Paris were putting together.

The only catch was that this was to be an ALL JEWISH tournament and I would have to play under an assumed name.

BOBBY LANE now became MARTY SCHULMAN!

In one of the games I managed to hit two home runs.

While I was trotting out my second round-tripper, I evidently dropped my "Miraculous Medal" between second and third base.

At the end of the inning, as we were switching positions and taking the field, the other team's Jewish shortstop approached me.

He handed me back my medal to my chagrin and embarrassment.

After a moment or two he said to me:

"Don't worry, we have a couple of "GOYS" on our team too!"

We wound up winning the tournament and took home the team trophies.

Paulie had the good sense not to have mine engraved with my Marty Schulman "Nom de Guerre" and to this day it remains blank.

Once I became a "Hitter", I would often buy a "Clincher" softball on my way home from work and take batting practice at 197.

A couple of young local kids would pitch to me for about an hour. These youngsters loved to see me hit balls over the leftfield fence and sometimes halfway up the apartment house across the street. How I never broke someone's window I'll never know.

In fact, my good friend, DAVEY LOWELL, happened to be walking behind a couple of those kids on Kings Highway one afternoon when this conversation took place between them.

One of the urchins said, "Do you know that if Bobby Lane (me) gets the right coaching he could be the greatest ballplayer of all time". His friend concurred.

Davey couldn't wait to tell me that he almost broke out in hysterical laughter right then and there.

Note: You're no "hero" to your friends.

Davey and I formed our own team to challenge some of the area's local teams, most notably the "Blackhawks".

We called ourselves the "Cobras" and we were pretty good in spite of being the new kids on the block.

Davey was our pitcher, Johnny Cotter our catcher, Anthony Imbriale played first, Ronnie Zollo second, Vinnie Wade short, Joe Schwegler third, Pat Quinn leftfield and our rightfielder was Davey's younger brother, Jimmy, who later became a priest.

When we didn't have a game, we would play "Automatics" with a "Spaldeen" in one of the smaller school yards at 197.

It kept us out of trouble.

We even ventured down to Bay Ridge to play some of my old friends, including Terry Hatch, at PS 102. (We lost)

Eventually I began to play some organized basketball and softball when I got a job at Remington Rand/UNIVAC in the city.

As far as basketball went, I still couldn't shoot...at first.

I happened to take one of my co-workers and good friend, LOIS PERLOWIN, to a game one evening.

Seeing what a horrible shot I was, Lois suggested that instead of shooting with two hands I try shooting with one.

All of a sudden, the ball started going in the basket and I was cured. Thanks, Baby Lois!

Note: Lois and I are still good friends to this day.

My Univac team used to play a game against our Blue Bell, Pennsylvania installation every year.

I was fortunate enough to be chosen as the Most Valuable Player in the contests for two years in a row.

The Remington Rand/UNIVAC softball squad was already pretty good when I joined them in 1961.

We played our games up on Randall's Island and it was the first time I'd ever played on grass.

In 1962 we managed to win the New York City Championship which was played in Central Park.

We actually won it on a suicide squeeze bunt by Dick Bender (1B/RF) that scored Vinnie Carbonetti (1B/OF/SS) from third base.

The rest of the team included pitchers Joe Carrano, Doug Welsh and George Feeney, Mal Hoffman (1B), Don Sturm (2B), Al Adornetti (2B/3B), Ben Thomas (SS), John McGuire (3B), Joe LoBianco (LF), Bobby Holm (OF), Frank Turner (IF) and Charlie Virga was our catcher. Incidently, Joey LoBianco is the brother of Tony Lobianco, the wellknown actor, who appeared in "THE GODFATHER" and also co-starred in "THE FRENCH CONNECTION".

Our pitcher, Joe Carrano, once managed to beat Eddie Feigner and his "King and His Court" touring 3-man team in an exhibition game years earlier in his career.

Through AL ADORNETTI I migrated back to Bay Ridge to play on a team sponsored by "Leemark Lanes".

This eventually led me to a team that played in the infamous "Dust Bowl" on 65th Street and 8th Avenue and in Sunset Park overlooking New York Harbor.

That came about because I had met PETE MARCHESE in my National Guard Unit and he asked me to join his "Channel 14" squad.

Channel 14 was a local "Den of Iniquity" (bar) frequented by some questionable characters of the Italian persuasion.

The bar sponsored the team and if we won, the losing team would have to return to Channel 14 and spend the afternoon drinking there.

We won quite a bit, but if we did lose, we would have to go to the other team's bar instead and drink there.

Some of my Channel 14 teammates were: Frankie Cuozzo (P), Johnny Phillips (P), John Mazzilli (1B) (Lee's uncle), Peter Saad (2B/SS) Tony Lupo (SS), Rocky Aiello (3B) and Dennis Kelly (C).

Our outfield consisted of Pete in left, me in center and Tony Mazza in right, but Bobby Cetta eventually joined us too.

When Channel 14 folded, I joined the Celtic Tavern team.

Ralph Marano, who I had met while playing for Leemark Lanes, was responsible for the switch.

Again, we were a really good team and won a lot.

Bruce Hannaway was our pitcher while Al Paturzo and Bobby Hanover handled the catching duties.

Al became a truly GREAT football coach at Susan Wagner High school over on Staten Island and has won many PSAL Championships.

The rest of the team included Jack Powers (2B), Ray Scotto (SS) while Ralph played third and Joe Maher (P/1B) filled out the roster.

The outfield changed from time to time, but I was a fixture in center.

Another team I played for was called the "ADANACS"
("ADANAC" is really" CANADA" spelled backwards)
The team was primarily made up of some older Bay Ridgers, including:
Jack Kiel (P), Richie Petrie (C), good buddy, Jerry Harrington (C)

Jack Bourgheri (1B), me at 2B, (Don't ask me how that happened), John Woods (SS), Tommy Mulligan (3B), Bob Byrnes (CF), (Another good friend), his brother Charlie (LF) and Al Dumar (RF).
Even though ground balls were an adventure for me, I could turn the double play pretty well.
As a matter of fact, we once turned five twin killings in a seven-inning game.

HOCKEY, as I said, was nowhere to found once we moved to Flatbush.
For the first four years (1954-58), I ran X-country and track for La Salle. It kept me busy and out of trouble for 10 months of the year.
I didn't start playing hockey again for nine years after I left Bay Ridge.
Finally, in 1963 I began to skate once more and I had a lot of catching up to do.
The reason I started playing again was due to the fact a couple of guys from my National Guard unit (Bobby Donnelly, Artie Santa Maria and Charlie Sacco) encouraged me to do so.
Artie and Bobby actually were playing on teams at the time, while Charlie was a big time New York Rangers fan.

Charlie and I initially bought season tickets to the Ranger games at the old Madison Square Garden on 8th Avenue and 49th Street in NYC.
In those days, you could buy those tickets 10 games at a time. (Imagine that!)
Our seats cost $3.00 apiece and we sat in the Side Mezzanine.
The only problem was that from our location you couldn't see the main scoreboard/game clock that was suspended from the roof at center ice.
This was due to the fact that the side balcony overhung our seats obstructing our view.
We held those seats for one year and then moved down to the "End Promenade" at ice level behind the 8th Avenue goal.

(Section W, Row E, seats 13 and 14)
I could almost hold my breath from the time I entered the building until I got to our seats.
Our seats were wooden folding chairs (cost $4.00) while the folks behind us in the "Loge" section had padded seats which cost $6.00.

Oddly, you were allowed to leave and re-enter the Garden between periods to go and get hot dogs at the NEDICKS store outside the main entrance on 8th Avenue.

This was due to the fact that there were not enough concession stands on the main floor of the building.

In those days there was also a hat check room just inside the lobby for the high rollers.

At about the same time, ARTIE SANTA MARIA invited me to start playing again on his team, the BLACKHAWKS.

I was amazed how far behind I was compared to the rest of the guys in the league.

It had been 9 years since I had played and at twenty-two years of age I needed to re-educate myself.

I needed to learn to take a slap shot since all we used back then was the wrist shot. (It took a while)

I was basically a left wing/center, but I had to play right wing on a line with Artie and old pal, RALPH MARANO.

I had a great deal of difficulty receiving passes on my backhand and my stick handling left a lot to be desired.

Our line, however, was very successful.

Ralph was our center and goal scorer, while Artie was a fine two-way player.

We only gave up 4 goals for the entire 12 game season and scored 40.

I got 7, Artie got 10 and Ralph got the rest (23)

A couple of seasons later, I caught up.

I learned to take a slap shot and also started to score some goals.

I started playing with a right wing named FRANKIE LUZIA and our styles meshed at once.

It was because of his fine passing, vision and knowledge of the game that I blossomed into a goal scorer.

After a number of seasons in roller hockey, one of my new co-workers, ED TOPOR, got me involved in ICE HOCKEY.

I was reluctant at first because I had never ice skated.

An old friend, JIMMY DUNLOP, had given me a pair of his old Hyde Hardware ice skates a few years prior to that and I started to play on ice with Ed and his friends.

As it turned out, we began to play every Friday night during the season for the next 19 years. (Usually at 1am)

Fortunately, I made the transition from roller skates to ice skates rather quickly.

My style of skating and stopping lent itself well to ice skating.

Back then there were no roller blades, just skates with four wheels.

In roller hockey I could turn to either side (a lot of players only turned one way) and stop by turning my skates and sliding to a stop.

(Many players stopped by dragging their toe)

In ice hockey you do it the same way.

I got so I could stop on one or two skates using either the inside or outside edge of my blades.

(In roller hockey it was the inside or outside wheels.)

Once we started playing on ice every week, I wound up skating with JIMMY DOMINIQUE as my center.

We seemed to know instinctively where each other was on the ice and how to find one another with our passes.

Later on, I played with JOEY BUONACORE and we had the same instantaneous on-ice chemistry.

It was because of these three guys, Frankie Luzia in roller hockey and Jimmy and Joey in ice hockey that I emerged as a goal scorer.

Thank you, gentlemen!

Other teammates during those 19 years included: Ed Topor (G), John Kaiser (D/RW), Jimmy (Flutters) Kearney (D), the Sherwood brothers, Donny and Ray (D), "Butchy" Knapik (RW), the Moriarity cousins Richie (G), Kenny (RW), Steve (D), Neil (LW), Donny Wallace (C), Frankie Lukasic (D), Barry Farher (D), Bill Weitzel (LW) and defenseman Vinnie Valente We occasionally would skate with New York City Fireman Bobby Higgins, the father of NHL player Chris Higgins. (Chris would also skate with us while he was still just a little kid.)

Bobby was at least a cut or two above us skill-wise, but he would play as just one of the guys unless you embarrassed him.

Then, Bobby would take over the game and show us how really good he was.

Unfortunately, the few times I skated with Bobby on the same line, our styles didn't complement one another and we were very ineffective.

(That is to say, I wasn't very good as his line-mate.)

One evening in December I hadn't been to the rink for a couple of weeks due to an injury.
When I arrived, I found out the single guys had challenged the old married guys to a game.
Jimmy Dominique said he was glad I had showed up since we married guys needed a goal scorer.
Jimmy and I skated with Donny Wallace on the same line.

The single guys knew they were faster than we were and were really full of themselves.

On the opening face-off, Donny won the draw, passed to Jimmy who skated down the right boards and fed me in front of the net for an easy tap in goal.
Next face-off, same thing; pass, pass, goal.
Third face-off, we did it again.
The score was 3-0 and the single guys hadn't even touched the puck yet.
We then made sure that we told them that hockey was a basically simple game.
You take the puck, pass it around and put it in the net.
No problem!
That shut the smart asses up.
I don't remember the final score, but we had proved our point.

The few times I skated against Jimmy over the years, I realized what a nasty little S.O.B. he could be.
No wonder why opponents disliked playing against him.
One game, very early in the first period, Jimmy got me from behind and gave me a pretty good shot which wasn't totally clean.
I skated next to him for the rest of the game never trying to even things up. (I wanted him to sweat and worry)
With about a minute left in the game, I ran Jimmy into the boards pretty hard and also not totally clean.
Jimmy popped up with a smile on his face yelling "Payback, Payback!"
He told me after the game he wondered why I hadn't retaliated right

away and he had spent the whole game looking over his shoulder and waiting.

We both laughed about it since we knew what had to be done sooner or later.

One night during the 1980 Christmas school break, I took both of our kids, Christine and Bobby to one of our games.

I had promised Christine that if I scored a goal, I would give her the puck.

Talk about pressure.

Luckily, I got one early in the second period and threw the puck to Chrissy over the glass.

I could see, however, that Bobby was a little jealous and disappointed that he didn't get one too.

Now the pressure was REALLY on!

Later in the third period, I managed to score again and got Bobby his own puck.

Whew!

The last baseball game I ever played was with a team run by my good friend and family lawyer, FREDDY SCHWARTZ.

The team was called the Braves and we competed in an over 40 years of age wooden bat league.

At the age of 67 I was one of the oldest players in the league.

I hadn't played ball of any sort in over 10 years and I was reluctant to give it a try since I had no desire to embarrass myself.

My knees were shot and I couldn't run anymore, but I could still hit.

Before the season, the team had gone to an indoor batting cage in Smithtown and I found I still had my stroke.

That last game was supposed to take place on the SUNY Old Westbury field, but it was flooded.

As a result, the contest was shifted to a local high school.

The SUNY field had a fence all around the outfield, while the high school field was wide open.

The first time up, I struck out on 3 curve balls and looked really bad doing so.

By my second time at bat, the other team had removed the pitcher who had made me look so foolish and brought in a new one.
On his second pitch, the new hurler threw me a waist high fast ball right in my wheelhouse.
I put a good swing on the meatball and hit it really well.
In fact, I didn't even feel the ball hit the bat.
(Always a good sign)
I looked to see where the ball had gone and was pleased to see the centerfielder's uniform numbers when he turned to chase the ball as it sailed over his head in distant left-center field.
(I've hit more than a few home runs in my life and I knew that this one had the distance)

Unfortunately, as I said, this high school field had no outfield fence so the ball just rolled and rolled instead of leaving the park.
Since I could no longer run, I barely got to second base before the ball was retrieved and thrown back to the infield.
Still, it sure was a nice way to end my ball playing career.

It's been fun.

Chapter Twenty-Six

UMPIRING

P rior to my last season, I hadn't played ball more than once or twice for almost 20 years.

I had busied myself coaching my son's Little League teams, managing some tournament and College Summer League teams and umpiring High School and various summer youth baseball leagues.

Umpiring was the best part time job I ever had.

I got to watch baseball while getting paid for it.

Whenever I used to tell my wife I was going to work a game, she would tell me, "You're just going out to watch baseball".

Yeah, but I still got paid!

Sometimes the local Little League would ask me to do a game if they thought there might be trouble.

I put up with no nonsense and everybody in town knew it.

One evening, the League Director called me at home at the last minute and asked if I could help him out and do a girl's-softball game since they couldn't get anyone else.

It was the first and last girl's game I ever did.

I foolishly had figured I didn't need my cup or shin guards.

How bad could it be?

The first two pitches banged into my shins and the third hit me where my cup should have been.

I called "time", went back to my car and put on the rest of my equipment.

One other thing about that wonderful game.

On every pitch, one team or the other would scream/shriek.

If it was a strike, the team in the field would scream.

If it was a ball, the team at bat, not to be outdone, would follow suit. I never had such a headache in my life.

Just when you think you've everything that could possibly occur on a ballfield, something weird would happen.
I could write another whole book about that stuff, but I'll limit myself to just a few examples of the strange and mysterious.

On one occasion, I was doing the plate when the coach of the team at bat called for a suicide squeeze with the bases loaded and a 3-1 count on the batter. (Don't ask me why)
The catcher, seeing what was going on, called for a pitchout which would have been ball four, forcing in a run.
The young batter, because he had been ordered to bunt, crossed the plate, bunted at the pitchout and missed.
As a result, ball four became strike two.
The catcher caught the pitchout and tagged the runner coming home.
Had the batter touched the ball at all, fair or foul, he would have been out and all runners would have to go back to their bases.
It took me a second or two to realize what I had just seen and make the call.
(I got it right, by the way)

Once, while doing a game in an "Over 30 League" (Has-beens and never was'), I was confronted with the following predicament.
The third baseman on one of the teams was a throwback to the "60's", headband, long scruffy hair, dirty clothes and all.
About halfway into the game, this individual came into pitch.
After walking the bases loaded, he decided he didn't like my strike zone, let me know it in no uncertain terms and refused to throw another pitch.
I told him he had 20 seconds to resume pitching or I would start calling automatic balls.
20 seconds...ball one, 40 seconds...ball two, 60 seconds...ball three, 80 seconds...ball four, forcing in a run.
This non-pitcher now began to colorfully fill the air with some truly descriptive and nifty purple prose.

After he said the "Magic 'F' Word", I informed him his presence was no longer required and ejected him from the premises.
As he was walking off the field, his girlfriend, sitting behind the backstop, also started cussing at me.
When she too uttered the "Magic Word", I launched her as well.
At this point, the lovely (not) lady, turned her back on me, bent over, dropped her drawers and "Mooned" me.

Another time, I was doing the bases in a younger league (10-12), when the runner on first stole second.
His adult (?) first base coach began really yelling at the boy, saying no one told him to steal the base.
On the next pitch, the rattled young man proceeded to retrace his steps thereby "stealing" his previously occupied first base.
Can't do that folks, runner out.

About 10 years ago, I happened to umpire one of good buddy, FREDDIE SCHWARTZ's over 30 team's games.
It should be noted that Freddie is not only a good friend, but our family lawyer as well.
As luck would have it, Freddie came up with two runners on representing the tying runs with two out in the ninth inning.
The count went to two and two and on the next offering Freddie tried to check his swing on a high and outside pitch.
I didn't think he had stopped in time and called him out.
Game over!
When Freddie protested the call a little, I told him, "If you can't screw your friends, Freddie, who can you screw?"
To this day, Freddie still tells this story to anyone who will listen.

JIM ANNACONE was my fairly regular umpiring partner for years.
Jimmy was a good guy, fun to work with and a fine umpire.
We had a lot of good times together.
One evening we were doing a playoff game at Tanner Park on the South Shore of Long Island when all hell broke loose.
Jimmy was doing the plate for two teams that really didn't like each other.
Late in the game, a batter for the visiting team hit a 3 run home run over the left field fence tying the game.

After a discussion with the home team's manager, Jimmy came out to talk to me on the bases.

It appeared that the manager had appealed that the hitter had missed third base while trotting out his home run.

Jimmy asked me if the if the batter was required to touch all the bases even though the home run ball had left the park.

I told him, "Yes he does and if you saw it, you have to call him out."

Jimmy made the call and a riot ensued.

The fans behind the 1st base fence were livid and started yelling at me. I told them that it wasn't my call and if they were going to go after Jimmy, to make sure I got his car keys since he was my ride home.

That calmed them down, they laughed and now I could go help Jimmy. We broke up a couple of fights and restored order...sort of.

There were a few injuries to the players and one of the visiting team's coaches had a cut over his right eye.

Jimmy called the town police on his cell phone and we finished the game with them in attendance.

After the game ended, the boys in blue escorted us to the town limits, just to be on the safe side.

On another occasion Jimmy and I were working a game at Sachem High. The weather had been threatening during the entire game.

The odd thing was that one of the parents watching the game from behind the bench was constantly yelling at the coach of his own son's team.

As the game progressed, the weather continued to worsen.

Finally, in the last half inning it began to rain very heavily.

Since there were only two outs left in the game, we continued to play.

The final two batters hit a fly ball to center and a line drive to short. Game over.

Now the parent who had been criticizing his son's coach, even though they had won the game, began to yell at me.

He kept it up and kept it up until I finally had had enough.

I told him, "Listen to me big mouth, for a person who knows nothing about this game, you've got an awful lot to say!"

I ejected "big mouth" from the just completed contest after he got even worse, saying the magic word.

He told me I couldn't throw him out since the game was over.

I informed him I was still in charge until we left the area and if he didn't make his way to the distant parking lot in 3 minutes, his son's team, which had won, would forfeit the game because of his actions. (I really couldn't do that, but I figured it was worth a shot)

He continued to mouth off and threatened to meet me in the parking lot.

I replied that the LAST thing he wanted to do was meet me out there. It was now pouring big time.

He still refused to leave so I told the rest of the people in the stands (About two dozen or so) they could not leave until he departed.

Believe it or not, they all stayed where they were in the pouring rain. After all, I was the umpire and was in charge. (It's good to be king!)

Things eventually calmed down and Jimmy said to me on the way to our cars, "Way to go, Bob, you did it again!"

I once was supposed to do a game in one of those over 30 leagues. When I got to the parking lot over-looking the field, it was raining fairly heavily, but the two teams were down on the field ready to play.

I don't know why since the field was rapidly becoming unplayable.

I went down to the field and asked both managers if they really wanted to play the game.

I explained to each of them that it was their choice to start the game, but once it had begun it was my call as to how long we would continue.

I also told them if we even started the game, we two umpires would have to be paid the entire fee.

I hoped and figured this would dissuade them, but they insisted.

As usual, yours truly did the plate and managed to get into the third inning in spite of the fact that home plate was under water and muddy.

Note: I don't need a plate to tell me if a pitch was a strike or not. In the back of my mind, I told myself that when the first runner slips and falls into the quagmire or a bat flies out of a batter's hands, I would call the game over for safety reasons.

When a bat landed in the third base dugout, I said, "That's it, we're done!"

One of the managers fully understood that we had done the best we could, but the other one went ballistic.

He said that all we wanted was the money and were looking for any excuse to end the contest.

He complained long and loud in the downpour and said that he would report us to the umpire's association and make sure that we would have to return all the money.

When he did call, he was told that they were surprised that we had managed to even get three innings in the storm and NO OTHER GAME on Long Island had even tried to play.

Every game on the Island was rained out and called off before even starting to play.

Most of the teams were told by phone not to even report to their fields, since the weather was so bad.

I never got a call, so it was my duty to show up regardless.

After trying to be nice and give this manager a chance to play, all I got from him was grief for acceding to his overwhelming demand that we play.

(No good deed goes unpunished)

P.S. We got to keep the money.

There are times when some managers/coaches make fools of them-selves because they have never read the rule book.

I've had managers try the hidden ball trick after a foul fly ball that wasn't caught. (Can't do that either, folks)

The ball is dead until I put it back into play which I wouldn't do until I see the pitcher has the ball on the mound and is ready to pitch.

I've also had coaches berate us for not awarding each runner one base when a ball is caught and the fielder continues out of bounds with his next step.

Note: Some high school fields on Long Island have a lot of room in foul territory so that a player, in theory, can run all day to try and catch a foul fly-ball. To prevent this a line is drawn parallel to each foul line about 40 feet away and declared "out of bounds" beyond which no catch can be made.

The coach involved failed to comprehend that the catch in question constituted the third out of the inning and there were NO runners on base in the first place.

(What would you like me to do coach?)

P.S. It was HIS TEAM in the field that he wanted me to penalize!

Fascinating!

Every so often I would have to work with partners other than Jimmy.
This could sometimes prove to be a tedious exercise.
In the summer, teams would play double headers on weekends.
After a while you would get to know some of the players pretty well
either from school ball or from just having often seen them over
the years.
As I've mentioned before, my games behind the plate usually went
rather quickly since I tended to call a lot of strikes.
If I had the slightest reason to call a strike ("Big Zone Bob"), believe
me, I did!

I never cheated anybody (except maybe Freddie), but I felt it moved
the game along and kept it fun.
My seven-inning games usually took an hour and forty-five minutes
or so to complete.
It usually was my thought to do the plate in the first game of a twin
bill, hoping to set the tone for my new partner in the second.
The advantage of that approach was to encourage the batters to
swing the bat and also convince the pitchers that they in turn could
throw strikes and not worry about a lot of walks.

Too often, I worked with partners who had really small strike zones.
As a result, there were a lot of deep counts and walks.
On one noteworthy occasion, I had done the plate in the opener and
was the base umpire in the nightcap.
(By the way, there were instances where I worked alone and did the
plate in both games)
My partner for this particular day had a very small and inconsistent
strike zone and as a result his game dragged on and on.
After two hours we were still in the fifth inning.
The kids were getting restless and frustrated wanting to get the hell
out of there.
After one particular pitch, the perplexed shortstop, Billy Oates,
who I'd known for years, asked me, "Mr. Lane, wasn't that last pitch
a strike?"
Before I could answer, Glen Roper, the second baseman, who I'd also
known for years, said, "Don't ask him, he calls EVERYTHING a strike!"

I didn't miss many calls over the course of my umpiring career, but when I did, I would get red in the face knowing I had blown it.
My goal was to compete against myself and do the best job I could by getting calls correct ALL THE TIME.

There were instances where I would bend the rules a bit to ensure things came out right after I had screwed up.
One thing that could be done was to get help from my partner after a manager requested it.

Note: A partner cannot volunteer his opinion on a given call.
I would gladly confer if I could. (Some calls cannot be reversed)
When conferring with my partner, I would quietly tell him, "Listen, I just blew that last call all to hell, so we're going to say you had a better look at it and convinced me to change the call and get it right."

While doing a game in Hauppauge, I called a pitch incorrectly.
It was clearly a ball, but I called it a strike. (Brain freeze)
On the next pitch, I mistakenly said "ball" when the pitch was a borderline strike.
I called time, turned my back to the pitcher and proceeded to dust off home plate.
While I was doing this, I looked up at the batter and catcher and informed them, "All three of us know that we're exactly where we should be in the count at one and one. Any problem?"
They said, "No sweat, ump."
Once again, problem solved.

As I've indicated, a lot of strange things have happened to me on the ballfields of Long Island, but the bottom line is that "umpiring" really was the best part-time job I could ever have hoped for!

When my knees finally gave out, I felt it was time to give it up.
Since I couldn't do the job up to my standards any more, I knew it was time to pack it in.
I had a lot of fun and collected a lot of great memories.
Baseball is a great game.
I was proud and happy to be a part of it for all those years!

Chapter Twenty-Seven

POKIE Q

~

I've saved the best for last.

One Friday in October, 1965, I got home from work and called up Pete Gardini to find out if there were any plans for the evening.

He told me that there was nothing special on tap, so I just got dressed in Bermuda shorts, tee shirt and moccasins and headed out to his house.

I lived on Avenue "O" in the Kings Highway area of Brooklyn and Pete's house was on Albert Road in South Ozone Park, Queens.

Albert Road is one of the exit roads from Aqueduct Race Track so you never wanted to be outside when the track let out.

All the horse racing bed-bugs would come flying up Pete's street at a frenzied pace trying to get to Roosevelt or Yonkers Raceway to re-coup their day's losses and get even.

It usually took me about 30 or 40 minutes to get to Pete's house, depending on the traffic on the Belt Parkway.

I pulled up in front of the Gardini house and saw Peter standing outside waiting for me.

He told me plans had changed and a bunch of guys were going to go to a place in Oceanside called the "Page Two".

I told Peter I had no desire to go and besides, I really wasn't dressed to go anywhere.

Pete said, "C'mon, it'll be fun" and told me I could borrow some of his clothes for the occasion. Reluctantly, I agreed to go.

That night changed my life forever.

When we arrived at the Page Two, Pete ran into an old girlfriend/enemy, Susan Boccio, who was there with some of her own friends.

Once we got there, all of the guys were in a particularly silly mood and I started doing the Army "low crawl" across the dance floor.

One of the young ladies, seeing this, said to me, "I've GOT to know, what are you drinking?"
I assured the pretty damsel that I didn't ever imbibe and was consuming only ginger ale.
We got to talking and in the course of the conversation she said her name was "Gail" and that she was of Cherokee and Swedish extraction.
I thought that this was an odd combination, but didn't question it.
We talked for a while and some sort of distraction separated us.
When I went looking for her, I was told she had gone to the "Little Girls" room.
I positioned myself outside the "Ladies Room", hoping to continue where we had left off.
I waited and waited and waited and waited, but Gail never re-emerged.
Finally, it was time to go and I asked Peter's friend, JOEY LOZITO, if he had seen the missing young lady.
"You mean Pocahontas Jorgensen?", said Joey.
I told him I had been trying to find her to no avail.
(It turned out that the elusive Gail had gone and hung out in the cloak room with the coat check girl)
Fortunately, I had the foresight to have gotten "Pocahontas" last name and I called her a few days later.
It was a relatively easy task since her family name was "Damm" and I knew from talking to her approximately where she lived.
There weren't very many "Damm's" in the Brooklyn phone book anyway.

I called Gail a few nights later and we spoke for quite a while.
She later told me that she remembered that there were two guys named "Bob" at the "Page Two" the night we met and she was hoping I wasn't the other one who was kind of creepy.
I knew who she was talking about.
He was an acquaintance of Peter's whom I had never met before.

I must say that Gail's assessment was correct, he was kind of creepy.

I made my first call from a phone book in my local candy store. (Dubin's) I didn't think it was good idea to use my home phone for a number of reasons. (No need to go into that) I asked Gail out and she accepted.

On our first date in November, Gail and I agreed to meet at the midtown Park Avenue, Manufacturers Hanover Bank building where she worked.
Later on, I found out that her parents didn't care for the fact that they had never met me prior to our date.
Gail, however, told them that I had gone to La Salle like her brother, Al, and that made things somewhat acceptable.
Al was a year in front of me at school, but our paths had never crossed.

When I arrived at Gail's building, I was hoping that we would be able to recognize each other.
As it turned out, Gail was having some last-minute misgivings about going out on a semi-blind date.
We had only seen each other that one time.
Gail later told me that one of her co-workers, Freda Kump, just about pushed her out of the elevator to meet me.

We first went to dinner at the Hawaii Kai Restaurant and then went to see the movie "The Sound of Music" with Julie Andrews at the Rivoli Theater.
We finished up the evening up at a little spot in Kew Gardens, Queens called "The Rumpus Room".
It was a dark little store front place that featured a three-piece combo in the back, a tiny little dance floor in front of the bar and a few booths by the front window and the side wall opposite the bar.
I've always wanted to open a place like that.

Years later we found out that the "Mob" took over the place, broke through the wall into the adjoining Laundromat, installed inflatable dolls, a small Ferris Wheel and some piped in music.
What a mess!

It didn't take me too long to realize that Gail was someone very special.
I proposed to Gail on my birthday, January 17, 1966 and she accepted.

We waited a couple of months, however, to ask her parent's permission since they might have thought it was too soon.

Once that was taken care of, we went to the Queens Borough Hall to get our Marriage License.

To my embarrassment, I only had two dollars in my pocket and the license cost three. (It was the day before payday)

Luckily, Gail had the extra dollar and we got the license.

We decided that May 20th 1967 would be our Wedding Day and every time we saw each other after that, we would count down the days remaining.

After one of our dates, I told Gail that we were going to take a ride on the Staten Island Ferry which she had never been on.

About halfway across, I presented my bride to be with her engagement ring.

One of the guys in my National Guard Unit, Bob Naughter, worked for a jeweler in the Diamond District downtown and helped me get the ring.

The day of Gail's Bridal Shower, I took her to "Willie's" the local ice cream parlor in Gail's neighborhood.

I loved Willie's tuna fish sandwiches and we went there often.

While we were sitting there, I told Gail I had a surprise back at her house.

When she tried to get me to tell her what it was, I finally gave in and said, "It's round, made of glass and bounces."

(To the best of my knowledge, there is no such object in our universe!) We went back to Gail's house and were greeted with the mandatory, "SUPRISE!"

The shower went well, but in the midst of the festivities, some of Gail's friends came over to her and said, 'Bob's sister is nothing like Bob, is she?"

I have never gotten along with my sister and only re-initiated contact with her at Gail's behest.

I had warned Gail about my sister, but she chose not to listen.

A year or so after we got married, Gail got her tail feathers nipped by my beloved sister.

I then reminded her, "I told you so!!"

We haven't spoken to my sister since. (50 years)

Our wedding took place at Gail's home parish, Blessed Sacrament on Euclid Avenue in Cypress Hills, Brooklyn.
We couldn't have asked for a nicer day.
Gail couldn't have looked lovelier and her Wedding Dress was and is THE most beautiful I have EVER seen.
My Best Man was Tom Callamari and my ushers included Ed Chanda, Pete Gardini, Joe Lozito and Gail's cousin Dave Weitzel.
Gail's Matron of Honor was her brother's wife Lorrie Damm and her Bride's Maids included her cousin, Kathy Cahill, Elvira Ragazinskas, Susan Boccio and the "Lovely" Dorothy Sauer.
(Gail's Mom always referred to Dorothy that way)
Our Reception was held at the Regency House on Jamaica Avenue in Queens.
Gail and I had been there before.
When my sister got married a year earlier, I was in the Bridal Party and I naturally asked Gail to accompany me.
Unfortunately, Gail was in the Bridal Party of one of her friends on the same day and she was about to ask me to accompany her.
Believe it or not, both receptions took place at the Regency House.
As a result, we spent the entire afternoon going back and forth between the two receptions.
The people at Gail's reception couldn't figure out who I was. (different tuxedo)

We spent our Honeymoon at the Carlton Beach Hotel in Bermuda. When we arrived at the hotel, the concierge greeted us with: "Welcome Mr. and Mrs. Lane."
When I heard, "Mrs. Lane" I thought, "Good grief, what's my Mother doing here?"

The hotel was great and we had a wonderful time touring Bermuda. One day while Gail went shopping, I ventured down to the hotel's sandy volley ball court.
I got involved in a game with some really crazy guys with British accents. They were a lot of fun.

That evening we went into Hamilton to a night club called the "Forty Thieves".

Appearing at the club was the English rock and roll singing group, "Freddie and the Dreamers".

When I saw them take the stage, I told Gail, "Those are the guys I was playing volley ball with this afternoon."

Freddie himself wasn't one of the players (I would have recognized him), but the rest of the group was.

When we got back from our Honeymoon, we moved into a first-floor apartment in a two-family house on Hillside Avenue in Kew Gardens, Queens and settled down to begin our married life.

In May of 1968, Gail called me at work to tell me she had gone to her doctor and had dispatched a bunny rabbit.

She was pregnant.

On January 2nd, 1969 we welcomed our daughter, Christine, into our lives.

Gail later told me that her doctor feared Chrissy would never make it, but she kept that information from me.

Fortunately, the Good Lord was looking out for us and in spite of some problems, "Peanut", as the nurses called her, came through with flying colors.

She was a "Tough Little Cookie."

We stayed in Queens for three years until my job(s) took us to the wilds of New Jersey.

We settled in the little town/hamlet of Bogota, south of Teaneck and across the Hackensack River from Hackensack itself.

As nice as our garden apartment complex (Pamela Gardens) was, there were a few problems.

First and foremost was the commute back into the City once my newest job took me back to Manhattan.

Next was the water supply.

The water was brown and it was impossible to get clothes clean and white unless we went to the local Laundromat.

The commute necessitated daily bus trips to the Big Apple and back.

Going in was not too bad, but the return trip required long waits in the Port Authority Bus Terminal on Eighth Avenue.

The Public Service Busses that served our general area operated on a strict timetable, but the Manhattan Line, which specifically serviced Bogota, would fill every last available inch of a bus before releasing a vehicle.

As a result, dozens of people would have to suck up all that Carbon Monoxide while waiting to be sent on their way by the company's starter.

I really hated that guy.

He would merrily delay the bus's departure until he was sure that no more sardines could be crammed into his iron-lung. Passenger comfort be damned.

It was nothing but pure greed on the company's part to delay a bus until they were good and ready, sometimes 10 or 15 minutes later than the scheduled departure time.

Bogota was a nice little town and we met some really fine people there. One of them, Linda Pirretti, and my wife remain friends to this day even though Linda has moved all around the country some forty odd years after our meeting her family in Bogota.

After three years in Jersey, we paid a weekend visit to the home of one of my co-workers, GENE ASSANTE, in Commack, Long Island.
Gail and I immediately liked the area.
We told the Assante's that if any homes should become available to please keep us in mind.

The following Tuesday after our visit, Gene's wife, Ginger, called me at work and said that a house on Whitetail Lane was for sale.
I went home with Gene that evening to check on the availability.
Unfortunately, by the time we got to Commack the house had been sold.
Luckily, Ginger knew of another house directly across from the first one which had not gone on the market as yet and was for sale by the owner.

It didn't take long to realize that this second house was a good fit for Gail, Chrissy and I.
So, in spite of the fact that Gail had not even seen the place, I put a small deposit on the house at 10 Whitetail Lane.

As mentioned in a previous chapter, we moved in on July 4th weekend 1973 and have lived there ever since. (46 years!)
A little over a year later Gail gave birth to our son, Robert Lane III.
My Dad was Robert Lane I, I'm II and Bobby III would eventually have a son of his own, Bobby IV.

The ensuing 46 years have been filled with joys, hardships, ups and downs, but all in all, I can't complain.
I certainly married the right person, that's for sure.
Gail has put up with my myriad antics for all these years.
She has been a truly wonderful life's companion and I couldn't have asked for a better Wife, Mother, Lover and now, Grandmother.
I can't imagine life without her.

We have been blessed with two children of our own, six grand-children and six pussy cats over the years, Grubby, Tubby, Glimpy, Dreadful, (or as Gail preferred to call her, Princess Munchkin), Bucky and Wednesday.

(Oops! We now have recently adopted cat number seven, "Samantha")

Christine and her husband, Richard Snyder, now have two children of their own, Richie, age 16 and Paige, age 13.

Bobby and his wife, Dawn, are the parents of four offspring, Bobby IV (16), Olivia (14), Lizzy (12), and little Mikey (7).

In recent years, Gail and I have begun to travel.

Gail did an Alaskan cruise with two of her friends and the two of us have done a National Parks tour, a trip to California leading to a cruise of the Hawaiian Islands, a tour of Italy (including Rome, Florence, and Pompey), a 4th of July weekend cruise on the Queen Mary II to Nova Scotia, Canada,,a bus/train tour of the Canadian Rockies and most recently, a Mediterranean cruise that took us to Venice, Dubrovnik (Croatia), Corfu, Katakolon, Athens (Piraeus), Mykanos, Kusadasi (Ephesus), Santorini and Naples.

When I think of all the people both Gail and I have known who have not weathered life's storms well, I realize I've been one lucky son of a gun.

I could never have managed it without the love of my life, Pokie Q.

Thank You, God, you did good!

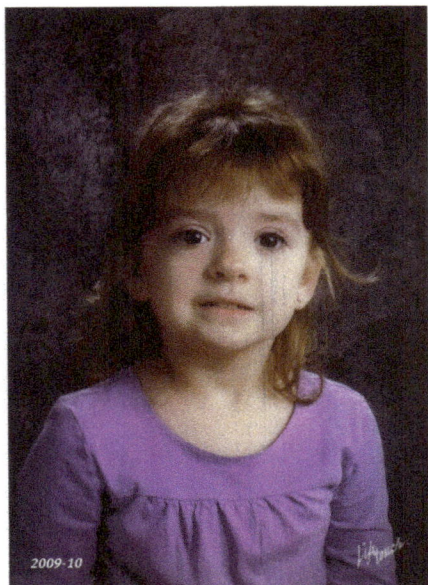

Appendix A
PHOTO INDEX

FRONTPIECE
Robert Lane II – Age six months

CHAPTER 1
Page 2 My Dad – Firemen Robert Lane
Page 5 Bob "Babe" Lane – Center Field
Page 6 The Brooklyn Visitations of 1936
Page 7 My fabulous high chair/stroller
Page 8 Christmas 1945 – Mom, Betty and I

CHAPTER 2
Page 23 Graduation photo – Our Lady of Angels – June 1954

CHAPTER 3
None

CHAPTER 4
Page 37 Glenn "Rocky" Nelson -Jim Busby-Jim Wilson
Page 39 The Boys of Summer
Page 40 (top) Brooklyn Dodgers' Sluggers
Page 40 (bottom) The 1956 Brooklyn Dodgers

CHAPTER 5
Page 46 Joe Adcock
Page 50 Ted Williams (2)

Appendix B

LIST OF MY OLA TEACHERS

Our Lady of Angels School
Bay Ridge, Brooklyn, New York
Robert Lane
1946-1954
Sisters of Charity
of
Halifax, Nova Scotia
List of My Grammar School Teachers
From Ann McCormack (Lento)

1A – Sister Marie DePaul
1B – Sister Rita Therese
2A – Sister Claire Theresa
2B – Sister Edward Josephine
3A – Sister Agnes Virginia
3B – Sister Francis Dorothea
4A – Sister Lawrence Marie
4B – Sister Anna James
5A – Sister Elizabeth Marie
5B – Sister Marie Francis
6A – Sister Anita Therese
6B – Sister Marie de Montfort
7A – Sister Marian Rita
7B – Sister Miriam Agnes
8A – Sister Mary Arthur
8B – Sister Mary Arthur

Our Lady of Angels School

BARBARA HOEY — GAIL GALLAGHER

EDWARD PHELAN · PATRICIA VANCE · MARGARET McSWEENEY · PATRICIA COLE · VIRGINIA JERRO · VERONICA WOLFE · EILEEN O'REILLY · CAROLA WADDLE · ANN ROGGENKAMP · KATHLEEN RIORDAN · MICHAEL ZAMPARDI

ROBERT GANNON · ELIZABETH SHAY · PATRICIA HOBBS · BARBARA BARRETT · CATHERINE WILLIAMS · ALICE COLL · KATHLEEN O'CONNELL · IRENE PURCELL · JOAN VERHOOGEN · JOAN MOLONEY · PATRICK MAHER

JOSEPH CALABRO · REGINA FOLEY · AUDREY MOFFITT · HELEN McGREGOR · DOROTHY DE NAVE · MARIAN KANE · VERONICA REID · SHEILA McDERMOTT · MARY LENTO · MARCELLA McCARTHY · DAVID O'CONNELL

WILLIAM ELIAS · JAMES FALLON · JOHN MALLOY · WILLIAM RYAN · JOHN DOWD · WILLIAM DeMARIA · JOHN KEENAN · RICHARD KOVATS · RICHARD GIUSTRA · JAMES LUNDRIGAN

MATTHEW MONAHAN · WILLIAM IRWIN · JAMES CLINE · RONALD KELLEHER · WALTER HARTMAN · BRIAN FLYNN

Class of June 1954

311

Graduating Class of June, 1954

GIRLS

Barbara Barrett	Margaret McCormack
Carol Brereton	Sheila McDermott
Hope Browne	Helen McGregor
Sheila Butterly	Margaret McSweeney
Patricia Cole	Eleanor McTiernan
Alice Coll	Audrey Moffitt
Mary Dell'Accio	Joan Moloney
Marina Dell'Aria	Kathleen Murphy
Barbara DeMarco	Mary Ann Nastro
Dorothy DeNave	Madonna O'Brien
Margaret Dunphy	Kathleen O'Connell
Elizabeth Fay	Eileen O'Reilly
Sharon Fay	Joanne Petrino
Geraldine Fitzgibbon	Irene Purcell
Regina Foley	Veronica Reid
Rosemary Fox	Kathleen Riordan
Gail Gallagher	Anna Roggenkamp
Carolyn Gregorio	Elizabeth Shay
Patricia Hobbs	Barbara Timony
Barbara Hoey	Maureen Treanor
Patricia Intorcia	Eileen Tubman
Virginia Jerro	Patricia Vance
Marian Kane	Joan Verhoogen
Mary Ann Lento	Carola Wadle
Barbara Lorenz	Catherine Williams
Marcella McCarthy	Veronica Wolfe
Cecelia McCormack	Elaine Zisk

Saint Brendan's Diocesan High School

Geraldine Fitzgibbon	Carolyn Gregorio
Regina Foley	Marian Kane
	Kathleen Murphy

FOR GOD AND COUNTRY

Commencement Exerc

School of Our Lady of A
Brooklyn, New York

in the

Church of Our Lady of A
SUNDAY EVENING, JUNE 27, 19

Eight o'clock

Rt. Rev. Msgr. EDMUND J. REILLY, V. F.

Assistants
Rev. JAMES J. McKENNA
Rev. THOMAS P. CAMPBELL
Rev. JAMES J. HAGGARTY
Rev. JAMES E. SULLIVAN
Rev. FRANCIS J. LABITA
Rev. ROBERT J. ECKER

Program

PART I

1. Festal March .... *Clarke*
2. Veni Creator .... *Himmel*
3. Graduation Exercises .... *Distribution of Diplomas*
4. Graduation Honors .... *Class of June, 1954*

The Archbishop Molloy Award for Religion was won by
Thomas Nacinovich
The Father Loftus Memorial Award for Religion was won by
Geraldine Fitzgibbon
The Father Flynn Memorial Award for Religion was won by
Dorothy DeNave
The Monsignor O'Hara Memorial Award for Religion
was won by .... *Michael Zampardi*
Medals for General Excellence were won by
Elaine Zisk 8B1
Patricia Cole 8B2
Medals for Highest Regents Honors were won by
Kathleen Murphy 8B1
James Fallon 8B2
Medals Donated by the American Legion for Social Studies
were won by .... *William Elias and William Royall*
Medal Donated by Catholic War Veterans (Father Stedman
Post) for Social Studies was won by .... *Irene Purcell*
Catholic Action Award Donated by the Bay Ridge Catholic
Action Guild was won by .... *Brian Flynn*
Scholarship to Regis High School was won by
Thomas Nacinovich
Athletic Scholarship to Holy Trinity High School was won by
James Lundrigan

5. Graduation Exercises .... *School of Religion*
6. Address to the Graduates .... *Rev. Thomas P. Campbell*

PART II

7. Benediction of the Most Blessed Sacrament

Ave Verum .... *Gounod*
Tantum Ergo .... *Silas*
Adoremus Laudate Dominum
8. Recessional: March .... *Elgar*

Music under the Direction of Professor Frederick T. Short

Graduating Class of June, 1954

BOYS

Charles Byrne	John Keenan
Joseph Calarco	Ronald Kelleher
James Cline	Richard Kovats
Thomas Convey	Frank Kush
William DeMaria	Robert Lane
William Donovan	Albert Lipari
John Dowd	James Lundrigan
William Elias	Patrick Maher
James Fallon	John Malloy .
Kevin Farrell	John McCann
John Fitzgibbons	John McGuirk
Brian Flaherty	Matthew Monahan
Raymond Flood	Thomas Nacinovich
Brian Flynn	David O'Connell
William Galloway	Raymond O'Hare
Robert Gannon	Arthur Peck
Richard Giustra	Edward Phelan
Walter Hartman	Victor Raimo
James Hass	Stanley Rashid
John Hassett	Patrick Reilly
James Herr	William Royall
William Hobby	William Ryan
William Irwin	Dennis Smith
John Johnson	Robert Williams
Michael Keane	Michael Zampardi

St. Michael's Diocesan High School

Charles Byrne	Robert Gannon
James Fallon	William Royall
	John Fitzgibbons

313

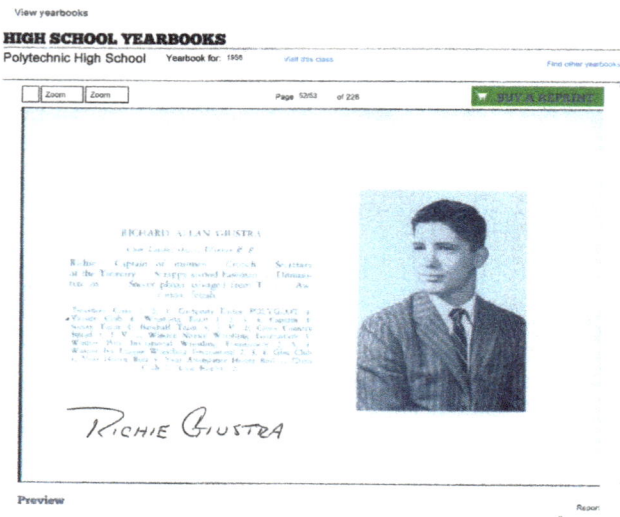

HIGH SCHOOL YEARBOOKS

Polytechnic High School   Yearbook for: 1956

E-YEARBOOK.COM   St. Joseph's College

E-Yearbook Home Quick Search Advanced Search Quick Browse

St. Joseph's College - Footprints Yearbook (Brooklyn, NY) - *Class of 1962*   Page 59 of 224

Page 59	Page 92	Page 94	Page 119
Text from page 69:	Text from page 92:	Text from page 94:	Text from page 119:
". ■ " REGINA MARY FOLEY, L Committee 55 "	"DOROTHY ELLEN MONTUORI, Study Club Varsity 88 "	"KATHLEEN MURPHY, B.A. ENG Glee Club 90 "	"ELAINE VERONICA ZISK, B.A. Prom Mercier Circle 115 "

9 781662 806377